DUBAI MILLENNIUM

DUBAI MILLENNIUM

A Vision Realised
A Dream Lost

Rachel Pagones

A **RACING POST** COMPANY

Published in 2007 by Highdown
an imprint of Raceform Ltd
Compton, Newbury, Berkshire, RG20 6NL

Raceform Ltd is a wholly owned subsidiary of Mirror Group Limited

A catalogue record for this book is available from the British Library.

ISBN 978-1-905156-32-0

Cover designed by Tracey Scarlett

Interiors designed by Fiona Pike

Printed in Great Britain by William Clowes Ltd, Beccles, Suffolk

CONTENTS

ACKNOWLEDGMENTS

This book could not have been written without the help of numerous people from Godolphin and Darley who generously shared their memories and time with me. Sheikh Mohammed and Princess Haya sparked the flame for the project when graciously showing me the unraced Dubai Millennium two-year-olds in the summer of 2004. I would also like to thank Simon Crisford, Saeed bin Suroor, Frankie Dettori and Brian Powell from Godolphin; Tony Proctor, who is no longer with Godolphin but gave me invaluable insight into life with Dubai Millennium; former Godolphin trainers David Loder and Tom Albertrani; John Ferguson, Liam O'Rourke, and Ken Crozier of Darley; and their chief vet James Crowhurst, of Greenwood Ellis & Partners, for his patience in explaining Dubai Millennium's battle with grass sickness. In that area I also owe a great debt to Dr Ken Smith, formerly of the Animal Health Trust, now with the Royal Veterinary College, and Katherine Whitwell, consultant to the AHT, for their obsessive attention to detail and wonderful hospitality, and to Dr Ulrich Wernery of the Central Veterinary Research Laboratory in Dubai for elucidating the current state of grass sickness research.

Many other people from the breeding community also helped the story come alive, including Philippa Cooper, David Mullins, Nick Nugent, Pat O'Kelly, Chris Richardson, Michael Russell and Ron Wallace, as did Simon Hart and Jim Kempton from Madame Tussauds.

Clare Balding and Clive Collins of the BBC generously provided access to archived video footage. *Thoroughbred Times* kindly allowed me to use its averages for the breed statistics. *Racing Post* journalists filled in all kinds of background: Tony Morris and Alastair Down were particularly helpful with pedigree and social context respectively, while *Racing Post* photographer Ed Whitaker was always ready to share his colourful recollections.

Special gratitude goes to my family for their encouragement and tolerance, always. Jonathan Taylor, my editor, has been a constant positive force. Finally, I would like to thank Brough Scott for believing in this book from the beginning. Without him, it really wouldn't have been written.

PREFACE

The party was already in full swing when the main event arrived. It was night, and the sky was black above the warm breath of the desert and the pulse of the Persian Gulf. Had the revellers looked up, they might have made out an especially bright star flickering in the inky darkness.

But they didn't look up. They peered forward into a blaze of artificial lights. Did they hear something? This was what they had been waiting for. They dropped their drinks and sandwiches and cigarettes, their hookah pipes and pizza. Those with small children raised them overhead to see, and dark-skinned men in white robes who had been picnicking on the ground jumped to their feet as the thunderous sound of hoofbeats pounding through an ocean of sand roared louder and louder. The frenzied voice of the crowd joined with the hoofbeats; the noise was a cresting wave, threatening to drown out the track announcer's excited voice.

"As they swing into the straight Dubai Millennium two lengths clear as they stretch out for home …"

Into view now swung a herd of swift-galloping horses, their limbs churning up the dirt. Leading them was a huge dark horse, his shadow looming larger than life under the electric glare. His coat glistened with the sweat of battle, his nostrils flared like those of one of his Arabian ancestors as it ran for its master's life across unforgiving sands. Unlike his ancestors, this horse was not fine-framed and lithe; he looked more like a broad-shouldered boxer as his legs dug into the earth, forcing his way down the long, relentless stretch of Nad Al Sheba racecourse.

Despite the horse's size and powerful action, he moved with amazing speed. Upon his back, a jockey in royal blue silks was perched high in the irons. His hands rested steady on the horse's neck. Behind him, other riders were a mass of frenetic movement, whips flailing, exhorting their grit-covered mounts for one more burst of energy.

The blue-clad jockey was still sitting chilly, a picture of calm. Another furlong marker passed, and silently, he crouched low in the saddle; the horse beneath him accelerated. He pulled out his whip, and smacked the dark haunch once, right-handed. The horse took off again. The jockey gave him another slap, then waved the whip a few times for good measure before glancing over his left shoulder. The rest of the field was dotted behind them.

A mass of white robes thronged against the rail running alongside the track, programmes waved ecstatically in the air. The announcer's voice was barely audible now above a cacophony of cheers and whistles.

"With just under a furlong to go it's Dubai Millennium, he's absolutely pulverised this field, he's eight lengths in front and going further ahead, Dubai Millennium, a superb performance to win the Dubai World Cup, the world's richest horse race ..."

The crowd had just witnessed an extraordinary moment in sporting history. The winning horse had been singled out by Sheikh

Mohammed two years earlier, as a gawky, unraced two-year-old, and stamped the best young horse in the sheikh's stables. The colt's old name, Yaazer, had been changed to Dubai Millennium, in the hope that he would win this race, the Dubai World Cup, in the year 2000.

How unlikely was it that the dream would come true? Throughout history, the dreams of horsemen have run hard aground on the reefs of reality. Many foals, no matter how well bred, never make the racecourse. Physical flaws, injury, illness or bad luck have put paid to countless careers. Many runners never win, and most are not much good.

Such is the nature of any athletic enterprise, but thoroughbreds, unlike humans, are bred to excel at running. Nonetheless, the breed is highly unpredictable. The ugly duckling who miraculously succeeds against the odds is as common a theme in racing as the born-and-bred champion.

But Sheikh Mohammed's faith in this particular dream was so strong that he made it public. If the name weren't enough of a hint, six months before the race he had caused jaws to drop when proclaiming that Dubai Millennium was the best horse his Godolphin racing stables had ever owned. Godolphin was one of the most powerful owners in the world. Its haul of big-race trophies in Europe, since its formation in 1992, was formidable, its list of top runners a roll call of racing's heroes. Godolphin's best horse ever – that was no throwaway statement, and the public knew it.

Here in Dubai, Sheikh Mohammed had put it all on the line for the world to see. If he failed, it would have been a supremely well-documented failure.

Just what the crowd, an eclectic mix from the cultural melting pot of Dubai combined with members of the global racing elite and their entourages, made of Dubai Millennium's victory at that moment is hard to say. For the professionals, there were international rankings to consider – times and distances, the quality of the competition. Later, most racing professionals who were on hand to witness it would hail the performance one of the greatest they had seen.

To the locals, it was a chance to let loose, and celebrate a homegrown victory for no less than the Crown Prince.

To the Godolphin trainers, managers, riders and stablehands – and for their retained jockey, the irrepressible Italian Frankie Dettori – it meant everything. They may have had hundreds of horses and unlimited finances, but to conceive of such a bold plan and then execute it with such perfection – that was a rare and sweet success indeed.

Most of all, this was a triumph for Sheikh Mohammed. Dubai was his country and this was his party. The Dubai World Cup was his baby, and ten years after its birth it had come of age in just the way he had planned. The night was the culmination of so many things, not least of which was the quest to breed the perfect thoroughbred. That was a central part of the story, if not the whole story.

CHAPTER ONE

DUBAI PLC

DUBAI: Where many created attractions appear to say:
'Look what we have achieved'.

Frankie Dettori was beaming. His trademark luminescent smile was captured hundreds of times as cameras flashed incessantly, giving the room the frantic strobe-like feel of an all-night disco. The crush of fans around him jostled for space as those without cameras raised their mobile phones to snap the moment into immortality.

Behind Dettori was a horse. The horse was in full stride, right front and left hind legs stretching into space. His left front pastern sunk deep into the reddish sand beneath his hoof, causing his left knee to hyperextend ever so slightly. Flecks of sand clung to his hooves and coronet bands, the bit of flesh just above the hoof. His muscles rippled beneath a taut bay coat which shone under the artificial lights. The horse leaned into the bridle, his dark nostrils flared, a knowing look in his radiant eye. On his back a jockey was just starting to raise his whip in victory, his mouth wide open in a yell of delight. The jockey was Frankie Dettori.

The horse and mounted jockey were not real, although every detail of the figures was so cunningly crafted you had to reach out and touch them to believe it. They had been created by Madame Tussauds for Dubai International Capital (DIC), which had commissioned the sculpture as a gift to Sheikh Mohammed bin Rashid Al Maktoum, formerly Crown Prince and now the ruler of Dubai since the death of his brother, Sheikh Maktoum bin Rashid Al Maktoum, at the beginning of the year. The sculpture was unveiled at the Godolphin Gallery, a museum devoted to the accomplishments of Sheikh Mohammed's thoroughbred racehorses, three days before the 2006 Dubai World Cup, the world's richest horse race.

The sculpture was a gift, but like so many things in Dubai – skyscrapers, ski slopes, theme parks, islands – it had the imprint of the country's ruler on it. As one of Dubai's primary government investment firms, DIC ultimately answers to Sheikh Mohammed. Since its founding in 2004, it has rapidly compiled a portfolio of diverse international assets – several of them, like Madame Tussauds, quintessentially British institutions.

DIC bought the 200-year-old London waxwork museum for £800 million in the spring of 2005. The following May it paid £691 million to acquire the engineering firm Doncasters Group, and three months later it announced the acquisition of another British icon, the budget hotel chain Travelodge, for £675 million. It became DaimlerChrysler's third largest shareholder, and in the winter of 2006 it made a bid to acquire Liverpool football club for £450 million.

Another Dubai government-owned investment company, DP World, quickly became the third largest ports company worldwide, but provoked an international storm when buying the London-based Peninsular and Oriental Steam Navigation Co. (P&O) for £3.3 billion in 2005. The sale ended 168 years of independence for P&O, but that wasn't the cause of the controversy. Some members of the United States government furiously protested Dubai's acquisition of a subsidiary controlling numerous American ports included in the deal, on the basis that it increased the threat of terrorism. The US nearly thwarted the sale; in the end, DP World agreed to sell off the US operations to an American buyer.

It was a rare case of rejection for Dubai World (DW), the holding company which owns DP World. DW is more used to an open-armed welcome, the unbounded optimism of its directors summed up in the name of its property development subsidiary, Limitless, among whose plans is the construction from scratch of a new Russian city outside of Moscow.[1]

The government plays a central role in funding and driving every major project emanating from the country. It is as true inside Dubai, where everything is on a larger-than-life scale, as it is outside of it.

"In Dubai, it's all Dubai PLC," said U. Balasubramaniam, the chief executive of Dubai Sports City.[2] Although the partners in Dubai Sports City, a $2.5 billion, 50 million square foot project, are private entities, the government subsidised the land purchase and the royal family is set to receive around ten per cent of the profit. They also retain ultimate control over its development.[3] The set-up is typical of projects in the emirate.

Dubai Sports City was designed to attract the world's biggest sports clubs along with their fans. One club needed no prompting – the International Cricket Club moved its headquarters to Dubai in 2005, abandoning 96 years of history at Lord's Cricket Ground in

London. The ICC, along with British football club Manchester United and David Lloyd Tennis, was expected to open an academy in Dubai Sports City. Plans also called for a state-of-the-art sports medicine centre and a giant sports-themed shopping mall.

Most telling of all were plans for the construction of a multipurpose outdoor stadium with capacity for 60,000 fans – reportedly grounds for a bid to host the 2020 Summer Olympics, as well as a middle-eastern World Cup in 2018 or 2022.

Sports City is just one of a constellation of Dubai 'micro-cities'. Also in the works are Aviation City, Aid City, Exhibition City, Festival City, Healthcare City and Silicon Oasis, all centres of free trade.

There are the cities, and then there are the worlds. Eco-Tourism World, Auction World, Virtual Games World, Themed Leisure and Vacation World – all are part of a larger plan to move development inland as Dubai's coastline becomes saturated with hotels and tourists. The frontline of the plan is Dubailand, where 200 development zones will incorporate the various worlds, along with the seven wonders of the (real) world in life-size replication.

The promotion of fun and recreation are clearly high on Dubai's agenda, as the country bids to outdo, well, everything that's been done before. Another Dubailand project is a dinosaur park populated with the closest thing to the real animal since the Cretaceous period.

The middle-east is not a natural skiing destination, but what with the Alpine glaciers melting and Val d'Isere still bare in December, why not? Dubai already has one indoor ski slope, built into the end of the Mall of the Emirates and thereby combining two of the most popular Dubai themes, sport and shopping. From the outside, it looks like a giant, partly squeezed tube of toothpaste rising skywards from the long, rectangular body of the mall. The proposed new ski slope in Dubai has a twist, literally – it will revolve. Skiers will then be able to recover their equilibrium in an iceberg-shaped hotel.

There is another plan afoot to counteract the problem of crowded coastlines. These projects are among the most audacious in the history of humankind – constructing islands in the Arabian Gulf. Not just any islands, they are an unlikely fellowship of aerial artwork, ingenious engineering and luxury living, conceived in some possibly unprecedented permutation of folly, arrogance, boldness and vision – and built of sand.

Their exotic novelty was marketed to celebrities such as English football stars David Beckham and Michael Owen and the Pop Idol judge Simon Cowell, all of whom reserved homes on the first island, Palm Jumeirah.[4]

Due for completion at the end of 2006, Palm Jumeirah is an island in the shape of a palm tree. Because of its size, the Palm Jumeirah's symmetry is best appreciated from the sky. In fact the developers – Nakheel, another DW offshoot – found the only way to construct it was to use a cosmic surveyor. The eye of God did not map out the island, so the developers used the next best thing: a satellite employing GPS (global positioning system) technology.

The size and scale of materials that it took to build the island, which consists of a trunk and 17 fronds surrounded by a crescent-shaped breakwater 11.5 kilometres long, is staggering. The engineering required to put it all together is incomprehensible to a layperson. The breakwater took six months to construct. Its curve required that each one of two and a half million rocks used to build it had to be individually positioned, using cranes and specialised equipment guided by GPS technology.

To source the rocks, 16 quarries were sent into 24/7 mode across the UAE, ultimately producing enough material to build two Egyptian pyramids. A round-the-clock floating conveyor belt carried the rocks, each weighing up to six tons, into rough position.

Even sand posed a problem. Dubai's sand is too fine to support the island, so dredgers were sent miles out to sea, where they dug up enough coarse ocean-bed sand to turn the island of Manhattan into a sandbox a metre deep.[5]

Fascinating as the island's construction is, once the 32 beachfront hotels, the 220 upscale boutiques and cafes, the 1,350 villas, the 1,500 marina berths, the 2,500 shoreline apartments and the monorail are up and running – not to mention the Trump Tower and Hotel and the Atlantis, an "ocean-themed destination" featuring 1,539 rooms, a waterpark, an "archaeological experience" called the Dig and the largest open-air marine habitat in the Middle East – few people will care how it all got there.

Indeed, Dubai residents may become downright blasé about palm-island construction as two more of them, each bigger than the last, are planned. The second, the Palm Jebel Ali, will have as its unique feature more than 1,000 elevated retreat homes. Wooden houses built on stilts, they will form a chain linking the palm's fronds and crescent, and will spell out a line of Sheikh Mohammed's poetry in Arabic, visible from up to 10,000 feet above. The line has been translated variously as "Take wisdom from the wise people/ Not everyone who rides is a jockey", or "Take wisdom from the wise/Not everyone who rides a horse is a great jockey." The rest of the verse goes: "It takes a man of great vision to write on water/Great men rise to great challenges."[6]

All of these plans are ultimately under Sheikh Mohammed's control. Ian Parker, a *New Yorker* journalist, spoke to Mohamed Ali

Alabbar, the founder and chairman of the real-estate company Emaar, which is erecting the world's tallest building, the Burj Dubai. How tall will it be? Nobody knows; the height is top secret, just in case someone decides to build a taller tower.

Emaar was valued in 2005 at $25 billion dollars. Nonetheless, Alabbar described himself as another horse in Sheikh Mohammed's stable. Asked about the competition among developers in Dubai, he told Parker: "His Highness is smart. He created the others to compete. He said, 'I'll put three horses in the race, they'll all run, they are all my horses.' I like that."

Alabbar said he did not mind being Sheikh Mohammed's horse. "I am a horse, but a horse is very valuable to Sheikh Mohammed."

He also gave an insight into the extent of the Sheikh's personal role in Dubai's development. "I'm not – excuse me – licking ass, but the sheikh taught us to be daring," Alabbar said. "This guy is beyond belief. He calls you every day. He says, 'Where is the crane? Show me the crane!"

In February 2006, Sheikh Mohammed ordered a slowdown on Dubailand. The original plan called for the mega-playground to run to the size of Singapore, but the Dubai ruler was worried that too much was happening too fast.[7]

Such concerns are the exception, however. Salem bin Dasmal, Dubailand's chief executive, compared Dubai to a teenager: "It's hungry, eats seven meals a day, runs around for 17 hours a day bouncing off the wall full of energy. A 70-year-old tends to be calmer and doesn't like so much excitement," he said.[8]

The adolescent energy has been fed largely by Dubai's oil reserves. Currently they produce enough income to provide the hungry kid's multi-meals, but they are expected to run out by 2016; hence the investment in tourism, an alternative black-gold rush.

The country, which hosted half a million tourists in 1996, attracted 6.7 million of them in 2005. It aims to more than double that number by 2010.

Since September 11, 2001 there has also been an influx of middle-eastern cash diverted from the US, a response to fears the money could be frozen in case of another terrorist attack on the country.[9]

It is hard to understand, logically, how the modern Dubai evolved. For much of its history, it was a small port whose main business, aside from trade, was pearl diving. That changed after the Second World War, when Japan's cultured pearls took over the market.

The loss of the pearl trade was not as devastating to Dubai, long a centre of maritime trade, as it was to the rest of the Trucial States – British protectorates which later formed the United Arab Emirates.

In 1971, the UAE was founded, with Dubai one of the federation's six member states (a seventh, Ra's al-Khaimah, joined in 1972). The de facto leader of the group was Abu Dhabi, which was the largest emirate and had the greatest oil reserves. Everything had already begun to change with the discovery of oil in Abu Dhabi in 1958, especially after commercial production began there in 1962. The emirate possesses four-fifths of the UAE's oil reserves, and more than a fifth of the world's oil supply.

Abu Dhabi's ruler, Sheikh Zayed Bin Sultan Al Nahyan, was president of the UAE from its founding until his death in 2004. It was he who first saw the potential for oil revenue to transform the region, and he who directed the flow of money into national infrastructures, health services and education. The transformation gained rapid momentum with the huge hike in oil prices following the 1973 Arab-Israeli war.[10]

Dubai ruler Sheikh Rashid Bin Said Al Maktoum became the first

UAE vice-president. Like Sheikh Zayed, he was a visionary and it was he who set in motion Dubai's propulsion into the modern world, his own drive presaging that of his third son, Sheikh Mohammed. Both Dubai Airport, which has become one of the world's busiest and most opulent aviation stops since the founding of Emirates Airlines in 1985, and the Al Maktoum Bridge spanning Dubai Creek, were built under the reign of Sheikh Rashid, who had a reputation for personally touring each of his projects with near-obsessive regularity and attention to detail.

Upon his death in 1990, the eldest of his four sons, Sheikh Maktoum, succeeded him as ruler of Dubai. Sheikh Mohammed, the third son, was appointed Crown Prince in 1995. He had long held a leadership role, though.

Endowed with his father's restless energy and relentless ambition, Sheikh Mohammed once said: "I do not know if I am a good leader, but I am a leader. And I have a vision. I look to the future, 20, 30 years. I learned that from my father, Sheikh Rashid. He was the true father of Dubai. I follow his example. He would rise early and go alone to watch what was happening on each of his projects. I do the same. I watch. I read faces. I take decisions and I move fast. Full throttle."[11]

In the 1990s, Dubai began its rapid upward curve into the ultra-modern world. Part building spree and part marketing blitz, it was fuelled by a tax-free regime to which expatriates from the colder climes of Europe and North America flocked. They brought in technical know-how and stimulated the local economy. Many of them settled in Dubai semi-permanently, landing lucrative contracts as planners, engineers and corporate heads.

At the other end of the socio-economic spectrum, workers from south Asian countries came in droves to do the actual labour.

Calling them expatriates may be a stretch, as they do not have a right to permanent residency, although foreigners such as the Beckhams have been allowed to buy freehold property in some areas since 2002. The labourers are unlikely to buy luxury condominiums, though.

Everywhere along the roads, in the faint light of morning, under the blazing midday sun, or by the harsh glare of artificial lamps through the night, slightly built, dark-skinned men can be seen, digging like ants in the dirt between the giant glass-and-steel towers. They come from Pakistan, Sri Lanka, India and Bangladesh, and they wear scarves beneath their construction helmets, which they wrap around their heads and faces to protect them from the incessantly blowing dust. They don't move quickly and sometimes they don't seem to move at all, but still the buildings rise up. To a visitor who leaves and returns a year later, the buildings seem to have risen with miraculous speed.

It has become a cliché to say that Dubai is a modern city which sprang from nothing. It is more surprising to hear Sheikh Mohammed propound the view himself. Creativity and hard work in order to create something from nothing are virtues extolled often, and passionately, by the sheikh.

In March 1999, Sheikh Mohammed sat before a phalanx of BBC cameras. He had just returned from a day-long endurance ride through the searing desert heat, but he seemed energised by the experience. The sheikh, who was born in 1949 and wears his age well, has one extraordinary physical characteristic – his eyes. When he looks directly at the person he is speaking to, the eyes are almost hypnotic; but often, they seem to be looking straight through what is in front of him. It is almost as if, instead of seeing the thing, he is seeing the idea behind the thing. Or what it could become.

The interview took place in a pale blue tent, the sheikh seated on a red oriental rug woven with geometric patterns. On his head was a royal blue baseball cap, which he jauntily wore back to front, and he had on a matching royal blue T-shirt. The juxtaposition between past and present hovered in the arid air. BBC television journalist Clare Balding trod carefully, trying to straddle the two worlds while determining which one the interview was being held in.

Sometimes it became a tricky balancing act. As they chatted about the endurance ride, Balding suggested: "Forty years ago, this is what an awful lot of people in this country would have been doing – they'd have been riding their horses through the desert."

"Yes," said Sheikh Mohammed, nodding.

Balding was taken with the idea of a romantic past, and pressed the theme. "Is it like sort of returning to your roots?" she asked.

Sheikh Mohammed shifted, reaching one hand behind himself to rest his weight. "Well, you see, Dubai, and the United Arab Emirates, is now working hard. People are working harder, to get to the place where we want. So therefore this is a holiday for me, a day out, and I enjoy it. I'm happy, I'm going to have a shower, and then be working tomorrow," he finished, sitting up and swinging his fist energetically, as if to demonstrate his enthusiasm for the sheer notion of work.

The message was clear: Dubai was no longer a backwater where Bedouins rode their dusty horses and pearl divers plied their trade. It was a modern metropolis where people worked hard to advance their lot – not only their own lot, but that of their country.

Everyone in racing knew that Godolphin, Sheikh Mohammed's elite string of racehorses, operated as a team; but fewer noticed that the sheikh also had a tendency to refer to his country as a team, and its modernisation as a team effort. Indeed, he extended the analogy to make Dubai a team player for the United Arab Emirates.

Referring to Sheikh Zayed, the late president of the UAE, Sheikh Mohammed said: "He had an aim and a focus, and we have to follow that, to focus and try to keep up with that. Now we are not stopping. Like Godolphin, we have no finishing line."

Godolphin was Sheikh Mohammed's elite racing team, which he established in 1992. Prior to that the sheikh's horses were spread among a number of British and French trainers, but he wasn't entirely happy with the result. Not that his horses didn't win races; it was the loss of control he didn't like. He liked having all of his horses together, where he could see and touch and speak to them, and he did not like having to bow to one of his trainer's decisions.

It was the Godolphin line, repeated in a public interview later that year, which the racing world picked up on. "There is no finishing line for Godolphin" became the slogan that defined Sheikh Mohammed's racing ambitions. But the public missed the broader message, which was cut during the BBC's editorial process; as went Godolphin, so went Dubai. The two were part and parcel of the same mission for Sheikh Mohammed.

Speaking of Dubai, he said: "We hate routine. Imagine if somebody just goes to the office every day, and comes back, and goes back again, and does the same thing. Kick him out! The routine will kill him. He must create something, he must come and bring something new; he must change, and not be frightened of the change. That's what I believe."

A year later, when interviewed by Balding for a television special before the Dubai World Cup, he applied the same language to both Godolphin and Dubai.

"None of my people have reached how good they are," he said, this time wearing a traditional white robe and red and white headdress held by a black band. His robe flapped in the breeze. Balding hugged her hands over her bare elbows, the desert wind tugging at her sleeveless shirt.

"They have to give me 100 per cent, 110 per cent, and then I want more," the sheikh continued. "And then I want more. You have to create something, not just do your job and sit at home. We must strive together, we must go forward; we must invent something – even from nothing. That's what Godolphin is about, that's what Dubai is about, that's what me and my brothers are about."

One of Sheikh Mohammed's inventions was the Dubai World Cup. The showpiece of Nad Al Sheba, one of five racecourses in the UAE, the race has been the world's richest since its inception. Prize-money for the first running in 1996 was $4 million. Ten years later, the pot had grown to $6 million.

Like the rest of Dubai, Nad Al Sheba had humble beginnings. Its ground was broken in 1986, but the modern era of Dubai racing did not begin until late 1992, when the first race staged paid $2,700 to the winner.[12]

In the summer of 1995, an American horse named Cigar began drawing international headlines. A five-year-old, Cigar had been a moderate horse while racing on turf as a youngster, but when his trainer Bill Mott switched him to dirt, the results were stunning. By July, the colt was on a seven-race winning spree, having captured the big North American weight-for-age and handicap trophies of the spring and summer – the Gulfstream Park Handicap, the Oaklawn Handicap, the Pimlico Special and the Hollywood Gold Cup. Cigar's form was all American – there was no reason to take him abroad for a Japan Cup or an Arc, as he was a proven nobody on turf.

But Nad Al Sheba was a dirt track, Cigar was the greatest dirt horse in the world, and Sheikh Mohammed had an idea. He called his advisers and put forth his plan, the name of which spoke the size of his vision: the Dubai World Cup. The race would be nothing less than a world championship, run over a Classic distance, timed to avoid clashing with the main regional events of other racing nations. And it would offer, as Sheikh Mohammed was wont to do when buying horses, so much money that it would be almost impossible for owners to turn it down.

The sheikh's advisers were keen, and suggested a start date of 1997. The sheikh told them: "Now."[13] Only in that way could he assure Cigar's participation.

The next step was to woo Cigar – or rather, his owner. The colt was owned by Allen Paulson, a self-made tycoon from Clinton, Iowa, who had worked his way up from the bottom of the aviation industry to found Gulfstream Aerospace Corp. Next to Sheikh Mohammed, Paulson probably had a greater investment in the thoroughbred industry than anyone in the world at the end of the millennium. He also had an adventurous streak, and in 1990, he and a Gulfstream crew manned two around-the-world flights on Gulfstream jets, establishing 35 international records. His horses' distinctive names were derived from aviation checkpoints.

Sheikh Mohammed believed he could win Paulson over. Cigar's owner had been in Dubai already: twice while circumnavigating the globe he had landed at Dubai International Airport, where he was given exceptional treatment – a runway was cleared for his team to allow them their fastest turnaround on the tour.[14]

The Crown Prince and the aviator had also done horse business together, when Paulson sold the sheikh 50 per cent of a two-year-old colt named Arazi for $5 million. Racing for the partnership, the colt went on to record the most spectacular win in the history of the Breeders' Cup Juvenile, in 1991.

Finally, if Cigar bagged the $2.4 million winner's prize, he would become the highest earning horse of all time, surpassing Alysheba's income of $6,679,242 – and Paulson liked to set records.

But flying his prize horse halfway across the world, to a little-known track in the middle of the desert, for a race which, due to international rules, could not even be awarded Group or Graded status, was something else again. Some fairly urgent diplomacy took place during the latter half of the year.

Just when it all seemed assured, Cigar suffered a bruised hoof. It was a month before the World Cup, set for March 27, and the colt was forced out of an intended start in the Santa Anita Handicap on March 2. Mott was in a race against time to have him ready for Dubai, and he and Paulson remained non-committal as the clock ticked.

The bruise healed, and, with a sigh and a prayer, the entourage winged into Dubai in late March. To their surprise, the desert sand was hidden beneath vast lakes of water. Dubai had been inundated with seven times its normal yearly rainfall over the winter, and the track, which was covered by ten centimetres of loose sand, had turned into a slog. There was even talk of postponing the race.

Luckily, Sheikh Mohammed knew how to throw a good party. Casting off the spectre of more rain, he showed his guests the time of their lives. A total of seven foreign horses had been gathered for the race, including Danewin from Australia, Lively Mount from Japan, Cigar, L'Carriere and Soul Of The Matter from the US, and from Britain, Pentire and Needle Gun. It was not hard to see why they came: the Dubai Racing Club paid round-trip airfare, stabling and veterinary expenses for the horses for up to 30 days, while owners, trainers, jockeys and spouses received first-class air travel and a week's accommodation in one of Dubai's finest hotels. Stable hands, too, were transported and put up gratis, albeit in economy class.

In the days leading up to the race, the guests were treated to tours of Al Quoz and the Dubai Equine Hospital, taken camel-riding, entertained by Simply Red at a gala on Jumeirah Beach, and spirited into the desert for the Arabian Nights bash, where the native themes included a tent serving mock hashish.

It would have been a shame, after all that, if the race didn't live up to the hype. Against the odds of human, horse and weather, it did, and the right horse won. Cigar, who somehow emerged clean from his mile-and-a-quarter trek around a rain-soaked Nad Al Sheba, was declared a world champion. He also became the world's leading equine earner, the winner's prize swelling his bankroll to $7,669,015.

The other American horses, Soul Of The Matter and L'Carriere, finished second and third respectively, emerging caked in sand and covered in glory. They were also several hundred thousand dollars richer each. The virtue of the race, at least to Americans, was assured. And it was all due to Sheikh Mohammed's determination in drawing Cigar to Dubai.

"Cigar saved the race. Period," wrote Jay Hovdey in *The Blood-Horse*, a Kentucky industry magazine, a week after the World Cup. "Without Cigar, the World Cup would have been nothing more than a multi-million-dollar commercial for a booming Arabian economy. With Cigar, Nad Al Sheba became the center of the sporting universe."[15]

Hovdey was a racing expert, but he spoke as an American racing expert. Europeans were still largely suspicious of the race, partly because it came at a time of year when the top trainers were reacclimatising after their winter holidays, while their horses were still trying to shed their winter coats. Americans, though, couldn't resist the idea of the big money and the all-expense-paid trip to a place most of them had never even heard of. When the silver-haired California trainer Bob Baffert took Silver Charm over to win the 1998 World Cup, he had to apply for the first passport of his life – at the age of 45.

The inaugural results only boosted American enthusiasm, and although Sheikh Mohammed's Singspiel, trained by Sir Michael Stoute, won the second running, Siphon and Sandpit, two Brazilian-bred horses trained in California by Dick Mandella – who saddled Soul Of The Matter in 1996 – finished second and third. The third World Cup went to Baffert's Silver Charm, with Godolphin's Swain a nose behind him, but the next year Almutawakel, saddled by Godolphin trainer Saeed bin Suroor and owned by Sheikh Mohammed's older brother Sheikh Hamdan, took back the prize for the Maktoums.

By this time, although British trainers had only tentatively dipped their charges' hooves in Nad Al Sheba's sand, other European trainers – Andre Fabre from France and Andreas Schutz from Germany – as well as handlers as far flung as Gai Waterhouse from Australia and a clutch of trainers from Japan, had also made the trip. Everyone who went raved about the place, as well they might; the lavish pre-race celebrations of 1996 became an annual tradition.

The event was one more opportunity for Sheikh Mohammed to show off Dubai to the rest of the world. With that in mind, he was happy enough to award the trophy to foreigners, Americans as it happened; but then a new goal seemed to appear on the horizon.

The year 2000 was approaching. The millennium would be new, just like Dubai. And the whole racing world, or at least important representatives from the major racing nations, would be there. It would be the perfect coming-out party for Dubai, and the icing on the magnificent, multi-tiered cake would be victory by a Godolphin horse in the Dubai World Cup.

1. The Associated Press, "Developer based in Dubai will build a city near Moscow", *International Herald Tribune*, 4 December 2006.
2. Lorne Manly, "An ambitious sports city is rising on imported sand in Dubai", International Herald Tribune (*The New York Times*), 9 May 2006.
3. Ibid.
4. John Arlidge, "Dubai's building frenzy lays foundation for global power", *The Sunday Times*, 21 May 2006.
5. *National Geographic MegaStructure* series, "Impossible Islands", 2006
6. Ian Parker, "The Mirage", *The New Yorker*, 17 October 2005.
7. William Wallis and Roula Khalaf, " 'Adolescent' Dubai shifts focus of its energy inland", *Financial Times*, 21 May 2006.
8. Ibid.
9. John Arlidge, "Dubai's building frenzy lays foundation for global power", *The Sunday Times*, 21 May 2006.
10. Ramesh Shukla, United Arab Emirates – The first 30 years (*Dubai: Motivate Publishing*, 2002), p.22.
11. www.sheikhmohammed.com
12. Graeme Wilson, "Sheikh, Rattle and Roll", *The Blood-Horse*, 16 March 1996.
13. Jay Hovdey, "Horse of the World – Cigar Conquers Dubai", *The Blood-Horse*, 6 April 1996.
14. Ibid.
15. Ibid.

CHAPTER TWO

SHAREEF DANCER

Every story rests on a delicate turning point. How did your parents chance to meet; why did your great-great-grandfather set sail from his ancestral home? Without this fateful event, the rest would never have happened.

There would have been no Dubai Millennium were it not for a pint-sized, but very expensive package, called Shareef Dancer. Born in 1980, the little bay colt, who grew to be only 15.2 hands – four inches above pony size – would later become Dubai Millennium's grandsire, on his dam's side.

Shareef Dancer set sail, or more accurately took wing, from his homeland when he was just a year old, after Sheikh Mohammed bought him from the Keeneland July Yearling Sale in Lexington, Kentucky for $3.3 million (about £1.8 million at the time). The price was the second highest ever paid for a yearling; the highest, $3.5m, was spent at the same sale for a colt who went through the ring shortly before Shareef Dancer. Prices for young thoroughbred colts were just about to go through the roof, thanks in large part to a stallion called Northern Dancer. Both Shareef Dancer and the $3.5 million colt, later named Ballydoyle after the famous stables where he was trained, were sons of Northern Dancer.

What made the colts so valuable? A quarter century after Shareef Dancer's sale, Northern Dancer would be known as the most influential sire of his time – perhaps the most influential sire of all time. By 1981, he was already a legend, the sire of such luminaries of the turf as Nijinsky, Nureyev, Storm Bird and The Minstrel, all of whom became valuable stallions in their own right after their racing careers were over. If his yearling colts proved good enough to win a Classic race like the Derby or the 2,000 Guineas, their value as stallions would skyrocket.

Ballydoyle was a full brother to Storm Bird, and was conditioned by the same trainer, Vincent O'Brien, in Ireland. However, he proved a complete disappointment, earning less than one-tenth of a per cent of his purchase price in a brief career.

Shareef Dancer was not as obviously well bred as Ballydoyle, but he still had excellent bloodlines. His dam, Sweet Alliance, had won six races including the Kentucky Oaks. She was a daughter of the stallion Sir Ivor, who had won both the 2,000 Guineas and the Derby, and a mare named Mrs. Peterkin, who had won half a dozen races, came from a long line of good winners, and had produced several of her own winners from previous matings.

Between the purchase of Shareef Dancer and the colt's first start, in August of 1982, the colt's ownership was transferred from Sheikh Mohammed to Sheikh Maktoum. It didn't really matter to the public who the colt belonged to. He was trained by the eminent Newmarket conditioner Michael Stoute, and he was the most expensive horse ever to have raced in Britain. That ensured him abundant attention, whoever owned him.

Shareef Dancer was an enigma from the start. He won his first race, an 18-runner maiden at Newmarket – but not very impressively, considering he was an evens favourite. He was beaten on his second start a month later at Doncaster, and finished the year unheralded, in a season dominated by the outstanding juvenile colts Diesis and Gorytus.

At three, racing over a mile and a half, he was a different horse. Indeed, he put up the best performance of a three-year-old colt all year when winning the Irish Derby, from a field that included the Derby winner Teenoso and the Prix du Jockey-Club victor Caerleon. This, coming after a strong-closing win in the King Edward VII Stakes at Royal Ascot, made him the presumed champion of the European middle-distance colts' division.

But instead of accolades, disappointment and acrimony crowned Shareef Dancer's season. Sheikh Maktoum's colt never ran again, although his connections did not announce he was unsound or unhealthy. The bitterest accusations came after he was withdrawn from the Benson and Hedges Gold Cup, where he would have met Caerleon again. The prospect of a rematch had drawn large, enthusiastic crowds to York's traditional Ebor meeting opening day, who found out upon their arrival that Shareef Dancer had been withdrawn due to morning rains which had softened the ground. The public's suspicion that this was a bogus excuse was strengthened by the fact that no other runners were withdrawn, including Caerleon, who was widely assumed to need firm footing but won the race anyway.

Disappointment being one of the least pleasant emotions, there was a public backlash. Racegoers felt cheated. The word 'craven' was bandied about. Later, after Shareef Dancer was withdrawn at the overnight stage from the September Stakes at Kempton, reportedly due to an unsuitable weather forecast, they became cynical. No-one believed he would line up for his next proposed target, the Prix de l'Arc de Triomphe. They were right: he did not.

"Shareef Dancer had become the ultimate absurdity, a racehorse seemingly too valuable to race," claimed Timeform's *Racehorses of 1983*.

There were other suggestions to explain away the withdrawals. Unsoundness, a savage temperament, even Sheikh Maktoum's health – he was rumoured to worry himself sick at the thought of his horse getting beat – were mooted as possible reasons for Shareef Dancer's growing record of no-shows.[1]

Undoubtedly, the horse was valuable. By the end of the year he had been retired to Sheikh Mohammed's Dalham Hall Stud, where his stud fee was quoted in dollars: 150,000 of them, a transparent effort to woo Americans. His syndication value was a world record $40 million (about £26.6 million at the time).

There may have been a grain of truth to the rumours about Shareef Dancer's savage personality. Ken Crozier was the stallion man who looked after the horse during his 13 years at Dalham Hall, before he was put down on May 6, 1999, after breaking his right hind leg while twisting awkwardly as he dismounted a mare. (By this time his stud fee had been reduced to £3,500.)

Shareef Dancer was far and away Crozier's favourite stallion, but "he was a sod," the slightly built handler recalled. "He would just knock you over and bite you and kick you. He put about two or three people in hospital. But he and I got on really well, and I thought the world of that horse."

Shareef Dancer may have passed on his tough-guy personality to his grandson, who won his second race three days before the stallion's death. Or maybe it was just coincidence that Dubai Millennium also made a habit of chasing people out of his box. Exactly what traits the exquisitely well-bred and vexingly talented Shareef Dancer passed on to Dubai Millennium is something we will never know. But such genes as he did contribute went through his daughter – Dubai Millennium's dam – a mare named Colorado Dancer.

The Maktoum family sent a number of high-quality mares to Shareef Dancer, but Colorado Dancer's dam was not one of them. Sheikh Mohammed paid 200,000gns for Colorado Dancer as a yearling filly at the Tattersalls Highflyer Sales in September, 1987. She was a bargain compared to her sire, especially considering that her dam, Fall Aspen, would turn out to be as good a mare as the 20th century would see.

Fall Aspen, like Shareef Dancer, began life in North America. Unlike Shareef Dancer, she was not immediately marked for greatness. No-one would have paid a tenth of her future mate's purchase price for her when she was a yearling.

Fall Aspen came from three generations of stock cultivated by New Jersey resident Joe Roebling. Her origin was an inauspicious purchase Roebling made in 1937, named Sunfeathers. Although Sunfeathers did not win for Roebling, two years after he bought her she produced a daughter named Carillon, who later gave birth to the 1948 champion American two-year-old colt, Blue Peter, and, five years later, the colt's full sister, Portage.

Portage was nothing like her brother on the track, winning a single race from 15 starts. However, she became quite a useful producer, her foals carrying names – Rainy Lake, Pack Trip, Black Mountain, Wyoming Wildcat – that harked back to their breeder's fondness for Wyoming, where he had made his fortune in cattle ranches.[2]

Portage's last foal, and one of the least successful, was the cleverly named Change Water, by 1955 Kentucky Derby winner

Swaps. Change Water won only a single race from a dozen starts, but Roebling's decision to cycle her back into his breeding band produced a treasure trove of a mare – Fall Aspen.

Fall Aspen was Change Water's third foal, and the best runner the family had produced since Blue Peter. She won the Grade 1 Matron Stakes and the Grade 3 Astarita Stakes as a two-year-old, and recorded another stakes win at three, eventually rounding out three years of racing with a tally of eight wins from 20 starts and nearly $200,000 in earnings. Unfortunately, Roebling did not live to see the next generation. It was a shame, because it would have been the culmination of all he had worked for over the decades, but Fall Aspen was sold as a four-year-old at the Saratoga sales in upstate New York. Brownell Combs, a renowned Kentucky breeder and proprietor of Spendthrift Farm, paid the grand sum of $600,000 to get her.

Four years later, Spendthrift sold Fall Aspen, at the Keeneland breeding stock sales in Kentucky to a group called International Thoroughbred Breeders for $900,000. By this time she had produced her first two foals, both fillies – Northern Aspen and Elle Seule – and was carrying her third, a colt eventually named Native Aspen. The fillies would both go on to win the Prix d'Astarte, a Group 2 race in France, and Northern Aspen later won at Grade 1 level in the United States. Elle Seule became a top-class matriarch, with her best foal the Irish 1,000 Guineas winner Mehthaaf.

Fall Aspen's foal of 1985 was another colt. Named Mazzacano, he too was a high-class racehorse, who won the Group 3 Goodwood Cup and was second in the Group 1 Gold Cup.

In 1986, Colorado Dancer was born, the first product of two matings between Fall Aspen and Shareef Dancer. A plain bay, she was a rangy individual, unlike her sire. But like him she showed a talent for middle-distance racing. She won three of ten starts for Sheikh

Mohammed, most notably the Group 3 Prix Minerve and Group 2 Prix de Pomone, the latter over a distance of nearly a mile and three-quarters.

A year after Colorado Dancer's birth, Fall Aspen again went through the Keeneland sales ring. Once again she was pregnant to Shareef Dancer. This time her price was $1.1 million, the buyer David Jamison of Westerlands Stud.

She would pass through Keeneland one final time, carrying a foal by Danzig in 1994. By now she was worth $2.4 million. John Magnier of Ireland's Coolmore Stud was the buyer, but Jamison later bought back a 20 per cent interest in her.[3]

Fall Aspen died in 1998, a result of haemorrhaging after producing her 14th foal. Incredibly, she had compiled a better record at stud than Shareef Dancer did, with four Group or Grade 1 winners and nine stakes winners among her foals, and many more among their descendents.

Colorado Dancer joined Sheikh Mohammed's broodmare band upon her retirement. With her bloodlines and racing history, she was a good bet to make a fine broodmare, but her first three foals were nothing noteworthy. The third, a son of Triple Crown winner Affirmed named Colorado Prince, did not even race.

The vagaries of breeding horses are the most democratic aspect of thoroughbred racing. No-one, prince or pauper, has mastered the whimsical interplay of genetics and environment. Colorado Dancer's record is an excellent example of this frustrating truth. The mare's fourth foal was the outrageously talented Dubai Millennium, by the Claiborne Farm stallion Seeking The Gold; but six years after her exceptional son won the Dubai World Cup, Colorado Dancer's nine other foals of racing age had earned less than $250,000 among them, and had yielded not a single stakes winner.

Although Colorado Dancer was effectively married to Seeking The Gold after Dubai Millennium came along, the champion racehorse's brothers and sisters were nothing like him.

The first was Dahjee, conceived the spring that his brother won the Dubai World Cup. The second, Philae, was bred the following year. Dahjee ran once for Godolphin, finished in mid-pack, and earned £428.

Philae ran twice in Sheikh Mohammed's maroon and white silks while trained by Andre Fabre in France. She was unplaced but earned a total of €900.

Colorado Dancer was mated to Seeking The Gold again in 2002, but came up barren. She returned to the sire again in 2003, and this time she produced a chestnut filly, who as a two-year-old of 2006 was quite backward and had yet to race. She also had a 2005 filly by Seeking The Gold, this time a dark bay. But after coming up barren to the stallion in 2006, she was bred to Shamardal, a four-time Group 1 winner who was in his first year at stud.

Colorado Dancer had moderate success when bred to other stallions. Most of them, like Seeking The Gold, were sons of the great North American sire Mr Prospector, although a few other crosses, to the Kentucky sires Pleasant Colony and Affirmed, French stallion Highest Honor and the British sire Groom Dancer, were tried too. However, the four foals produced from these matings won just two races among them.

Next to Dubai Millennium, Colorado Dancer's best foals were Denver County, a colt by Mr Prospector who was third in the Group 2 Prix Greffulhe in France; Hobb Alwahtan, who won six races in the UAE; and Dubai Vision, who won four races in the UAE. Both were sired by Mr Prospector's son Machiavellian.

Although the reflected glory of Dubai Millennium gained several of his half-brothers places at stud, none is located anywhere near the northern hemisphere epicentres of breeding, Newmarket, England, and Lexington, Kentucky. Colorado Dancer had a spell in Chile and finally fetched up outside the hamlet of Torrecilla de la Abadesa in central Spain. Dahjee was sent to a minor stud in Japan, Hobb Alwahtan went to stand in South Africa, and Dubai Excellence arrived at stud in Australia after an identity mix-up saw him detoured to the Ukraine for a couple of months in 2005.

March 20, 1996 was an unexceptional day at Dalham Hall Stud. Mares were mated with stallions; foals were born. In a corner box of the foaling unit, set back from the main breeding activities of the stud and not far from the graveyard where Dalham Hall's most beloved stallions and mares were buried, Colorado Dancer gave birth to a bay colt.

It was her fourth foal, and the mare knew what to do. A day earlier her udder had swelled and tightened, and a waxy substance had formed on her teats. Now, as the heaviness in her belly became unbearable and the contractions started pulsating through her distended uterus, she groaned and let her legs fold, collapsing heavily into the deep straw piled around her.

Dimly through her pain, she could hear human voices speaking in soothing tones. The box door clanged lightly as it slid open and shut, and the scent of humans and something else, the sharp tang of iodine, wafted through her nostrils. She turned her head, glanced towards her tail, lifted it as something pinkish and elastic began to emerge. Then with another heavy groan she dropped her head and stretched out in the straw, her flanks steaming in the chill air.

An hour later her foal, all legs and whiskers, was balancing comically atop four spindly limbs, his body swaying as if a sudden gust of wind had blown through the insulated box. He made a lurch towards a teat, from which an enticing bauble of warm milk was suspended, and landed flat on his face as his two front legs abruptly splayed out of control. A startling sound: human laughter, then the soothing tones returned along with his dam's guttural nicker, and hands were reaching out to support him. Finally his lips closed over a teat. He let his eyes fall shut as he drew in the rich, life-giving colostrum.

Aside from being a good size, although angular, and having no white markings, the colt did not stand out among the 65 foals born on the stud that winter and spring. As he grew, he quickly learned to control his limbs, to run and twist and buck. But he did not become particularly graceful.

Instead of filling out into a tidily proportioned frame, he grew tall and gangly. He wasn't an ugly little horse, but by no stretch was he a pretty one, what with his strong body and a large head perched on a delicate, swan-like neck. The head didn't seem in sync with the rest of his body, somehow. And his front legs still turned out slightly.

Dalham Hall's stud manager, Liam O'Rourke, had been watching foals develop ever since his childhood days in Ireland, when his father, a vet, kept a few mares of his own. Periodically throughout the spring and summer, O'Rourke took notes on each foal born at the stud, grading them like schoolchildren on their physical conformation and development. To Colorado Dancer's colt he initially gave a grade of C+. But the weanling foal steadily improved, finally earning a B before he was sent to Ireland for his second year. O'Rourke noted that the colt had the frame to make a nice yearling, but at the moment he was just a big, gangly foal who was behind the curve in his development. There was nothing special about him at all.

1. Tony Morris, Thoroughbred Stallions (*Swindon, Wiltshire: The Crowood Press*, 1990), p. 206.
2. Tony Morris, "Fall Aspen was one in a million", *Racing Post*, 10 February 1998.
3. Ibid.

CHAPTER THREE

HORSE WITH TWO NAMES
HOW YAAZER BECAME DUBAI MILLENNIUM

David Loder's first impression of Dubai Millennium was singular. "He's too big," the trainer thought. "You get a great big horse like that, mostly they're no good. It might make a nice jumper or something. But normally they're just too big to cope with Flat racing, or to be any good at it."

There was, in fact, no Dubai Millennium in March of 1998. The big colt who disembarked in Loder's yard was named Yaazer, and it didn't help that he, like the other Godolphin two-year-olds that shipped into Loder's Graham Lodge and Sefton Lodge stables in Newmarket in March, promptly grew a heavy winter coat. The youngsters had wintered in the hot sun of Dubai, and arrived on Newmarket's wet, wind-whipped heaths with sleek summer coats. Their systems reacted swiftly to the change, kicking into survival mode by growing thick natural blankets. But while a warm coat can mean the difference between life and death in the wild, in an English racing stable it calls a halt to serious training. Unfortunately, in

Yaazer's case the survival instinct was particularly strong, and the colt was still furry in July.

Loder could not get over his size. The colt was phenomenally large for his age, and with his thick coat he reminded the trainer of nothing so much as a hunter ready to pack a 12-stone rider and his flask across a frosty winter countryside. One evening in mid-summer Loder was showing a visitor round the stables. They stopped at Yaazer's box, and Loder peered in, but did not open the door. "He was standing there, a great big horse, carrying plenty of condition because he hadn't done a lot of training," Loder remembered. "And I said 'Look, I can't tell you anything about this horse, because he looks like a heavyweight hunter at the moment'."

On top of it all, Yaazer, like the other Godolphin juveniles coming from Dubai, was in soft condition when he arrived on Loder's doorstep. The trainer knew he had his work cut out for him the first time he sent a string of them up Warren Hill, the hillside gallop on the north-east side of town. Trainers usually send their horses up the hill in twos or threes in an easy canter; then the horses walk back down before repeating the exercise at a brisker pace. The Godolphin two-year-olds were all winded before they reached the top.

This was an important year for Loder, and he intended to get these horses into shape. An ambitious 34-year-old with a round, boyish face beneath thinning blond hair, he was now in his sixth year as a fully fledged trainer, and he had already developed a fearsome reputation for his ability to churn out two-year-old winner after two-year-old winner. Not only did he produce winners – these were high-class winners. The first horse Loder ever saddled as a licensed trainer won a Listed race at Newmarket. That signalled his intent: to win, and to win big.

Driving ambition, early success, and a tendency to go your own way do not necessarily win you friends in the staid confines of Newmarket, but Loder did not much care. He had respect, powerful clients and good horses. And he was winning races right, left and centre.

In the late 1990s, Loder's success with two-year-olds dovetailed with a plan of Sheikh Mohammed's, which had taken form at roughly the same time as Godolphin's birth in 1992. Known as 'the Dubai experiment', it involved moving all of the Godolphin horses into Sheikh Mohammed's Al Quoz stables in Dubai over the winter, from the end of one British Flat season in November to the beginning of the next in March.

The start of the Dubai experiment caused something of a local uproar. It meant that top British trainers such as Henry Cecil, Luca Cumani and Sir Michael Stoute, who had promising young horses belonging to Sheikh Mohammed or his brothers in their yards, would lose them to Godolphin's new trainer, Saeed bin Suroor, a soft-spoken man in his 30s who had been handpicked by Sheikh Mohammed from his job in the Dubai police force. While most trainers muffled their discontent, the Dubai experiment initiated a high-profile rupture between Sheikh Mohammed and champion trainer Cecil, following a spat with the trainer's second wife, Natalie, in 1995.

"Henry Cecil is a very good trainer," said the sheikh at an impromptu press conference at Ascot racecourse, when the break-up was announced. "But I want *him* to train my horses, not someone else, and not someone who knows very little about thoroughbred horses."[1]

It wasn't just the control. The sheikh loved his horses, and he wanted to have all of them near to him. "It gives me great pleasure here," he said at Al Quoz one winter, five years after the split with

Cecil. "I can see them from my house. Train them and then come to see them, in the afternoon, or in the evening ... and feel them and touch them and talk to them. This is a great pleasure."[2]

Whatever the effect on the Newmarket trainers, the early racecourse results of the Dubai experiment were so positive that Timeform, the venerable chronicler of British and Irish racing, deemed in its book *Racehorses of 1995* that: "The experiment, to see how horses would react to spending the winter in a warmer climate, has been an unqualified success."

The most memorable result of the 1994-1995 experiment was Lammtarra. Although he raced for Sheikh Mohammed's young nephew Saeed Maktoum Al Maktoum rather than for Godolphin, Lammtarra was trained by bin Suroor under the Godolphin wing. His unbeaten run in the Derby, the King George VI and Queen Elizabeth Diamond Stakes, and the Prix de l'Arc de Triomphe, following a winter in Dubai after he won his only start as a two-year-old for the late trainer Alex Scott, spelled unqualified success for the experiment. Three months in the desert air clearly gave horses an edge, or so it seemed. "Lammtarra confirmed that Sheikh Mohammed's personal project, the 'Dubai experiment', has proved a major breakthrough in the training of racehorses," trumpeted Timeform. "The success of the Godolphin-trained horses worldwide was one of the stories of 1995."

By 1998, Loder, still a private trainer, was receiving all of the Godolphin two-year-olds in his yard. He had handled the early careers of such classy Sheikh Mohammed-owned runners as Blue Duster, who won the Cheveley Park Stakes for two-year-old fillies, Diktat, a top sprinter/miler and later a successful stallion at Dalham Hall, and Starborough, who won the Prix Jean Prat and was retired to stud in France. Loder's reputation for hammering out top-class two-year-olds made him a natural choice for Godolphin, which had only

60 boxes at its Newmarket base at Moulton Paddocks – enough space for the older horses, but not for the youngsters.

In April of 1998, news hit the racing press that Godolphin was to install Loder as the operation's private two-year-old trainer at Evry, a disused racecourse in France, the next spring. It was to be another bold experiment, in line with both Sheikh Mohammed's predilection for such things and with Loder's freethinking tendencies. It also reflected the success the trainer was having with Maktoum-owned horses, and others.

The success continued that summer and into the autumn, when Sheikh Mohammed's Lujain won the Middle Park Stakes, effectively the sprint championship for two-year-old colts, to cap a memorable season for the yard. "They had 60 two-year-olds, and I think ten to 15 of them ended up either winning or placing in Group 1 races," Loder recalled. But the best of Loder's runners that year was Desert Prince, who belonged to his other main client, Edward St George's Lucayan Stud. The colt won the Irish 2,000 Guineas, the Prix du Moulin and the Queen Elizabeth II Stakes, and despite a last-place finish in the Breeders' Cup Mile at Churchill Downs, ended the season as the internationally top-ranked three-year-old miler.

Loder, who has the dry wit of the English public school boy and a habit of cloaking cogent thoughts in a low-key delivery, said he does not know exactly why, sometime between July and September of 1998, he became convinced that the big, furry, unraced colt in his barn was better than Desert Prince – better, indeed, than any horse he had ever laid hands on. It was illogical. To begin with, he was disinclined to trust any horse that size. Second, although the colt had the same sire as Lujain, he didn't particularly like the stallion, Seeking The Gold. Loder thought the sire tended to throw disparate types whose main similarity was a predisposition to unsoundness. Finally, the colt had not done any serious work yet, as Loder had refused to pressure him until he was sleeker and fitter.

However, the trainer didn't need a watch to spot this horse's talent. "I don't judge them on the work necessarily," he said. "I judge them on the canter and work up Warren Hill."

Yaazer, who had earned a reputation as a bit of a Jack-the-lad, was ridden by one of the yard's biggest, strongest work-riders. By August, he was plenty fit to climb the hill at a good brisk pace. "He had one of my head lads on, a big heavy Irish lad," said Loder. "We had a pretty top-class bunch of two-year-olds that year, and when you've got one that's carrying a bit of weight, and it's going with horses that are carrying less weight ... you could see pretty well that he was well above average."

Loder knew he would lose the horse to Godolphin over the winter. Then he would be off to Evry to condition a new pack of unvarnished recruits, while bin Suroor took over the training of this surreally gifted colt. That was the way the deal worked, and Loder accepted it. He was sure Yaazer could win for him first though, and his sharp competitive drive would not allow the horse to leave his yard without that win. "It's always disappointing if you know you're looking down the barrel of a winner and you can't get it," he said when trying to explain his singular focus to score a maiden victory with the colt. "I like to win *every* race."

One thing about Loder – he did things his own way. His method was to start small; then when he knew he had the weapons, he would fire with all chambers loaded. As a general rule he preferred to send his debutants to a quiet racecourse like Nottingham, Leicester or Yarmouth, where they could have a nice easy introduction. Just occasionally, though, he felt one was good enough to make its debut at a splashier course, like Newmarket, Ascot, or Newbury.

Loder had a plan for Yaazer. Newbury held a three-day meeting in late September, highlighted by the Mill Reef Stakes, one of the more prestigious autumn contests for two-year-olds, on the final day. Two of the races on the opening card were sponsored by Dubai businesses – the Dubai Duty Free Cup and the Dubai Airport World Trophy. Although they were only Listed races, they carried just about as much prize-money as the Mill Reef. The first race on the card was the Racing Welfare Charities, British Sporting Art Trust Maiden Stakes, and it too was unusually valuable for the type, worth more than £11,500 to the winner – about three times as much as an average British maiden. Loder's plan was to win the hefty maiden prize. His heart was set on it, and he waited anxiously for the Saturday before the race, when he could submit the colt's entry.

But like so many well-laid plans, this one met with a hitch. Sheikh Mohammed had also been laying plans, and on Friday he arrived in the yard with a question for his trainer. Bypassing the small talk, he walked straight up to Loder, directed his mesmerising gaze upon him, and asked: "Which is the best two-year-old you've got in the yard?"

Loder may have liked to start his horses cautiously, but he was also given to bold predictions. He did not hesitate. Pointing to Yaazer, who had finally shed his winter coat and was growing into his generous frame, he replied: "He's not only the best two-year-old here, he's the best horse I've ever had."

Without skipping a beat, Sheikh Mohammed told Loder: "In that case I will change his name."

The trainer's heart sank. He knew that it would take at least two working days to register a new name, and that the horse could not be entered the next day as Yaazer if his name was going to be changed. Once a horse races, it is stuck with its name forever, in all but extraordinary circumstances.

Sheikh Mohammed knew this too, which was why his question to Loder was so important. If he gave this name, a special, gifted name, to the wrong horse, the mistake would be irrevocable. Despite the gravity of the moment, the sheikh showed absolute faith in his trainer's judgement.

The owner's trust was especially remarkable because this was the first time he had visited Yaazer since he arrived at Graham Lodge. "He hadn't seen the horse before," Loder said. "He had come up to the yard before, but I hadn't shown him the horse because he was just too backward to bother looking at."

Sheikh Mohammed had either uncanny prescience or a huge helping of luck that evening. Either way the naming of Dubai Millennium happened by virtue of one thing – the sheikh's bold and uncompromising vision. Nothing was more characteristic of him than that audacious leap into the future. Gambling for money may be forbidden in Dubai, but gambling to win is a natural act for Sheikh Mohammed, whose reward, if he wins, is being proved right.

The Crown Prince of Dubai left the yard and returned to his house, where he called a meeting with his advisers in the majlis, a traditional meeting area, of his Newmarket home. The question was what to name the special horse. According to his racing adviser Simon Crisford, "There was no indication at any time prior to that meeting that he was going to call a horse Dubai Millennium. There was just no indication. It was that horse in particular. When his talent had been identified, Sheikh Mohammed decided at that point that he wanted to change his name. So the question was, 'Well, what are we going to change his name to?' We were all sitting around, and Sheikh Mohammed came up with the name Dubai Millennium."

Crisford was not at all surprised that the big colt called Yaazer had been marked out for greatness. He remembered him as a charismatic yearling. Recalling the previous winter in Dubai, he said: "Even at that stage, he had an incredible presence about himself. He looked very aristocratic, he looked incredibly noble, he looked incredibly bright, in his demeanour and his attitude to life. He had a very joyous disposition, quite playful."

Crisford had also visited the colt with Loder in Newmarket, and had been impressed by his action on the gallops. "He'd always been a very powerful horse. And he was one of those types of horses that when he was working, you would just see that he would devour the ground. He was so powerful that you knew certainly that the ability was there. The question was how much – how far could he go?"

Sheikh Mohammed was convinced that the horse could go at least a mile and a quarter – the distance of the Dubai World Cup. He chose the name Dubai Millennium with the idea that the colt would win the world's richest race, his creation, before an enthralled international crowd in the year 2000, when the colt was a four-year-old. "It's not the only reason he was called Dubai Millennium," Crisford said. "But it tied in very neatly with the idea that he was always going to be a better four-year-old than a three-year-old, and it tied in very neatly with everything that Sheikh Mohammed thought about the horse. He would have had it in his mind, no doubt about that."

Now David Loder had a problem. His vision was on an altogether different scale to the sheikh's; it was smaller. When his employer told him of his plan, "all I remember is being bitterly disappointed because I wasn't going to be able to run him on Saturday," he recollected. "That was all I cared about." His immediate response to Sheikh Mohammed was not what the boss was accustomed to hearing. "I wouldn't do that sir, because I want to enter the horse," he said.

His plea was to no avail, but still he wouldn't give up the idea of the Newbury maiden. That night Loder rang up Crisford. "Oh, please talk him out of changing the horse's name, because he'll win next Thursday," he begged.

"No, no, no, no, the boss wants to change his name," Crisford replied in a voice that brooked little sympathy. The racing manager knew there were bigger fish to fry than a maiden race, whatever the prize-money.

As luck would have it, the next morning, Saturday, the colt soon to be known as Dubai Millennium came up with a set of sore shins. There would be no Newbury race for him anyway. Instead Loder entered a colt named Berlioz. Such was the stable's form that Berlioz, making his first start, went off at odds of 1-2, while 14 horses in the 23-strong field were valued at 50-1 or greater. Canyonlands, a colt owned by Sheikh Mohammed and trained by Sir Michael Stoute, finished second, and Loder was pleased that he had bagged the prize. "We won with Berlioz, so it didn't matter about the name change," he said, single-minded as ever.

Nonetheless, he was still going to send Dubai Millennium out a winner. After giving the colt's shins time to cool out, he selected a race at Great Yarmouth, a placid track by the beach resort of the same name on the Norfolk coast. The race, the South Norfolk Caterers Maiden Stakes, was scheduled for late October, and the added month's training only bolstered Loder's belief that this horse was the real deal. So confident was he that the night before the race he called up Richard Evans, the racing correspondent for the *Daily Telegraph*.

"I think you want to take a price about this horse for the Derby," he told Evans, "because I'm pretty sure he'll win it."

All went swimmingly as Evans availed himself of big double-digit odds for an ante-post Derby bet on the unraced colt. October 28 was a blustery day on the coast, and the trees clung to their last leaves in the wan autumn sun. The few people who turned up at Yarmouth racecourse wore padded jackets and caps. They tucked their cold knuckles into their pockets, oblivious to the outrageous dreams that were clip-clopping past them.

Wearing a shadow roll – a round of faux sheepskin that fits over the noseband of the bridle and is supposed to prevent horses from being distracted by things on the ground – Dubai Millennium was loaded into the starting stalls. He was carrying Godolphin's stable jockey Frankie Dettori, who for the first time ever had been allowed off a Godolphin runner, Blue Snake, at the urgent behest of Loder. The jockey was wearing Sheikh Mohammed's maroon and white silks, and carrying a mighty load of hope.

Blue Snake, a colt who had shown a penchant for making the running in two previous starts for Godolphin, immediately flashed to the lead and cut out a strong early pace. A quarter-mile from home, Dettori set Dubai Millennium down for the drive. The result was like throwing a Ferrari into gear amid five lanes of Volkswagens. His muscles bunching, the colt shot past his rivals. If there had been any dust, they wouldn't have got close enough to eat it.

Dubai Millennium's official winning distance was five lengths, but he could have doubled the margin according to the *Racing Post*'s analyst Tom Goff. His verdict sent happy shivers up Evans's spine: "Dubai Millennium simply destroyed his rivals here, and could have won by more than ten lengths if he was not eased down by Dettori in the closing stages. He looks like a serious Derby horse."

1.   Robert Henwood, "A Kingdom for Their Horses", *The Blood-Horse*, 16 March 1996.
2.   BBC video archives, Sheikh Mohammed interviewed by Clare Balding, 25 March 2000.

CHAPTER FOUR

WINTER

A week after his romp at Yarmouth, Dubai Millennium was flown to Dubai to join Godolphin. At Sheikh Mohammed's Al Quoz stables he would be prepared, under the meticulously watchful eyes of Saeed bin Suroor, the Dubaian trainer's American assistant Tom Albertrani, and Simon Crisford, to win the British Classics, starting with the 2,000 Guineas at the beginning of May.

That was the plan, anyway. Within days after his arrival, the plan was already going wrong. On November 18, an ultrasound scan revealed that the colt had a lesion and some scar tissue on a tendon. While the injury was considered minor, any tendon lesion is potentially career threatening, and so Dubai Millennium's introduction to Al Quoz was an unexpectedly quiet one. The colt was put on the easy list, and it was only in springtime that he was allowed to do more than light work under rider Lee Roebuck.

By this time the Guineas was only a couple of months away, but such was the team's faith in the colt that the British Classic race was not ruled out.

To bin Suroor, Dubai Millennium was an exceptionally beautiful animal, the kind that comes along only rarely. The trainer first saw the colt shortly after they had both arrived in Dubai, and he immediately broke into a broad smile – an expression which is never far from bin Suroor's friendly, bearded face. Unusually for a horse trainer, whose quotidian experiences with the fragile animals in their care tend to make them prone to bouts of cynicism, bin Suroor has an even temperament and a sunny disposition. This is just as well, given the unique pressures that are brought to bear on Godolphin's head trainer.

One of the tribulations bin Suroor initially had to contend with, ironically, was that some people whispered he was not under any pressure – at least not the normal day-to-day decision-making pressures of a racehorse trainer. He was, they said, a mere figurehead for Sheikh Mohammed, a puppet picked from the police force to be dangled in front of the public, opening his mouth to speak only the boss's words.

Bin Suroor's answer to the rumours was to ignore them. He was grateful for his job, grateful most of all to have a leader like Sheikh Mohammed. He believed that Godolphin had the best owner in the world. "Sheikh Mohammed understands horses, and he understands his people," bin Suroor said one morning in his office at Godolphin Stables. "He knows everybody tries to do their best for his company, and we do try to do the best for our boss."

It was the vision the Godolphin leader instilled in his team that the trainer appreciated most. "Even if you lose, he gives you confidence about the future. You may lose the race, but he doesn't think only for this moment, he thinks for the future. He gives you a chance – not chance, something more than chance. Something like confidence to plan ahead. And that makes our job easy."

So he continued training and let the results speak for themselves. Perhaps the reason the whisperers were so sure bin Suroor was not under strain was that he always showed up in public with this smile – his response to both happiness and pressure. However, he was not immune to the latter.

"The pressure is always in racing," he said, trying to describe his feelings. "You can hide it, you can put on a smile, like I do, but the pressure is in the heart. It's inside the body. You can't hide it from yourself."

But when he saw Dubai Millennium, his natural optimism couldn't help but flow through. The horse was only a maiden winner, he cautioned himself. There are millions of horses that win maidens everywhere in the world. Nonetheless, while admiring the colt's statuesque frame, his striking head and his extraordinarily bright eye, he thought: "He will be a special horse one day."

"It's not easy to find a horse who, before he runs, just looks like such a beautiful animal," he said. "His eyes, his ears, his face, his neck, his body, his legs – he looked like something special. When he was cantering, the way he moved, he looked like he would be something really good."

Tom Albertrani, too, noticed something out of the ordinary about the big colt. The 41-year-old had been hooked by the racing game at the age of 13, when he started hanging out at the Belmont Park track in his native New York. He would lead the horses around after they came back from exercise until they cooled out – walking hots, they called it. Later he graduated to grooming, and learned the most important skills a racing horseman can have – how to detect the first signs of heat or swelling in a leg, and how to apply the myriad potions and bandages to keep the delicate front limbs in working order.

What Albertrani really wanted to be was a jockey. He was just small enough, and when he was 18, he turned to race-riding, but by the time he was in his early 20s he was back on the ground, eventually landing a job as assistant to trainer Bill Mott. The years he spent with Mott were a seminal period – he met his wife, Fonda, who was Cigar's exercise rider, there. And of course there was Cigar. By the time the great horse won the inaugural Dubai World Cup, though, Albertrani was already working for Godolphin. He had flown to Dubai two days after Cigar won the Breeders' Cup Classic at Belmont Park, Albertrani's old stomping grounds.

Dubai was completely new territory to him – he had to dig up an atlas to find out what part of the world he was moving his young family to. Once there, he found it didn't really matter where Dubai was in relation to anything else. It was unlike any other place on earth. Al Quoz, though, was similar to any other top-class racing stable, and Albertrani brought many of his American touches with him – fitting insulated boots filled with ice on the horses' legs before and after training, rubbing them with alcohol, and wrapping them in protective bandages at night.

Dubai Millennium was one of the horses who would get ice boots on his legs, before he went out with the first lot each morning. Right from the start, he caught Albertrani's eye. He was a magnificent looking horse, and he had a presence about him, something that jumped out and grabbed you, even just walking past his box.

The winter days in the desert passed uneventfully. Stables live by simple routines, and Dubai Millennium's schedule did not vary much. Breakfast came before the sun rose, then the nightwatchman would come and take the feed tubs out of the boxes. At 5.30 the grooms would pull off the bandages and meticulously check the horses' legs. At 6.30 first lot would head out for a warm-up jog, with riders and trainers again checking for the least sign of lameness. Then a canter around the sandy oval track, followed by half an hour of hand-walking to cool out. Finally the horses' all-important legs would be massaged and wrapped up again.

In the evenings, the horses would be taken out for a breath of fresh air. In England, they would have had a pick of green grass, but in the desert, they had to settle for a walk. So it went, day in and day out. Beneath the placid and well-organised routines of Al Quoz, though, something raw and passionate was brewing.

Sheikh Mohammed had always been a hands-on horseman. Like many racehorse owners, he enjoyed not only racing but the animals themselves. He and his brothers had been taught to ride by Sheikh Rashid when they were young, and horse riding had always been his favourite sport.

More than sport, though, horses were a heritage. To Sheikh Mohammed, they symbolised a history both personal and cultural. When he looked at Dubai Millennium, he saw the horse's Arabian ancestry in his head in particular. It was a fine, pretty head, not big and coarse like some animals.

The sheikh also admired the colt's sloping shoulder, his generous deep girth and the powerful muscles extending down his hindquarters. This was a horse who embodied the athleticism, the strength and finesse that three centuries of thoroughbred breeding had strived to perfect.

Finally, there was the colt's personality. Dubai Millennium was fiery, but he also had a playful side, and he was clearly intelligent. He liked to stick out his tongue and let Sheikh Mohammed pull on it. It was a little game they played, and the colt would become downright cantankerous if the sheikh didn't join in. But once pacified, he was content to stand for hours with his owner, seeming to take comfort in the human presence. In this, too, he was like his Arab ancestors.

The sheikh's equine advisers and trainers all noticed the blossoming relationship. Most remarkable of all was the way the horse, who had been known to pin people against the wall in his box or come after them with his teeth bared, would calm down when his owner entered. They had never seen anything quite like it before.

In April the Godolphin trials rolled around. While the British press marked these as an event on the calendar, Crisford, a former journalist whose many responsibilities included handling Godolphin's relations with the press, played down their significance. This was just "a little run round Nad Al Sheba".

Fitness-wise, Dubai Millennium was way behind schedule. To gauge just how far behind – and whether his sheer physical superiority might see him through a Guineas campaign anyway – he was put in the stalls at Nad Al Sheba with a group of Godolphin runners including Island Sands and Adair, two recruits bought privately at the end of the last season.

Island Sands had come from a shrewd trainer named David Elsworth. The colt, no earthshaker in terms of looks or pedigree, had originally cost Elsworth just 18,000 Irish guineas as a yearling. He had won both of his races as a two-year-old, and Elsworth had spoken of him as a Guineas horse from the time he won a maiden race at Salisbury, a minor track in the south of England, in August. No wonder, then, that Sheikh Mohammed had snapped him up for Godolphin.

Adair had won his only race, a maiden at Belmont Park in New York, in October. There were only three horses in that race, but Adair came with other credentials: he was owned and bred by Cigar's owner-breeder, Allen Paulson; he was ridden by top US jockey Jerry Bailey, with whom Godolphin had a close working relationship; and he was by Theatrical, an outstanding runner in both Europe and the US, suggesting that he would thrive on European turf.

Island Sands was Godolphin's leading Guineas hope, while Adair was the pick of the Derby contenders. In spite of Crisford's valiant effort to downplay the trial, it was clearly more than a regular gallop. Frankie Dettori chose Island Sands as his mount, underlining the team's increasing doubt that Dubai Millennium would make the starting line-up at Newmarket.

Jockey Daragh O'Donohoe was aboard the big colt. "Just pop him out of the gates, get him in between horses and then take him easy," he was instructed.

The gates opened, the horses burst out and Dubai Millennium took a strong hold as expected. But after five furlongs he buckled. He was beaten by four horses, including the favoured pair. Island Sands was the 'winner', with Adair two and a half lengths behind after finally revving into gear off a slow start. Crisford, Albertrani and bin Suroor, watching, could read the writing on the wall: there would be no Guineas for Dubai Millennium.

"We knew he was going to go four furlongs and get tired," said Crisford, shrugging off the suggestion of disappointment. "And that's what happened."

Back in Britain, the public was anxious to hear the results of the trial, but to their frustration, no-one was able to watch it.

"We didn't release a video of the trial, because unless we issued a 1,000-word essay on exactly how every horse had wintered, the bare viewing of the video would be misleading to most people," said Crisford in excuse.

His statement rang with, if not irritation, a somewhat frustrated resignation that comes from the constant interplay between the public's need to know and the trainer's need to train. With a big operation like Godolphin, the public scrutiny was relentless, and while publicity after a big win was welcome, the intrusion into training hours could be irksome. When the general public was fed morsels of information on what went on behind the scenes, it inevitably re-proved the maxim that a little learning is a dangerous thing. Such had been the case with racehorses, their trainers and the public from time immemorial. After Seabiscuit threw in a slow workout at Belmont, for instance, the *New York Daily Mirror* demanded an investigation by racing officials.[1]

The problem had not gone away with the advent of high-tech, high-speed communications. The Godolphin website duly published updates on its horses, but these were controlled, of course, by Godolphin. The press was as hungry as ever for a good story, the public still ready to believe the wool was being pulled over its eyes. The issue of the April 1999 Godolphin trials was a minor one in the scheme of public/trainer relations, but it showed how uneasy the relationship could be.

Thirty Godolphin horses, including all of the Guineas contenders, winged back to England on April 25. The seven-hour flight from Dubai to Heathrow airport was followed by a two-hour road trip to Newmarket. Disembarking on the softly green English turf at Moulton Paddocks, the string of horses, their coats sleek and fine after six months in the middle-eastern sun, seemed immune to the change in climate. Some of them raised their heads and whinnied as they sensed the new surroundings. It was good to stretch their legs at last, and one or two pranced sideways, although most were leg-weary from the trip and walked docilely as they were led to their spacious new boxes.

Most of the work-riders made the trip too, but Lee Roebuck had gone on to the US, where Godolphin was fielding its $5 million colt Worldly Manner in the Kentucky Derby. The headstrong Dubai Millennium needed a skilled new rider, someone with strong arms but sensitive hands, who wouldn't bully the colt or be bullied by him. Tony Proctor, a former jockey who had been with Godolphin for a year, was selected as the man for the job.

At 28, Proctor had spent more than half of his life riding racehorses. Born in Newbury, he began riding out for David Elsworth, the former trainer of Island Sands, when he was 13. It was a natural progression for Proctor, whose father Brian had been a jockey and work-rider for Major Dick Hern, and now rode out for Godolphin. Although Brian Proctor had not encouraged his son to follow in his steps as a boy, he had long since accepted Tony's career, and it was he who had put in an application for his son to join Godolphin.

For Tony, there was never any doubt what he would do. Horses were a calling, not a choice, and his father was his hero.

"If I rode half as well as he did, I'd be happy," he said, proudly describing his father's career. Brian Proctor had ridden work on some of the all-time greats – Troy, who won the 200th Derby in 1979; Henbit, who won the 1980 Derby; and the great Nashwan, who swept England's most prestigious Group 1s in the summer of 1989.

Tony Proctor's early path took him to an altogether different neighbourhood. Although he got on some good horses, and for Elsworth rode the famous stayer Persian Punch to his first race victory, he soon found his career going the way of too many others: riding lots of bad jumpers, concerned mainly with whether he would get round the course in one piece or not.

His problem was partly one of size; he was a couple of inches too tall to easily make the weight of a Flat-race jockey, but too slight in build compared to the more robust jump jockeys. When he rode a jumper, the trainer often had to pack his horse's saddle with lead to make up the weight. Trainers prefer the weight of a live jockey, which can be intelligently redistributed, to dead weight.

All in all, Proctor wasn't having much fun. Beneath an earnest face, he had a quietly playful side, but that was being squashed under the weight of, face it, failure. He was feeling disillusioned and worried that, before he hit 30, he was losing the enthusiasm that had fuelled his whole life up to now.

Then the phone rang. "Tony, you're going to get a call from Godolphin," Brian Proctor told his son. "I've put in your application and they want you."

This would be a life-changing course of events – Tony knew that immediately. He had a steady job with trainer Roland O'Sullivan and was fond of the man, but there was no doubt about his answer to Godolphin. The afternoon of the call-up, he went outside to look for O'Sullivan. Spotting him, he sat down on a wall that bisected the yard. "Roland, we need to have a chat," he told his boss.

"It's bad news, isn't it?" answered O'Sullivan.

"Well, I'm leaving, but it's not all bad," said Proctor.

To most jockeys in most situations, a move from race-riding to work-riding is a step down in the world. Not so for Godolphin's work-riders, most of whom are ex-jockeys. They ride some of the world's best racehorses each day, and that is all they do. Unlike the typical English stable lad, they do not muck out, groom, cool out or otherwise care for their horses aside from returning some evenings to take the horses out for hard-grazing. In the American style, their job begins and ends with riding the horse – the difference being, that Godolphin's 30 work riders get on just two horses each day. American exercise riders typically have five to ten mounts per day.

There was no job in racing that compared to it – Proctor knew that. It was easy money, and although he missed the thrill of race-riding at its best, he did not miss the slow and wayward horses, the bad weather and the spills. His life had taken a steadier turn; he was engaged now to Sam, whom he had met while working for O'Sullivan, and the adrenalin rush of racing was a thing of the past. Or so he thought.

One morning soon after the team returned from Dubai, bin Suroor and Albertrani took the horses to the far side of town, called the racecourse side gallops because of their proximity to Newmarket's two racecourses. A thick fog blanketed the land, which stretched out flat and unprotected for miles. People often joked that the wind blew straight from Siberia to Newmarket, so cold did the exposed Rowley Mile racecourse often feel, even in summer.

Dubai Millennium, with Proctor aboard, was to have his first extended gallop since arriving in Newmarket. His workmates were Blue Snake, who had finished 20 lengths behind Dubai Millennium at Yarmouth, but was a useful workhorse with good speed, and Mukhalif. Ridden this morning by Tom Manning, Mukhalif had won both of his starts as a two-year-old and had been Godolphin's first runner of the year, when he finished a good second at Newmarket to Beat All, a leading Derby fancy.

Blue Snake's rider John Phelan and Manning were both seasoned work-riders. The plan was to let Blue Snake set the pace, while Dubai Millennium dropped in behind the other pair. Swallowed by the fog, Phelan let his horse set a brutal clip. It was fast, too fast, all three riders knew, but they were hidden from the eagle eyes of the trainers, and horses and riders alike were relishing their speed through the cold morning air.

They roared into the 'Dip', the beginning of an uphill climb that notoriously separated the men from the boys at Newmarket races. Proctor, feeling a mountain of strength under him, urged his colt forward. The result was electrifying. Dubai Millennium went from a stiff gallop into running-away mode, swinging between Blue Snake and Mukhalif and leaving them for dead.

When they finally pulled up, a breathless Phelan turned to the other two. "Don't tell them I went too quick," he pleaded. He and the other riders knew you could set a horse's programme back, even injure it with too fast a gallop, especially with inexperienced horses so early in the year.

Manning had something else on his mind. "What is that?" he said to Proctor, indicating the big colt, who was barely winded. "I've never seen anything come upsides me after going so quick like that did."

As the three drifted back across the heath towards the rest of the string, their horses blowing great breaths of steam now in the chill air, Proctor's mind was humming. "Yeah," he thought, "this horse is a little bit special."

1.   Laura Hillenbrand, *Seabiscuit*, (London: Fourth Estate, 2001), p. 209.

CHAPTER FIVE

OVER THE EDGE IN THE DERBY

Nothing happened between winter and late spring to change the Godolphin team's belief that it had a gifted horse on its hands. But Dubai Millennium needed a race, and he was entered in a conditions contest at Doncaster, the Yorkshire racecourse famous for staging the St Leger, on 3 May.

The field for the race came up soft, but unfortunately the ground did not. The footing was good to firm, which didn't suit the big colt – his round action and heavy frame were more comfortable with some give underfoot. The timing at least was right, early enough that he could still run in one of the traditional Derby prep races, if he came through his blowout all right.

Tony Proctor, who was on board the colt every day and knew him intimately by now, couldn't see him getting beat. For a betting man, this was buying money. The public thought so too, and made Dubai Millennium the 4-6 favourite in a field of four. Despite the ground, he far outclassed his rivals, and sauntered to a nine-length win under Frankie Dettori, who needed to do little more than steer.

In the event, it really didn't matter that the only horse in the field to win subsequently was last-placed Adelphi Boy, who seven years later was racing over hurdles.

It was now time for step two, a more ambitious move up the ladder. Since Dubai Millennium had missed the 2,000 Guineas – won by Island Sands, his conqueror in the Godolphin trials at Nad Al Sheba – the obvious target was the Derby. However, the Godolphin camp was conflicted over the race. They were concerned he had too much speed, both in his style of racing and in his pedigree.

His sire, Seeking The Gold, was best known in Europe for siring two top horses: Godolphin's swift two-year-old Lujain, and the brilliant filly Seeking The Pearl, who shocked the European racing world by shipping in from Japan to win the Group 1 Prix Maurice de Gheest, a race run over barely more than half the distance of the Derby.

In the United States, Seeking The Gold had sired such horses as Heavenly Prize and Cape Town, Grade 1 winners over distances up to a mile and a quarter. But American races require less stamina and more speed than European races over similar distances, and the extra quarter-mile of the Derby, over Epsom's rollercoaster course, was something else again. It demanded stamina and balance as well as speed.

There was also the matter of Dubai Millennium's intransigence. The colt had a free-running style and a headstrong personality. It endeared him to some of the Godolphin staff, like Proctor, who began to live for the mornings and the buzz that came with riding the colt. To others, his grooms for instance, he could be a real chore to work with.

It was decided that the racecourse would have to be the ultimate testing ground in the speed versus stamina debate, and two weeks after his Doncaster romp, Dubai Millennium prepared to enter the stalls at Goodwood. He was entered in the Predominate Stakes, a race run over a mile and a quarter – a quarter-mile less than the Derby. The ground this time was more to his liking, and although the official going description was good, Dettori judged it was riding good to soft.

On a grey and otherwise lacklustre day, the pair faced five other runners, including Godolphin's Clodion, entered as a pacesetter. Clodion kept to his task of cutting out an honest pace under Daragh O'Donohoe, while Dettori assured Dubai Millennium was covered up at the rear of the field against the rail. Coming down the hill into the straight, O'Donohoe, still in the lead, snuck a quick look back to see where his stablemate was. Dettori had pulled his colt off the rail, but he was still near last position, with the speedy Coventry Stakes winner Red Sea to his inside.

Suddenly Dubai Millennium was looming on the outside, Dettori perched as high in the irons as if he were out for a morning breeze. They were inhaling horses, and as they passed Clodion, the jockey finally crouched down for the drive. His horse's momentum was already well under way, and he shifted sharply right towards the rail. Dettori felt that Dubai Millennium wasn't finishing properly, but he was far enough in front, three and a half lengths at the finish, that there was no point quibbling. You could make a case for him staying a further two furlongs if you wanted to.

The Godolphin team badly wanted to, in spite of a few lingering reservations. Excitement and optimism mostly succeeded in drowning these out. "At that time we all got sucked into making ourselves believe that he would stay and he'd be fine and get the trip," said Crisford later.

Unbeaten in three races, and with two winters in Dubai under his belt, the colt was still a big baby. The team had tried to give him various types of experience – the straight course at Yarmouth, a left-handed one at Doncaster and Goodwood's rolling right-turning course – but he was still prone to antics such as pulling too hard or drifting, both of which he'd done in the Predominate.

At Epsom, he showed a side Godolphin hadn't seen before, and hoped not to see again. Heading into the race, they were in good spirits. Six days earlier they had sent Mukhalif, Dubai Millennium's sometimes work companion, to the Capannelle in Rome to win the Derby Italiano. The victory represented another landmark for Dettori, whose father had won the race before him. He was a man with dreams fulfilled lined up like freshly minted trophies on the shelves of his young life. The Epsom Derby, though, was not among them – yet.

Dettori had been second aboard Sheikh Mohammed's Tamure when Walter Swinburn rode Lammtarra to his historic victory in 1995. The next year he was third on Sheikh Mohammed's Shantou, as jockey Michael Hills guided Shaamit to victory. In 1997 he finished ninth, 25 lengths behind Benny The Dip, on Godolphin's 20-1 shot Bold Demand.

Most depressing of all was 1998, when he was again a well-beaten ninth. He had entered the race amidst high hopes for Cape Verdi, Godolphin's wide-margin 1,000 Guineas winner. The Oaks would have been a more natural spot for the talented filly, who had won the Lowther Stakes at two and then spent the winter in Dubai.

Entering her in the Derby, a race won by only five fillies since its inception in 1780, was a trademark Sheikh Mohammed move: bold and iconoclastic to some eyes, bordering on folly to others. True, there had been a golden spell for female Derby runners in the early twentieth century, oddly coinciding with the suffragettes movement. Emily Wilding Davison threw herself in protest under

King George V's colt Anmer in the 1913 Derby, bringing the horse down and suffering fatal injuries herself, a year after the filly Tagalie became the fourth female to win the race, and three years before Sir Edward Hulton's filly Fifinella won.

But not one filly had won the Blue Riband since then. Entering Cape Verdi in the Derby was both a sporting gesture and an audacious one. The public believed in Godolphin, though, and they believed in Cape Verdi. They made her the Derby favourite, and it was deeply disappointing for Sheikh Mohammed's team when she did not stay the trip and was comprehensively beaten by High-Rise, owned by the sheikh's cousin, Sheikh Mohammed Obaid Al Maktoum.

High-Rise subsequently joined Godolphin. But to Dettori, the main upshot of the 1998 race was that the Derby remained the only British Classic not on his CV. He longed to fill in the gap in bold black ink.

Saturday 5 June 1999; dawned grey and chilly. A day earlier it had rained on the Oaks, won by Saudi Arabian Prince Fahd Salman's rapidly progressing filly Ramruma for the sizzling-hot trainer/jockey combination of Henry Cecil and Kieren Fallon.

Dettori had ridden Godolphin's Zahrat Dubai, the favourite, to a distant third place finish in the Oaks. Today he would be favoured to win again, as Dubai Millennium was already trading at 5-1, the shortest odds of the 16 Derby runners. Revenge would be sweet – but would the colt stay, after all? Or would Godolphin suffer another disheartening Cape Verdi scenario?

Cecil and Fallon were teamed up again, this time with Oath, owned by Prince Fahd's brother Prince Ahmed. The colt, who had cost his owner 450,000 guineas as a yearling, was also popular in the betting ring.

The runners gathered in the stable yard for a pre-parade before heading down to the parade ring proper. It was soon clear that Dubai Millennium was not going to behave like a well-mannered racehorse. Spring was in the air, and he had other things on his mind.

"He was thinking about the mares or something, and he was coltish," said bin Suroor. "In my heart I said, 'I hope I'm wrong'. But this is the Derby, and it's not an easy race."

"He got very, very horny," Proctor affirmed. "He was very on his toes, which he hadn't really ever been before. He was normally a fairly laid-back sort of horse in that sense."

"As soon as he walked into the paddock at Epsom it was obvious to all of us that the occasion had really got to him," said Crisford. "His eyes were popping out of his head and he was getting too warm and he was on his toes, and he was just a little bit buzzed up. Not a little bit, he was a lot buzzed up."

After moving into the parade ring, with fans piled along the paddock rail and the inner grassy area filling with owners, trainers and television cameras, Dubai Millennium seemed to calm down. Like most of the runners, he had two handlers, one on either side of his head. But he strode confidently and easily around the ring. The public continued to put their money on him.

In spite of that, a case could be made for many of the runners. Oath had sprung to prominence when winning the Dee Stakes at Chester a month earlier, in a style that promised he would stay the Derby trip. What's more, his trainer and jockey combination were on fire; they had already won two of the season's Classics, including the 1,000 Guineas with Saudi Arabian Prince Khalid Abdullah's Wince, as well as the Oaks.

Sir Michael Stoute had entered Saeed Suhail's Beat All, a lightly raced but promising American-bred colt who had beaten Mukhalif soundly in April. Unraced since, he had just recovered from a hoof problem and would be ridden by Gary Stevens, who was freshly arrived from California. One of America's top jockeys, Stevens was starting anew, with a new English wife and a new job as Stoute's stable jockey. A win in the Derby would get the ball rolling nicely.

Lucido had been re-entered at a cost of £75,000 after his owner, Hildegard Focke, and trainer, John Dunlop, had let his original entry lapse. The son of the Breeders' Cup Mile winner Royal Academy had redeemed himself from a drubbing in a German Group 3 the previous autumn with two wins in the spring, beating Oath in a conditions race at Newbury and then Daliapour in the Derby Trial Stakes at Lingfield.

Daliapour, saddled by last year's winning trainer Cumani, was also in the line-up. His French rider, Gerald Mosse, had put up 2lb overweight in the Derby Trial, but there would be no such problem today, with all the riders weighing in at 9st. Daliapour, who was dancing on his toes as the horses paraded around while waiting for their jockeys, was attracting fair support at 8-1.

Another likely prospect, if he stayed the trip, was Saffron Walden, winner of the Irish 2,000 Guineas for Aidan O'Brien. Owned by Sue Magnier, the wife of Coolmore maestro John Magnier, Saffron Walden had just been granted the unusual privilege of a name change midway through his career. It had nothing like the import of Dubai Millennium's name change, though; his owner had petitioned to have the 'e' in Walden changed from an 'o', as it had been registered, to match the spelling of the Suffolk market town.

Godolphin's Adair, who would be ridden by Daragh O'Donohoe, was one of the longer shots in the field. At even longer odds was All The Way, a son of 1978 Derby winner Shirley Heights. All The Way, who was trained locally at Epsom by Terry Mills, had finished second to the Oaks winner Ramruma in a maiden race in April. He returned in May to win a minor event, but the bookmakers were taking no chances so close to the Derby, and had slashed his ante-post odds from 100-1 to 25-1. Punters were not so keen on his chances now, though, and his price had lengthened.

The horses continued to circle the ring, most walking calmly now despite the palpable excitement in the air. Sheikh Mohammed, dressed in grey trousers, top hat and tails, stood anomalously alone in the centre, watching them go round. Although the skies remained grey he was wearing dark glasses, and as Dubai Millennium passed by, he rubbed his hands together, glanced around and removed the glasses, dangling them in his hand.

The riders arrived, were legged up and as the bugle call sounded, horses and jockeys began the final parade to post, walking past the stands before turning and galloping off towards the starting stalls on the far side of the course.

Dubai Millennium had paraded coolly enough in the end, but when Dettori let him into a gallop he immediately grabbed the bit. The colt seemed upset and he was galloping too freely, Dettori noted with some misgiving.

By the time they were met at the stalls by Tony Proctor, who had been summoned for extra support, Dubai Millennium was quite warm. So was Saffron Walden, whose odds had suddenly tightened, although the colt was now dripping with sweat. While this could have been due to a sudden injection of public confidence, a drop in odds was not an altogether unusual turn of events for horses owned by Coolmore, one of whose partners, Michael Tabor, was a former bookmaker renowned for his quietly audacious gambles.

Oath, wearing the distinctive white bridle that Ahmed Salman preferred for his horses, had been more stirred up in the paddock than anybody, prancing and sweating. Cecil and Fallon had decided to break ranks in the traditional parade and gallop him to post early, risking a fine from the Epsom authorities. Whatever the officials thought of it, the plan worked, and Oath was standing calmly now. He would be the last to load.

The handlers began leading horses into the stalls, coaxing or pushing as required. Dubai Millennium was one of the early ones loaded and he walked compliantly into stall two. Dettori, waiting as patiently as he could, reached down to adjust his left iron. Like the boss, he was wearing shades – dark goggles, actually. Finally, Oath was ushered into stall one, immediately to Dubai Millennium's left. Fallon fine-tuned the fit of his yellow goggles and secured his whip in his left hand as the back doors slammed shut behind him. They had been edgy before, but both horses were remarkably quiet now as they stood in the tight metal compartments. Nor did the two jockeys show any emotion, or even acknowledge each other, both staring intently ahead in the long moment before the stalls popped open.

It was a good clean break and the pair of colts raced side by side as the field tacked over to the right, towards the rail. All The Way, under Irish jockey Johnny Murtagh, sped up to set the pace. Right behind him ranged Salford Express, an entry from the Elsworth stable ridden by the most experienced Derby jockey in the field, Pat Eddery. Also looming were Housemaster, an entry from the Highclere Thoroughbred Racing syndicate ridden by Willie Ryan, and Sheikh Mohammed's Glamis, under Ray Cochrane.

Oath had taken a keen hold but had nonetheless settled for Fallon, and held a good position a few lengths off the leaders. Dubai Millennium, however, was already fighting his jockey, flipping his head up and down, trying to shake loose from the bridle's restraint.

As the field straightened out of the first turn, the Epsom stands were awash in the crowd's noise. At home, thousands pressed up to their TV sets, listening to Channel 4 race caller Graham Goode sound out the order : "It's All The Way, out in front, out of trouble, that has the edge here, to Val Royal on the inside of Salford Express, and then Daliapour and Oath. Behind these Dubai Millennium and then Zaajer, with Housemaster behind that now, Lucido midfield. Beat All is on the outside, out of trouble, Through The Rye one of the back markers is well out the back, Adair the big horse from America is nearer last than first. Saffron Walden is *well* down the pack at this stage."

Dubai Millennium was still pulling Dettori, who was vainly trying to settle his colt on the inside. The horse was in what Dettori thought of as his rhino mode. "It was like riding a rhino, sitting on a rhino without control," he said later. "If he decided we're gonna go today, I mean nobody could stop him." Now the rhino hauled his jockey all the way to the top of the hill, a 130-foot ascent.

"They're at the top of the hill now," the voice rang out. "Shortly past the halfway stage in the Vodafone Derby, with All The Way leading, to Salford Express in second and Daliapour in a good position, Val Royal, then five is Oath, sixth Lucido getting closer, Zaajer, Dubai Millennium, Beat All getting closer all the time, and then we have Housemaster followed by Compton Admiral, Glamis, Saffron Walden, on the outer, Brancaster is out the back and so too is Through The Rye."

Dettori was on a spent horse already; he knew it as they rolled down the hill on tired legs to Tattenham Corner, the final bend before the grandstand and the home straight.

"They begin the descent to Tattenham Corner now and All The Way still just has the edge, red cap of Salford Express running a big race, Daliapour and Oath with the white bridle, grey colours to the inside is Val Royal, Dubai Millennium still being shuffled down the pack, Zaajer holds a good position," Goode called, his voice gaining momentum as several of the horses lost theirs.

The field rounded Tattenham Corner, All The Way still on the lead with Daliapour to his outside. Eddery had Salford Express poised prominently, while Beat All began revving into gear under Stevens. Dettori, refusing to throw in the towel yet, looked vainly for room but found he was boxed in.

"From the back Beat All starts to run, Val Royal, Dubai Millennium looks for room but he can't find any." Suddenly the voice rose. "Here comes Oath under Kieren Fallon, on the outside of Daliapour they're head to head, Beat All starts to pick up and Housemaster a giant run, then All The Way and Glamis. They're in the final furlong now and I swear it's Oath on the lead! Oath is going to win the Vodafone Derby!"

With a remarkable turn of foot, Oath had swept past Daliapour, Fallon using his distinctive flailing style, which looked so awkward but was so effective, to coax the maximum effort from his horse. They crossed the line a length and three-quarters in front of Daliapour, with Beat All another length and a half behind, a short head in front of Housemaster.

Saffron Walden wound up seventh, three lengths in front of Dubai Millennium in ninth place. Adair had beaten only three horses, Lucido just one. The 100-1 shot Through The Rye, a maiden who had never got into the hunt, finished last.

Sheikh Mohammed was a gracious loser, greeting the ecstatic Prince Ahmed in the winner's enclosure and bestowing three kisses upon his cheeks. Prince Ahmed kissed Oath, and lifted Fallon into the air; the inscrutable Cecil scratched his head, looking bemused. It had been an unbelievable season for all of the victors – for Cecil, having saddled his third Classic winner of the year; for Fallon, who had been aboard all three and was bagging his first Derby; and for the Salman family, who had been in this very spot celebrating Ramruma's victory 24 hours earlier.

It was a very different scene in camp Godolphin. To finish last with a 100-1 shot may make you feel foolish; but to finish out of the frame with the favourite leaves a heavier, more bitter taste, even when failure might have been foreseen.

"By the time we got to the top of the hill I knew my fate," Dettori reflected. "No horse can pull that hard and finish the race. Of course I was disappointed, but I could see I was in trouble."

"It was a desperately disappointing day, because we knew how much ability he actually had," said Crisford. "Walking off the stands after seeing a beaten favourite is really hard. Especially when you know the horse didn't perform to his real ability. But we all knew, well that was it – a mile and a half was not a good idea, and we weren't going to be trying that one again."

Putting disappointment behind them, the Godolphin team regrouped. They would go back to square one – give the headstrong colt time to relax and calm down, then place him in an easy spot, preferably on soft ground.

Six weeks later Dubai Millennium found himself facing four rivals at Maisons-Laffitte in the Prix Eugene Adam, a Group 2 race over a mile and a quarter. This time he broke sharply and Dettori let him take the lead. Still in front two furlongs from home, the jockey pushed him out a notch and they quickened clear to win by an easy three lengths.

Godolphin decided to try an even shorter distance for his next race, the Group 1 Prix Jacques le Marois, run at the Normandy seaside resort town of Deauville. With its world-famous casino and thalassotherapy clinic – a spa to treat the ills of the privileged with seaweed wraps and mud baths – Deauville is a playground for the rich and idle, but its racing is serious and the Jacques le Marois one of Europe's premier mile contests. The August meeting is also prone to steady downpours, and the turf was bottomless as a field of five entered the stalls. The main threats appeared to be Slickly, winner of the Grand Prix de Paris for owner Jean-Luc Lagardere in June; and Prince Khalid Abdullah's Dansili, who had been second in the Poule d'Essai des Poulains, the French 2,000 Guineas, in May and later won a Group 3 race at Deauville. Both Dansili and Slickly were trained by France's perennial leading handler Andre Fabre.

The distance, the racecourse, and the names had changed but the race unfolded like a duplicate of the Prix Eugene Adam. Dubai Millennium went straight to the lead and never looked back, quickening in the straight and beating Slickly by an uncontested two and a half lengths, with Dansili a length behind him. It was time to go home and show British racing what Dubai Millennium was really made of.

Britain's premier late-season mile race is the Queen Elizabeth II Stakes at Ascot. It was here, in the waning days of September, that Dubai Millennium was sent to seal his reputation outside of Godolphin's inner circle. To the team, he was already the most important horse in the stable – and this in a season that already included 15 Group 1 wins and a superstar named Daylami. A striking five-year-old with a nearly white coat, Daylami had established himself as Europe's leading middle-distance performer with wins in the Coronation Cup, King George VI and Queen Elizabeth Diamond Stakes and the Irish Champion Stakes.

Dubai Millennium came through his final spin in fine form on the Wednesday before the race. With Proctor up, he impressed work-watchers while stretching several lengths clear of his companion Opera King over seven furlongs on Newmarket's Al Bahathri gallop.

There was always a good chance of soft ground at Ascot in early autumn, but heavy, thundery showers at the end of the week forced the course authority to cancel racing on the Saturday of the QEII. The prestigious meeting was moved to Sunday instead, leaving the team with a dilemma – what to do with a race-ready Dubai Millennium cooped up in Ascot's stables.

Midway through Saturday morning, Tony Proctor received a call. "We need you to drive down to Ascot and ride your colt this afternoon," he was told. So he jumped in his car and made the two-hour trip from Newmarket, arriving in mid-afternoon. Heading out on to the waterlogged course, he was surprised to find a small crowd of people who had somehow got wind of Dubai Millennium's impromptu appearance and stayed to watch the gallop, which was as restrained as he could make it.

Sunday dawned with a fresh rain, but by the time the first race was off, there was a brilliant autumn sun slanting down, giving the still-wet grass an emerald sparkle. Dettori had won the first race, the Group 1 Fillies' Mile, aboard Teggiano for trainer Clive Brittain and he was in high spirits as the field was loaded quickly into the stalls for the Queen Elizabeth II Stakes. The heavy ground had eliminated his prime challenger, the French-trained Sendawar, from the race, as well as the Sussex Stakes runner-up Docksider. Thus the field was depleted of much of its intrigue, and Dubai Millennium was the odds-on favourite.

Dettori had received pre-race instructions from Sheikh

Mohammed: "Don't mess about today, just let him stretch out." Unfortunately there was another front-runner, the improving three-year-old Gold Academy, and Dettori decided it would be pointless to take him on.

When the stalls burst open, he let Pat Eddery set the pace on Gold Academy. It was no easy task. After his easy day on Saturday, Dubai Millennium was all too eager to run, and Dettori had to anchor him with his full weight.

As the field tacked over under the trees, looking for better footing, he could feel the lactic acid building in his arms and he began counting off the furlong poles. The horses were moving fast but the poles seemed to go by agonisingly slowly – six, still ages to go, five, his biceps were burning, four, he could feel his breath coming more heavily, only two more furlongs and he could let the colt run, and finally the three-furlong marker passed by and he loosened his grip. Dubai Millennium sailed past Gold Academy as if he were standing still, idled momentarily upon finding himself in front and then took off again with a nudge from his jockey, storming six lengths clear of the late-running Almushtarak. Gold Academy was three and a half lengths behind him. The fourth runner, the Coronation Stakes winner Balisada, was tailed off by 20 lengths.

It was a thrilled team that greeted Dettori and Dubai Millennium in the winners' enclosure, where the jockey performed his trademark flying dismount and then animatedly filled in Sheikh Mohammed with a blow-by-blow description of the race. Within minutes the press, expecting an interview with bin Suroor, had descended on the enclosure. To their surprise, it was the sheikh himself who spoke.

"This horse, I think he's the best we have had in Godolphin," he told them.

"That's quite a statement," said a rather startled Jonathan

Powell, who was interviewing for the BBC. "When did you decide that, because you did of course run him in the Derby when perhaps he didn't stay, but you were harbouring hopes that he might be the best before then?"

"Yes, when we saw him working we called him Dubai Millennium. But he is just growing – he was a baby in the Derby and he's improving now," replied Sheikh Mohammed. "And I think, from my small knowledge, he's the best we have had."

"And on this ground, a lot of horses really don't like it – he seems to thrive on it," persisted Powell.

"No, he will be even better on better ground," the sheikh answered firmly.

"That's another, er, quite a statement," said the journalist, taken aback.

The bevy of reporters pressed in around them, some with recorders extended at arm's length to catch every word emanating from Sheikh Mohammed's lips, others scribbling furiously on notepads. It was the first they had heard of Dubai Millennium's greatness. Minutes earlier, they had been debating his standing among the miling division.

"He'd have to be one of the world's top milers," announced commentator Jimmy Lindley immediately after the race.

"I'm not sure I'd go as far as Jimmy Lindley, to say he's one of the best milers in the world, because I think Sendawar would have given him quite a battle on decent ground," Clare Balding remarked to her co-presenter, jockey-turned-pundit Willie Carson.

"Yes, well actually, you would say that Dubai Millennium would be the best horse on this type of ground, but not on ordinary type ground," said Carson. "Sendawar is another horse you would have to consider."

Now they were listening to Sheikh Mohammed saying that this horse was better than Daylami, better than Lammtarra (whom Godolphin claimed despite the horse's official ownership by the sheikh's nephew), better than Godolphin's first Classic winner Balanchine, winner of the Oaks and the Irish Derby in 1994, better than 2,000 Guineas hero Mark Of Esteem or Oaks heroine Moonshell, better even than Swain, who had scored a historic second King George VI and Queen Elizabeth Diamond Stakes victory on this very racecourse a year earlier. It was quite a statement, all right.

"Of course with a name like Dubai Millennium it wouldn't take a genius to work out that he'll be running in the Dubai World Cup next spring," continued Powell.

"Exactly," the sheikh nodded. The world would be coming to Dubai next March to witness Godolphin's best horse ever attempt his greatest feat yet.

CHAPTER SIX

THE NIGHT
THAT FANTASY
BECAME REALITY

The sun rose with a start over Dubai. It pushed abruptly above the edge of sand and sky, heralded by nothing more than a hot breath of wind insinuating itself into the cool dark desert dawn.

On the Al Quoz training track, in the sudden light, dark amorphous shadows resolved into legs, heads and bodies of galloping horses, riders perched high in the irons above them in an effort to contain the half-tons of energy barrelling over the sand beneath them. To Tony Proctor the gust of warm air felt like an appliance switched on by some giant hand as his mount, Dubai Millennium, raked across the surface, head low, in a rhythm, lob, lob, lob – that was the only sound in the rider's head as he let himself get lost in the moving air and the rising sun and the cadence of the moment.

The wind rose too as the big dark colt barrelled around the track's bend, and suddenly there was a shape that shouldn't have been there, a great low-flying thing tumbling and spinning towards them. "Masafi bottled water" its cardboard wings read. Proctor had time to see the printed words in the long, lucid moment before an abyss opened where his mount had been, and the earth rushed up to meet his face and outstretched arms. He tucked his head instinctively, letting his rounded shoulders take the brunt of the fall even as he stretched out his left arm in a last-ditch attempt to grab the reins. But it was in vain, and the colt, suddenly cut loose from human control, spun round.

Then he picked up his head and jogged across to the outside rail, where the riders customarily pulled up their mounts after exercise. Ears pricked and head swinging alertly, Dubai Millennium trotted back to the gap where the horses entered and left the track.

With their fiery star safely caught, the team made light of the incident. "Someone put an APB out on that box!" joked Tom Albertrani, relief seeping into his voice. The last thing they needed was Dubai Millennium galloping loose across the desert in literally unbridled enthusiasm. Luckily, the colt was smart – really smart, and domesticated in the way the Arabian horses who lived with their Bedouin masters in the desert once had been. For all his vigour and aggression, he seemed to truly enjoy human company.

At least, he enjoyed the company of selected humans. Some of the Godolphin handlers could hardly get near him. In fact, the comments made about him by head lad Brian Knowles were startlingly reminiscent of Ken Crozier's recollections of Shareef Dancer. "He was a bit of a miserable sod in the box. He wouldn't think twice about biting you, and you wouldn't trust his back end either."

Knowles thought the colt was arrogant. "He always had that air of presence about him. He was a big, tough colt who thought he was the bee's knees."

Simon Crisford and John Ferguson, Sheikh Mohammed's chief bloodstock advisor, whose jobs did not entail hands-on horsemanship, also found him a bit much to handle. That made the colt's almost-loving relationship with Sheikh Mohammed all the more remarkable to them. "He was like a lion," said Crisford, "but he would respond to the boss as a person. I don't think anyone else could get him to rest his head in his arm, because the horse would see you out of the box pretty quickly.

"He was tough, although there was nothing nasty about him. He had a lovely temperament in terms of being a kind horse, but he was playful, and he was tough. And he was big, and full of energy. Energy was just popping out of him the whole time."

Ferguson thought the colt was "a man. He wouldn't go in there and eat you, but he knew what he wanted."

He too was amazed by the rapport between the boss and the big colt. "It was absolutely extraordinary. He used to go talk to him – he'd just go stand in his box and mess around with him. He had this thing about messing around with his tongue, and Dubai Millennium used to just stand there."

It was in Dubai that Sheikh Mohammed's relationship with the horse became obvious to everyone. While the colt was "a man" to Ferguson, Sheikh Mohammed would tell people that he was still a baby. The image was apt. Sometimes when showing him off to people he would surprise them by suddenly leaning over to kiss the colt's face, as one would kiss a small child out of sheer spontaneous love.

He spent hours alone with Dubai Millennium, going into the colt's box after evening stables to feed him carrots, stroke his shining, sun-warmed coat and simply sit. Who knew what went through the minds of man and horse as they rested companionably in the warm desert evening? Maybe they found a rare relaxation, when both could let down their aggressively energetic public personas and just be. Perhaps they dreamed together.

Dusk would fall, then night, and Crisford would stop by. "Boss, you still here?" he would say. Sometimes Sheikh Mohammed would stand and shake the bedding from his clothes, give the colt one last pat and leave with Crisford. Other times he stayed on into the night.

Whatever dreams were dreamt under the stars, daytime held a definitive plan. That was for Dubai Millennium to win the Dubai World Cup before continuing his career from Godolphin's English base. Luckily there were no setbacks that winter, but still Crisford and the team felt that the colt's training regime required special management. It was his sheer power, the same electrifying turn of foot that had first impressed Proctor on the Newmarket gallops, that needed managing.

The colt may have been a baby in Sheikh Mohammed's eyes, but he had developed physically. Even bigger and stronger than he had been at three, he seemed not to know his own power.

"He needed an excellent guy riding him both in his fast work and in his slower paces," said Crisford. "And he needed controlling. There's no doubt about that, he needed serious controlling."

By controlling, Crisford didn't mean physical restraint – although there was that too. The trainers had taken to using a lip chain, placing the length of chain at the end of the leather shank used to lead the horses, between the colt's gum and upper lip as an added measure of control when he was being led.

The other sort of control was a meticulously executed programme of workouts, set up under the constant advice of Sheikh Mohammed. Dubai Millennium's works at Al Quoz were brilliant, perhaps too brilliant. One morning just after 6.00, when Proctor rode the colt out as usual with the first string, Albertrani told him: "Just do a piece round on the bridle."

Proctor duly let his mount out a notch, breezing nice and easy on the bridle. Albertrani was waiting for him when he pulled up to stand for a moment before walking out the gap. "On the bridle?" he asked.

"Yeah he's nice. Lovely."

"Well, you've just worked faster than most milers run."

Even Proctor, with all his experience, had been fooled by Dubai Millennium's extraordinary cruising speed. So Sheikh Mohammed, Crisford, bin Suroor and Albertrani mapped out a work campaign in which the colt would be matched with various Group winners from the stable, some sprinters, some milers, some with more stamina. On board would be Godolphin's best work-riders, able to accurately calculate fractions in relation to furlongs. In that way Dubai Millennium would become racing fit without being allowed to set his own pace.

No matter whom they paired him with, he won the work. "You didn't even have to click, you'd just pull him out and he was gone," said Proctor.

The Al Quoz track, like Nad Al Sheba racecourse, was sand. Dubai Millennium skipped over the surface like he was born to it. To Proctor he felt the same on dirt or turf – just switch him on to autopilot, show him an inch of daylight and he was gone. "Unreal" was the best word he could summon to describe the colt's action.

But he had never raced on dirt before, and Sheikh Mohammed decided that he should have a preparatory race over the surface. The Sheikh Maktoum bin Rashid Al Maktoum Challenge, Round 3, was chosen. Held over the same course and distance, a mile and a quarter, as the Dubai World Cup, it should offer a close enough approximation of track conditions on the big race day. The Challenge took place on the evening of 2 March, three weeks before the World Cup.

Godolphin entered two pacemakers, Comeonmom and Goombayland, to ensure that Dubai Millennium got a taste of kickback from the sandy surface. Without a leader, he might have shot to the front and never tasted dirt. The second pacemaker was there as extra insurance.

Frankie Dettori was given stern instructions to hold his mount up, and with some difficulty he managed to keep him behind the other Godolphin runners; the race was reminiscent of the QEII, when his arms were burning with strain halfway through the race as he tried to anchor the powerful colt. When he finally turned Dubai Millennium loose, the horse set sail up the Nad Al Sheba straight. He was still on the bridle a quarter-mile from home and won by an uncontested four and a half lengths from the overmatched Lear Spear. Comeonmom was another three lengths back, and Goombayland seven lengths behind him. The final time was a new track record of 1 min 59.6 seconds.

So that question was answered. Dubai Millennium could handle racing over a dirt strip. Now it was back to managing his pace – and fine-tuning some little things. First of all, Dettori and the horse would be kept apart until the final pre-race work. To leg the jockey atop the colt was like striking a match – instant ignition. Second, he would be loaded in the starting stalls every few days, to teach him to settle. Or so went the plan.

Dubai Millennium had two significant workouts before the World Cup. The first was too slow, the second too fast. That left the race itself for the team to get it just right.

Proctor was aboard for the first work. Goombayland, who had

set the pace in the Maktoum Challenge, led the gallop under the lad who had been the work-rider for the 1999 World Cup winner Almutawakel. Proctor set Dubai Millennium in tracking position, and when he pulled him out, the colt shot forward like a rocket. But as soon as he was in front of the other horse, Dubai Millennium's head came up and he fell back to a lacklustre gallop.

"He can't win the World Cup on that," said Steve.

"Don't you worry about this horse, he'll win the World Cup," shot back Proctor. "Not a problem."

Proctor wouldn't admit to the slight twinge of worry he felt. But really, he wasn't much concerned. To him, Dubai Millennium was saying, "Oh, that'll do; I've done my bit now. Let's go home, have a wash and a drink and I'll go back in my box and go to sleep."

"He was cute," said Proctor afterwards, "but the good ones are, aren't they? If you have a horse that's exceptional like him, and they work to their full potential every time, you'll have nothing left. Good horses won't work to their full potential every time. You don't want 'em to – there's no prize-money on the gallops, is there?"

But with Dettori aboard it was another story. The colt knew this was his race-rider, and he was fired up for the final pre-World Cup breeze five days before the race, with the press on hand to watch. On his own this time, he blistered five furlongs in 59 seconds, with Dettori helpless to slow him down.

The training crew, bin Suroor, Albertrani and Crisford, were incensed. All of that careful planning burned up in the last gallop. "People were chain smoking, saying you went too fast, you messed up," Dettori recalled. "Well, I couldn't stop him. But .59 for a good horse is nothing; .59 for another horse is killing material."

Of all the people who had invested their dreams in Dubai Millennium, Dettori may have had the biggest personal score to settle. He had finished dead last in the race in three of its four runnings, including the previous year on High-Rise. In his best World Cup result, he rode Kammtarra to an eighth place finish, beating two home in 1997. That was the year that Jerry Bailey rode Sheikh Mohammed's Singspiel to victory, the American jockey's second consecutive win in the race, following Cigar's landmark triumph in the inaugural World Cup.

Moreover, Dettori still felt the sting of his worst year ever. His infamous ride on Swain in the 1998 Breeders' Cup Classic, when the horse veered sharply right under seven cracks of the jockey's left-handed whip, losing the race narrowly to Awesome Again and Silver Charm, had not been easily lived down. The press and public reaction – and even, Dettori felt, some of the inside response from Godolphin – was unforgiving. However, Sheikh Mohammed remained supportive as ever and the boss's encouragement, combined with Godolphin's 18 Group or Grade 1 wins, 13 of them under Dettori, in 1999, helped the jockey regain his equilibrium.

He felt vengeance was fully his when he rode Daylami to win the Breeders' Cup Turf at Gulfstream Park in November. Few could forget his wild screams of "Come on me!" as he rode the grey horse back to the winners' circle. Now, four months later, the last two spent in the sun and fun of Dubai, he was tanned, fit and ready to take on the world.

He was still not convinced of Sheikh Mohammed's claim that Dubai Millennium was the best horse Godolphin ever had, though. In an interview with the BBC's Clare Balding early on the day of the World Cup, the jockey laid out his number-one goal: "Looking for the next Daylami. I still haven't found one. Still haven't found one, but I'm still looking."

When Balding asked him about the "Godolphin's best horse"

claim, he hesitated a moment before answering. "He is certainly one of the best horses I've ridden."

Balding also interviewed Sheikh Mohammed, who took her on a tour of Al Quoz. They entered Dubai Millennium's box, and she asked the sheikh specifically what he saw in the horse that made him superior to the rest.

"Look at his head, his eyes," said Sheikh Mohammed. "You can see his heart through his eyes. He's kind, he's a nice horse and kind, if you know how to handle him. He knows what he wants.

"And of course he's a very, very well-bred horse. And you see what I say about conformation, look at his head. It looks like an Arabic head, you know, not a big ugly head."

All the while the colt and the man kept up a physical dialogue, Dubai Millennium sticking out his tongue, Sheikh Mohammed taking hold of it, the colt tucking his head under his owner's arm as the sheikh stroked him. As Sheikh Mohammed concluded his description of the horse, he ducked his head and gave him a kiss on the right side of his muzzle, away from the camera. Then he turned and led the BBC crew out of the box, his face impassive.

It was time for the race. The international field had dropped to 13 after Malek, who had finished second and fourth in the two previous World Cups, was withdrawn on the eve of the race with a career-ending injury. His trainer Dick Mandella was still well represented by Chilean-bred Puerto Madero, winner of the previous year's Grade 1 Donn Handicap. Also from America came Behrens, fresh off a five-length win in the Grade 1 Gulfstream Park Handicap after finishing third in the Donn for trainer Jim Bond; the Elliott Walden-trained Ecton Park, winner of the Grade 1 Super

Derby the previous October; the California-based Saint's Honor, winner of the Grade 2 San Fernando Breeders' Cup for trainer Craig Dollase in January; and Public Purse, an ex-French runner trained by Bobby Frankel in California for Khalid Abdullah. Public Purse hadn't run since winning the Grade 2 San Marcos Handicap at Santa Anita in January.

From Japan there was World Cleek, not the country's best horse, perhaps, but a Japanese Grade 1 winner in December. Hong Kong trainer Ivan Allan sent Indigenous, an extremely busy and consistent, if not quite top-class horse who began his career in Ireland.

British trainer Philip Mitchell sent the globe-trotting Running Stag, while David Elsworth would saddle Lear Spear, who had recently begun a global campaign of his own, most recently finishing second to Dubai Millennium in the Maktoum Challenge, his first dirt race.

John Veitch had trained Alydar, the persistent gadfly of Triple Crown winner Affirmed, for Calumet Farm in his glory days. Those days were long gone, and Veitch was now based in Saudi Arabia, from where he arrived with the Argentine-bred Strudel Fitz.

The field was rounded out by two Godolphin runners, Worldly Manner and Gracioso. Both had been smart performers in their time: Gracioso beat the sensational Montjeu in the Prix Lupin, while Worldly Manner had been Godolphin's (ultimately disappointing) Kentucky Derby entry a year ago. Now, however, their main role would be as pacesetters. Jerry Bailey was on Worldly Manner, while French jockey Sylvan Guillot rode Gracioso.

The Dubai World Cup was the last race on the card, which began with an Arabian race in early evening, followed by six thoroughbred contests, ranging in value from the $250,000

Godolphin Mile to the $6 million Dubai World Cup. In all, the six races were worth $11,750,000 in prize-money. On top of that, the Dubai Racing Club paid transportation and housing costs for the horses and their human connections from abroad.

Darkness had fallen, but the World Cup horses walked under a blaze of artificial lights from the saddling area to the parade ring in front of the grandstand. Crisford's doubts, raised by the blistering pre-race work, began to evaporate.

"I remember watching the horse being saddled and coming into the paddock," he said. "He reminded me of a prizefighter – shrouded from head to toe in a towel, walking down into the ring. He was like that; he was pumped up like a prizefighter."

Tony Proctor, on the other hand, was too nervous to watch in person. "I think it was probably the first time I'd had butterflies since I finished riding," he said. He had spent the first part of the evening living it up – actually trying to drown out thoughts of the race ahead – in the Irish Village, a large area fenced off from the grandstand and given over mainly to one Irish pastime, drinking. But before the race he slipped quietly into the weighing room, after the jockeys had gone out. There he could be alone with his emotions.

Crisford, sitting with the royal family in the grandstand, had his eyes on the big screen behind the parade ring. As the stalls opened and Dubai Millennium tacked over from his outside draw in post 11 while rocketing to the lead, he had one thought: "Oh no."

The big colt was going too fast and he was taking Dettori for a ride. He meant business, all right. What was worse, he had hooked up with Worldly Manner.

Crisford could hardly believe his eyes. Here were two of Godolphin's own horses, and the pacesetter was taking on Dubai Millennium. Both colts looked ready to run for their lives. But that was the way the race was unfolding, and no-one could manage Dubai Millennium now.

Proctor, still in the weighing room, listened intently to the light Australian drawl of racecaller Jim McGrath on the television set. The crowd's noise outside was a muted roar.

"As they head down the back and Dubai Millennium is going like the wind in front, leads by a length and a half. Up on the outside is Saint's Honor and Worldly Manner is just tucked away on the inside as they continue their journey down the back."

"I remember thinking they're going too quick, and Frankie's going too quick, and Dubai Millennium is definitely going too quick," said Crisford. "I couldn't imagine seeing the horse get home halfway through the race, because I thought no horse can maintain this level of raw speed. That's what it was, raw energy and speed. And I thought the petrol tank was going to be flicking a bit when they got into the straight and Frankie asked him a question."

Alone in the weighing room, Proctor was having much the same thoughts. "They jumped out of the stalls, he's pinged the gates and he's tanking," he recalled.

Aboard the powerhouse that was Dubai Millennium, Dettori knew he had no option but to let him go. The colt was free, but he was in control, and he was doing the blistering splits in his own rhythm. He was finally learning to manage his own tremendous raw energy. Dettori was feeling confident. While part of him was hoping that they hadn't burned too much fuel, in his heart of hearts he felt that if they could escape the others until the straight, they would be in business.

"Indigenous is just behind them from Running Stag, he's very handy. Two lengths away then on the outside Gracioso is making some ground, Behrens is right there in the centre as well. Well back in the field is Strudel Fitz at this stage, in company there with Lear

Spear and Public Purse, they're followed by World Cleek and Puerto Madero is tailed right off."

The crowd shoved its way towards the rail. They were eight deep and wild with excitement, although most of them could scarcely see what was happening.

"Well Frankie Dettori is really taking a chance here on Dubai Millennium, he's blazing a big trail here, leads by a length and a half as they race towards the half-mile and towards the entrance to the home straight. On the outside Saint's Honor and just behind him Behrens is moving up in the centre, out wider Running Stag."

Proctor jumped to his feet in the weighing room. "As soon as he got to the front and Frankie sat up on him, I thought, there's only one winner now. It's game over now, nothing will get near this horse."

McGrath took the same opinion as his voice caught the excitement of the moment.

"Well he's going to set a record today if he lasts a record, as they swing into the straight Dubai Millennium two lengths clear as they stretch out for home, Behrens battling in second, Running Stag, but the cheering has broken out already halfway up the home straight, Dubai Millennium about four lengths in front of Behrens, then Running Stag, further back is Public Purse, Puerto Madero coming from last ..."

"It was remarkable," said Crisford, "because he floated over that surface so well that when he did turn into the straight and he changed his lead, it was almost like the horse lowered himself to the ground and changed gear – he went from fourth into fifth gear, and he just took off. And you knew immediately, even though it's a very long straight at Nad Al Sheba, and a lot of horses who have been in front get collared close home, on this occasion you knew, when you saw him take three lengths off the field early in the straight to make his move, you knew that nothing was going to catch him. However tired he got, you knew the race was all over.

"It's very rare when you see a move so far out that you don't even have to watch the rest of the race. That was one of those occasions. I'm sure everyone would agree with that. It was one of those electrifying bursts of energy and speed, and the acceleration was what was unbelievable."

Entering the straight Dettori knew he had managed to stay clear of the field. He could hear the crack of the other jockeys' whips, and he knew they were all in trouble. With three furlongs to go, he let the colt out just a notch and a wave of sound from the stands engulfed him. He decided to sit quiet and wait until after the two-furlong marker to ask for his effort. As they powered down the stretch into the artificial glare and the deafening roar, he finally crouched down for the drive, pulling out his whip and smacking the colt once, twice. Incredibly, Dubai Millennium increased his margin again.

McGrath's voice was nearly as frenzied as the crowd now. "With just under a furlong to go it's Dubai Millennium, he's absolutely pulverised this field, he's eight lengths in front and going further ahead, Dubai Millennium, a superb performance to win the Dubai World Cup, the world's richest horse race, Dubai Millennium by eight lengths, Behrens second ..."

The official winning margin was six lengths. The time for the mile and a quarter was 1 min 59.5 seconds. Dubai Millennium had broken his own track record.

"When I got to the wire, I thought now I can afford to have a look back," Dettori recalled later. "And I had a look and they were like little dots in the back. And I was able to enjoy the feeling."

"To me there was no second, there was no third in the race," said Proctor. "There was Dubai Millennium, and there was a completely different race behind him."

As the glistening dark bay horse and the jockey in Godolphin blue silks passed the winning post, the front and centre of the grandstand, where the royal family sat, erupted. Sheikh Mohammed, wearing a black robe and red and white checked headdress, embraced Sheikh Maktoum, lifted him from his seat and gave him a kiss. Both were beaming. Then they fought their way through the throngs to Dubai Millennium and Dettori.

They had a hard time of it. A melee had broken out among the 80 or so photographers jostling to get shots of the winner. It had started even before the race was over, as they fought for the best position from which to snap the horse crossing the finish line. The matter of press photographers was one area the racing association had overlooked; there was no organisation, not enough space and now the fight was turning ugly. Flash bulbs were smashed and lenses knocked to the ground, with the result that very few viable pictures were taken of the finish of one of the most widely publicised races in history.

Perhaps because of that scarcity, one shot has become iconic. Taken by Gill Jones, whose husband Trevor is the more widely known British racing photographer, it looks almost posed. Taken as horse and rider cross the finish line, it captured Dubai Millennium with his ears pricked and legs extended, Dettori high in the irons, just beginning to raise his whip hand in victory, mouth open in a jubilant cry. Behind them is a red-and-white board with the words "Dubai World Cup" written across its arch. "Fly Emirates" it says on either side. The photograph was later used as the basis for the wax sculpture of Dubai Millennium created by Madame Tussauds and displayed in the Godolphin Gallery.

Racing Post photographer Edward Whitaker was one of the lucky few to get a picture after the race. "It was pandemonium," he recalled. "It was the most tremendous scrum ever. Absolute chaos. You knew you had to do something."

Whitaker waited for Sheikh Mohammed and bin Suroor to reach the horse. Biding his time while hemmed in along the side of the crush, he waited until a small gap opened. Then he stepped in – and got out as quickly as he could.

A veteran photographer, he had seen his share of post-race skirmishes – when Desert Orchid won the Cheltenham Gold Cup in 1989, when Lammtarra won the Prix de l'Arc de Triomphe to remain unbeaten – those scenes were pretty wild. But this was something else again.

"It was dangerous," he said. "You have these 6 foot 4 inch, 20-stone bodyguards who didn't give a shit about photographers, they just wanted clear access.

"And the horse behaved impeccably. He was very well behaved."

Dettori, for one, didn't fight the publicity. Swallowed by the sea of press, he shoved his face into the cameras, yelling jubilantly, "Show me the money! Show me the money!" His face was lit up with pure joy, and it was impossible not to respond in kind.

Unaware of the war being waged among the press, Crisford too embraced the euphoria. "The whole of Dubai went ballistic," he said. "And the great thing about Dubai is they know how to have a good time. The Dubai World Cup is the biggest party in Dubai, because everyone loves going racing and it's great fun, a fabulous atmosphere. It was a huge, huge night."

Beyond the fun, this was Godolphin's greatest dream realised. They could finally let down their guard and celebrate.

"We thought he would win, but not necessarily this impressively," said bin Suroor.

"No words can describe it," said Dettori.

The race had changed his opinion of the colt, no doubt about it. "He is the best horse I have ridden," the jockey proclaimed.

"This result, this horse, this name, it is the greatest race in my life," said Sheikh Mohammed. "When I changed his name, I knew he was a good horse. Of course I was hoping he would come and win this race."[1]

Everyone in the operation felt they had reached a milestone. "The atmosphere in the yard was cock-a-hoop the next day," said Brian Knowles. "Because he was an extra-special horse. He was a true champion. You can get lucky and win Group 1 races with a horse that's not probably a true Group 1 horse, and you're delighted it won, but it doesn't give you the same feeling as one that you know is a proper champion. You know you're bloody lucky to have him, or to be around him."

Dettori said: "My career has been quite short by Lester Piggott standards, but I've been in racing over 12 years and my father 30 years before then and I've never seen a performance like that in my life. What was meant to be the greatest race in the world, it showed something that no horses have showed for a very, very long time, and it was amazing. It was amazing for me that I was on top and I was even more amazed watching the replay. He absolutely killed a top-class field, from the beginning, and I think it will take a very long time before we see a performance like that again."[2]

Crisford later summed up what the win meant to Godolphin. "That was the best, because it meant so much. For us it was the best, by a long way. It was the best race that Godolphin's ever won, really. It meant everything to everyone.

"Everyone had prayed that it would all work out like that, and when it did work out like that it was remarkable. But at the time, you don't really have time to appreciate it all, because things are happening so quickly, and there's a stable full of other horses, so things are moving along very fast, and much as you appreciate it, you don't have the time to stop and think about it. Because no sooner is that finished than you're thinking about the next event."

No-one could have imagined what the next event would be.

1. Dan Liebman, "Millennium Cup", *The Blood-Horse*, 1 April 2000.
2. Frankie Dettori video interview for Flat Racing Review 2000 (London: Satellite Sports Services, 2001).

CHAPTER SEVEN

THE MATCH
THAT NEVER WAS

March in Dubai had been an all-time high for Godolphin, but the beginnings of an English summer portended ill.

It was June 1, and Godolphin's sights were set on running Best Of The Bests, a progressive colt whom they had recently acquired from Mohamed Obaida and trainer Clive Brittain, in the Derby in nine days' time. The colt, who had been bred by Sheikh Maktoum's Gainsborough Stud, was to be Frankie Dettori's mount, and with the team on a roll it wasn't hard to entertain hopes that this could be the year Dettori finally broke his Derby duck.

Today there were more mundane matters at hand. Today, though, Dettori was flying to a bread-and-butter meeting at Goodwood in Godolphin's hired plane, accompanied by jockey Ray Cochrane. On a finer day Cochrane would take the trip down from Newmarket by motorbike, but today he wanted to avoid the drearily wet and windy weather that was whipping across the country.

Godolphin's regular pilot Patrick Mackey was manning the controls of the twin-engine Piper Seneca. Normally he flew Dettori to meetings in a Cessna Crusader, but the plane was being serviced, so they had been using the six-seater Seneca for the last week. Dettori didn't like the replacement much – the way it had seemed to take off early and then hop about before finally getting off the ground the day before had bothered him – but half of a jockey's life consists of getting to and from racecourses, and flying saved a lot of time. So he, Mackey and Cochrane all met at the improvised airstrip on Newmarket's July course about an hour before noon.

With Dettori seated behind the pilot on the plane's left side, and Cochrane sitting to his right, the plane began to taxi down the grassy runway. They were going to rise over the Devil's Dyke, an ancient but famously well preserved embankment and ditch which reaches four metres below ground and up to six metres above for more than seven straight miles. The dyke crosses the land between Newmarket's July and Rowley Mile racecourses, and is a popular spot for dog walkers. As the little plane gathered speed, several pedestrians looked up to watch.

What they saw first snagged their attention, then filled them with horror. The plane bumped and bounced as it accelerated; at last it became airborne, but after ascending steeply for perhaps seventy feet, it veered right and began a rapid descent towards the Devil's Dyke. Teetering precariously, its right wingtip struck the bank and the plane was pitched forward into a bizarre mechanical cartwheel.

Inside, as they careened earthwards, Dettori could see the right engine smoking. "We're gonna die," he yelled to Cochrane as they waited for the impact.

Astonishingly, Mackey managed to avoid the dyke. The machine slammed into the ground. Both jockeys were immobile for a moment, suspended in shock. Then Dettori heard Cochrane shouting something. The sounds assembled themselves into words in his battered brain. "Get out, get out," they were yelling.

Staggering around the smoking plane, the jockeys found a small opening; the baggage hatch in the left rear had swung halfway open. Dettori wondered if he had lost his right eye – there seemed to be blood pouring from it. At any rate, he could barely see, and he was moving in slow motion. Cochrane gave him a shove, sending him through the hole and to the ground. The engine was on fire and he was trying to get away from the plane, but after ten steps he collapsed, his ankle severely broken. He screamed for help.

Cochrane, who had been trying to reach Mackey, turned back, eased through the gap and dragged Dettori along the grass, away from the smoking machinery to safety. Then he headed back to the plane, which by now was burning fiercely. Fresh explosions added to the chaos, and Cochrane, by now suffering extensive burns as well as cuts, was eventually beaten back. Later, he would be awarded heroic medals for his efforts in saving Dettori and attempting to rescue Mackey, who died. But at the moment, he was frantic and inconsolable – no longer a jockey, just a human fighting to stave off sudden, violent death.

The men were airlifted to Addenbrooke's hospital in nearby Cambridge, where Dettori underwent surgery to insert two pins in his ankle and repair the deep cuts in his face, and Cochrane was treated for cuts and burns. Winning races was the furthest thing from their minds over the next several days, as family and friends – including Sheikh Mohammed – trooped in and out with their words of encouragement. They could not stop thinking of Mackey, who, they were sure, had saved their lives by avoiding the treacherous Devil's Dyke. The married 51-year-old, who had had 15 years of flying experience, had been piloting for Godolphin for three years and he and Dettori had become close during that time.

Besieged by the press, Dettori agreed to hold a press conference on the day of his hospital release, although his real hope was that the reporters would leave him alone to recover afterwards. The thoughts he issued gave them plenty to dwell on.

"Right now, the Derby means nothing to me," he said from a wheelchair in front of the hospital, his leg immobilised by a cast, his forehead puckered with stitches.

"If I never win a race again it doesn't matter. I've got my life and I've got that to look forward to. I'll probably come back and give it a go when I'm mentally ready. I have no plans to rush myself back into racing. Obviously, racing is the only thing I know and want to do. Physically, bones can be fixed, but there is also the mental aspect of it. I hope I can pull through and be strong enough to come back and enjoy what I was doing before this happened.

"Nobody wishes to die, and when it happens very suddenly like that and you have only two seconds to think about it, it's beyond scary. No words can explain that bit. It just makes you wonder why we get upset about things. We are forever rushing and chasing our tails, for what?"

To the crowd's relief, he added: "It went through my mind to give up, but I'm 29 and what am I going to do? I do love racing very much and I'm planning to do it for another few years."[1]

The shock of the plane crash affected everyone at Godolphin. And soon it became clear that something else was amiss: the horses weren't winning any races.

By the time Royal Ascot opened on June 20, more than three weeks had passed since the team's last winner. The dry spell began even before the tragic crash; Godolphin's last winner before the royal meeting was Broche, a Guineas also-ran saddled by bin Suroor to land the four-runner Rosehill Conditions Stakes at Doncaster on May 27 under Darryll Holland.

The first day of Royal Ascot, a rollicking summer's outing for the social and sporting sets, brought nothing but more disappointment for Godolphin. None of the four runners they sent out, ridden by Willie Supple and American jockeys John Velazquez and Cigar's rider Jerry Bailey, even made the frame. The depressing run started when Muhtathir, a Group 1 winner in Italy, finished sixth in the Queen Anne Stakes, six lengths behind the winner Kalanisi. Then Godolphin's Irish 2,000 Guineas hero Bachir was sixth, with UAE Derby winner China Visit, fresh from an unsuccessful run in the Kentucky Derby, tenth of 11 in Giant's Causeway's St James's Palace Stakes. Finally bin Suroor saddled Dubai Two Thousand to finish sixth in the two-mile Queen's Vase at 12-1 under Bailey.

It had been a long day. At the end of it, picking their way through the champagne tipplers now sprawled under Ascot's splendid trees in the dying sun, the Godolphin crew felt more apprehension than anticipation at the thought of loading their big gun into the stalls for the next day's Prince of Wales's Stakes. It would be Dubai Millennium's first run since his star-spangled World Cup triumph.

Perhaps basing their judgement on Godolphin's dry run, the absence of their beloved Frankie Dettori, and the fact that Dubai Millennium's outstanding moment had come on dirt in a far-away and exotic land, the crowd made Sendawar the 6-5 favourite for the Prince of Wales's, a Group 1 race over a mile and a quarter. Restricted to four-year-olds and up, the race is a strong factor in determining the top middle-distance performer among the older division in Europe.

The punters' opinion was really surprising. It was the first race of Dubai Millennium's life in which he would not be the betting favourite, and only once had he disappointed, when still an inexperienced young colt attempting an excessive distance in the Derby. Indeed, with his eight wins to date achieved by a combined margin of thirty nine and a half lengths, he certainly hadn't left punters in any doubt as to the extent of his abilities.

Not that Sendawar wasn't a worthy rival. The colt was bred and owned by His Royal Highness the Aga Khan, who had been much longer a fixture in the European racing and breeding establishment than Sheikh Mohammed. The Aga Khan's current pride and joy had won his last four starts, all Group 1s, with his most recent loss coming more than a year earlier at the hooves of the mighty Montjeu. These were the points in Sendawar's favour.

A potential drawback was the trip; Sendawar, a four-year-old like Dubai Millennium and his other four rivals, had won all of his Group 1s over nine furlongs or less. He had won a minor race over today's trip when younger, on very soft ground in a canter, but nonetheless was considered primarily a miler.

The rest of the field consisted of German invader Sumitas, who had won his country's 2,000 Guineas the year before; Beat All, the third-placed finisher in Dubai Millennium's forgettable Derby; King Adam, who looked a smart colt in the making for Sir Michael Stoute, but was unproven at this level; and Rhythm Band. The last-named horse, winner of the Group 3 Dubai Duty Free for Godolphin on World Cup night, was entered as a pacemaker for Dubai Millennium.

Jerry Bailey, who had been flown in especially for the ride, had never won a race in Britain. His two unsuccessful mounts the day before had at least given him valuable experience over the course, and the day before, Dettori had briefed him on the ins and outs of the horse during a three-way meeting with Sheikh Mohammed. The Italian cautioned the American jockey not to rush Dubai Millennium out of the stalls and to try to save some energy for the home straight. The advice was sincerely meant, but Dettori of all people appreciated what a hard task it would be to follow.

Today, against his wife Catherine's advice – "You're mad to go," she told him – Dettori had made a spontaneous decision to attend the race himself. He hastily borrowed a morning suit from a fellow jockey, then rang the boss to ask if he could hitch a ride in his helicopter.

Dettori's determination to make the trip, given his recent horrific experience and newfound fear of flying, spoke volumes of his deep feelings for Godolphin's best horse. He was having a tough time pulling through the trauma of the crash, both physical and psychological. The thought of riding Dubai Millennium again, specifically returning for the Prix Jacques le Marois in August, was the only thing that kept his interest in race-riding alive. This would be his first racecourse appearance since the accident, and he would have to face crowds and the press along with his own demons.

In the paddock, his broken right ankle encased in plaster under a plastic boot, Dettori was enveloped by well-wishers. It was the first time he had been out without his crutches, and he walked with a limp; but he was amazed and overjoyed by the reception he got.

The Godolphin leadership also had instructions for Bailey: "Just ride your race. He likes to gallop from the front, so if he wants to take you on, don't fight him too much. But try and keep a little bit up your sleeve for the finish – if you can."

At the eleventh hour they had decided not to use Rhythm Band as a pacemaker. There was no point taking on their own horse – after all, what if Dubai Millennium ran like he had in Dubai, fighting for control with Worldly Manner?

As it turned out, Bailey didn't have to fight. It looked as though he scarcely needed to do more than hang on for the ride, although in fact the jockey rode a canny race from the front, setting a stiff gallop that sapped Sendawar's speed – but not that of his own mount. Dubai Millennium, fresh from nearly two months away from the races, powered to the lead and never looked back. Turning for home, his massive dark bay frame was six lengths clear of an already struggling Sendawar, who was well in front of Sumitas, King Adam, Beat All and Rhythm Band.

Three furlongs out the race-caller exclaimed: "Sendawar – the distress signals are out – is making no impression."

At the furlong pole, Sendawar was obviously a spent horse. Dubai Millennium rolled on. He wasn't accelerating anymore, but he didn't need to. The rest of the field was in another zone as the announcer cried: "Sendawar can't live with him … Dubai Millennium took Sendawar on and broke his heart."

Up in the stands Dettori was watching the big tv screen as Sheikh Mohammed followed the race with his binoculars. Watching Dubai Millennium gallop past the post, eight lengths in front of Sumitas, he felt tears spring to his eyes. It wasn't sorrow that he was missing the ride, or envy; he was simply overwhelmed. All his life he had lived for racing, the urgent desire to win, the appreciation for a horse who could do it so easily. Watching such a great racehorse destroy a field like this brought on feelings he could scarcely put into words – and speechlessness was not something the loquacious Dettori normally struggled with.

The official winning margin was eight lengths, with Sumitas finally getting up for second, a half-length in front of Beat All.

Another two and a half lengths back, a humbled Sendawar was fourth, a neck ahead of King Adam, who was five lengths to the good of Rhythm Band.

For Godolphin, the delirious joy of the night in Dubai was back. In the parade ring, Bailey did his best imitation of a Dettori-style dismount and landed almost in the arms of the Italian, who smothered him in a heartfelt hug and then nearly smooched Dubai Millennium's muzzle before thinking better of it. Then he took a step back to gaze at the colt's face, his own as proud and wondrous as if he were contemplating his baby son.

With a good smattering of the world's racing press crushed haphazardly around him, Sheikh Mohammed repeated his claims, made previously after the QEII and Dubai World Cup: "He is the best horse we have ever had.

"You can wait 20 years and never get a horse like this," he added. "He is a true champion and I have never seen or owned a horse like him. He is quite outstanding. There is no horse like this horse."

"Today was a relief," said Crisford. "We were expecting to see what we saw, and if it hadn't happened we would have been devastated."

Then Crisford articulated Godolphin's new goal. "The most remarkable thing about this horse is he is a brilliant champion on turf and dirt. If he were to win the Breeders' Cup Classic, he would be crowned the first of that type ever. We think he can do it and we very much hope he will."

Bailey picked up his seven-year-old son Justin and gave him a hug. "Justin, you could have come with me on that one, buddy," he said.

With a southwest wind of 22mph blowing into the horses' faces as they headed out of Swinley Bottom, from where they emerged to make their final run to the finish, and the ground riding slower than the official good to firm rating would imply, the time was a quotidian 2min 7.48sec – more than two and a half seconds slower than the standard time for the course and distance. Nonetheless, Dubai Millennium's performance sent the pundits into rhapsodies.

"Sheikh Mohammed's proud boast that Dubai Millennium is the best racehorse in the world came a step closer to universal acceptance when the colt destroyed a high-class field, that included the brilliant Sendawar, in yesterday's Prince of Wales's Stakes at Royal Ascot," wrote Jim McGrath in a *Telegraph* article entitled "Royal Ascot: Dubai the destroyer on top of the world".

"Everything they have said about this horse has come to fruition – all those millions of pounds, the vast empire of horses somehow justified in the two minutes and seven seconds Dubai Millennium took to bash down the door and barge into the room where only the greats are allowed," wrote columnist Alastair Down in the *Racing Post*.

It was "a case of choose your own superlative for Dubai Millennium, who lived up to his pre-race billing as the star of this year's Royal Ascot, with a flawless performance – gradually sapping the spirit and stamina of Sendawar, before powering home in splendid isolation, to be full value for his runaway margin," ran the *Racing Post*'s Ascot analysis. "From a betting point of view the rest of his campaign could be a non-starter for most punters, but for the purist it should be a season to savour. In short, he looked every inch the potential world champion."

A world champion on dirt and turf. Dubai Millennium, if he achieved it, would be the first such champion. Cigar, winner of the inaugural Dubai World Cup, had come close to being acknowledged as the world's first international thoroughbred superstar; but Cigar had been a flop on turf, and he had not run in Europe. Sheikh Mohammed had been fiddling with the notion for years now, first with the creation of the Dubai World Cup, then of the Emirates World Racing Series, a loosely linked set of international Group and Grade 1 races. But never before had a horse come close to really earning the accolade.

To wear the title legitimately, Dubai Millennium would need to win the Breeders' Cup Classic – a race, like the Dubai World Cup, run over a mile and a quarter on dirt. A Breeders' Cup win this year was critical, because the sheikh had also revealed, in his impromptu post-race press conference, that at the end of the season Dubai Millennium would be retired to Dalham Hall Stud.

Some British wags, though, had been whispering that Sheikh Mohammed's colt needed to do more than win at Churchill Downs: he would have to prove himself against last year's Prix de l'Arc de Triomphe winner Montjeu, who already held five Group 1 titles. Owned by Coolmore partner Michael Tabor, Montjeu, unlike Dubai Millennium, could be restrained, allowing his jockey to place him tactically in a race. And he possessed a killer weapon – a devastating turn of foot. He had won the previous year's Irish Derby with such ease that it looked an insult to his nine rivals as he sauntered past them in a canter, jockey Cash Asmussen still high in the saddle, for all the world as if he were out trekking the Curragh's windswept green fields rather than setting down for the drive in a Group 1 race.

Before the sweat had been scraped from Dubai Millennium's coat after the Ascot race, the wags' whispers had turned to open and urgent calls from respected commentators. "Until the colt meets Montjeu, last year's Arc winner, at a mile and a quarter, claims of owning an undisputed world champion will have a hollow ring," wrote McGrath in the *Telegraph*.

"All the evidence suggests that only Montjeu could live with Dubai Millennium in this sort of form, and that really would be a race to savour," wrote the *Racing Post*'s Postmark analyst Paul Curtis.

Chatrooms turned to speculation over the outcome of a theoretical match. "Over a mile and two furlongs, who do you think would win a match race between Montjeu and Dubai Millennium?" Clare Balding was asked on BBC Online Sports Talk. It was July 28, the day before Montjeu was to take his show to Britain for the first time, as hot favourite in the King George VI and Queen Elizabeth Diamond Stakes, the country's premier middle-distance race matching three-year-olds against their elders. Dubai Millennium was not running, as the King George was contested over the Derby distance of a mile and a half.

Balding answered: "Montjeu has less to go wrong. Dubai Millennium still has his temperament problems and if he was to be taken on up front it's uncertain how he would cope. He is a bit of a bully. I feel if Montjeu had a pacemaker to take on Dubai Millennium then he would win with his finishing kick."

All eyes were on Montjeu on Saturday. With the summer ground riding good to firm and a field of seven, including that year's Coronation Stakes winner Daliapour – who had been runner-up in both the Epsom and Irish Derby a year earlier – the Tattersalls Gold Cup-winning filly Shiva and Japanese 2,000 Guineas winner Air Shakur, along with Godolphin's progressive four-year-old Fantastic Light, the race would be no walkover. Then again, it didn't look like there was a serious challenger to Tabor's monstrously talented colt either.

A tall bay colt with a sleekly muscled frame, Montjeu belied his kind expression with a hot-headed personality that made Dubai Millennium's pre-Derby antics look like child's play. As the horses were saddled up and walked from the pre-parade ring along the railed-off passage to the paddock before the King George, he refused to budge. He was led around again and refused again, led around again, and again refused. After half a dozen attempts to coax the unyielding horse out of the ring, trainer John Hammond finally called on Montjeu's work-rider Didier Foloppe to climb aboard. That did the trick, and the race could proceed.

The famously competitive mid-summer contest turned out to be a mere formality for Montjeu. Settled towards the rear by Irish jockey Mick Kinane, who had been struggling all summer with back problems, Montjeu never had to produce his trademark turn of foot. Still on cruise control, he began passing horses with the same scarily offhand speed he showed in the Irish Derby. Once again embarrassing his high-class opponents, he passed the finish line eased down, having never come off the bridle.

Afterwards the understated Kinane and Tabor exchanged jests. "Mick said I could have won on the horse," joked Tabor.[2]

Before the trophy was presented, calls for the two superstars to meet were already reaching a fever pitch. Almost immediately, Sheikh Mohammed, on hand to greet second place finisher Fantastic Light, poured cold water on the suggestion. As Hammond detailed the rest of Montjeu's year, including the Irish Champion Stakes in September and a return to Longchamp for the Prix de l'Arc de Triomphe, possibly ending with a trip to Tokyo for the Japan Cup, Sheikh Mohammed announced his own plans. They did not include the mile-and-a-quarter Irish Champion, the obvious showdown for the pair.

Instead, said the sheikh, Dubai Millennium would duplicate last year's campaign: first a trip to Deauville for another tilt at France's premier mile event, the Prix Jacques le Marois, followed by a return to Ascot for the Queen Elizabeth II Stakes. After that his training would be geared solely towards the Breeders' Cup.

Alluding to a racecourse clash between the two horses, Sheikh Mohammed said cryptically: "You don't light a candle towards the sun!"

He added: "Our target is the Breeders' Cup and we want to space his races. In any case, we beat Beat All further than Montjeu, and I am confident in my horse.

"We wanted to meet Montjeu – why didn't he come to Ascot for the Prince of Wales's? We want to give ours five weeks between races."[3]

He tossed in a casual challenge to Tabor along with the announcement, offering to pay Montjeu's entry fee for the Breeders' Cup race. That was immediately nixed by Hammond.

"Each horse has his own programme and ours might not be the same as theirs. At the moment, our horse is probably a runner in the Irish Champion. If Dubai Millennium is there, he's there. If he isn't, he isn't."[4]

The Chantilly-based Englishman spiced up his response with a veiled warning, remarking that Godolphin's horse had only one style of running, while Montjeu was versatile.

Although connections of both horses had sounded definitive – defiant, even – the press was unwilling to let the topic go. On Sunday, 24 hours after the King George, Alastair Down wrote under a banner headline on the *Racing Post*'s front page: "What everyone in racing wants to see is the showdown to end all showdowns between Dubai Millennium and Montjeu ... It is a clash that would cast a shadow far beyond our sport's casual domain of the racing pages ... And, crucially, neither side has anything to lose because neither Montjeu nor Dubai Millennium would lose any caste in defeat by the other ... Such a clash, in the highest of sporting traditions, would earn all concerned the racing public's lasting gratitude."

No more than 24 hours later, Tabor publicly picked up the call to battle, like Sheikh Mohammed using the racing pages to express his view. Voicing deep disappointment that the Godolphin horse would not be coming to Ireland, he said: "I wish there was some carrot that could be dangled to make Sheikh Mohammed change his mind – I'm open to suggestions and maybe someone will think of something."

But Tabor added: "In no way am I throwing down the gauntlet." Still, he couldn't resist commenting that a clash was what the public wanted. "It would be like Ali against Frazier."[5]

Crisford responded on his boss's behalf, reiterating his primary goal of producing the first world champion racehorse on both dirt and turf. "The goal is not to beat Montjeu or have a clash of two great champions," he told the *Racing Post*, which by now was running daily banner headlines on the notional clash.

Perhaps it was the lavish press coverage that gave Sheikh Mohammed the idea. Perhaps it was, as Down was to say later, that the sheikh "can't see a challenge without hurling himself at it". Whatever the catalyst, three days after Tabor's comments appeared in the press, Down was invited to the Carlton Tower hotel in London for a meeting with the Godolphin executive: Sheikh Mohammed, Simon Crisford and John Ferguson.

It was mid-evening when the journalist arrived at the corner of Cadogan Place and Sloane Street, in the exclusive Knightsbridge district. He was whisked up to the sheikh's private floor, although in effect the five-star hotel in its entirety was part of Sheikh Mohammed's portfolio; later, it would become part of the Jumeirah Group including the spinnaker-shaped Burj Al Arab hotel in Dubai, ultimately belonging to the government investment vehicle Dubai Holdings.

Seated on sofas in the living room, which was tastefully appointed with all the modern comforts subtly shaded in Arabic themes, the Englishmen were served a glass of wine. Sheikh Mohammed took a sip of fruit juice, placed the glass on a table in front of him and began to speak.

He proposed what would be the definitive sporting clash of the new millennium. Yet it would be in the old style of match racing, harking back to the very foundations of the game, when one sportsman pitched his best animal against another's. Forget meeting in the Champion Stakes or Breeders' Cup – this would be a one-on-one, winner take all showdown. The sheikh was putting $6 million on the table, and so would Tabor, if he took up the challenge.

The details were mapped out: the race would take place over a mile and a quarter, under regular Jockey Club rules, with a choice of three dates and venues: August 24 at York, two days later at Newmarket, or on September 23 at Ascot.

The idea would be presented in Saturday's *Racing Post*, splashed across the front page. Down, for one, did not take Tabor's earlier call for a meeting as a serious challenge – it had been a rhetorical gesture, a throwaway remark turned into a headline. But this would be a genuine laying down of the gauntlet. It would draw the attention of the sporting world beyond racing to these two equine champions, and all that they stood for. As far as Dubai Millennium was concerned, that was quite a lot. The strapping bay colt carried the history of racing, of the thoroughbred itself; the hopes of Godolphin; and the rise of Dubai in a new, hopeful and prosperous millennium. Godolphin stood for Dubai, the horse stood for Godolphin. But he was more than that too.

As Down saw it, Sheikh Mohammed's love of the horse as such had found its ultimate expression in Dubai Millennium. The colt was a near-perfect example of thoroughbred potential, his beauty and talent the chance synergy of generations of knowledge, hazard, guesswork and hope.

The atmosphere in the room was lighthearted, bubbling. Crisford in particular was buzzing with excitement, Down, another glass of wine in hand, was already mentally composing his front-page scoop. Sheikh Mohammed was at his best, sights on a target and full steam ahead. Only Tabor could stop the momentum now. Would he take up the challenge?

1. Jon Lees, "Frankie: my battle is only just starting", *Racing Post*, 6 June 2000.
2. Richard Griffiths, "No match to be found for Montjeu the magnificent", *Racing Post*, 30 July 2000.
3. Jon Lees, "Godolphin ace set for Deauville", *Racing Post*, 30 July 2000.
4. Richard Griffiths, "No match to be found for Montjeu the magnificent", *Racing Post*, 30 July 2000.
5. Matt Chapman, "'Think of something'", *Racing Post*, 31 July 2000.

CHAPTER EIGHT

BREAKDOWN

A fine warm summer sun was rising over Newmarket as heavy bundles containing hundreds of copies of the *Racing Post* were delivered to the High Street newsagents on Saturday, August 5. Hoofbeats rang their centuries-old cadence in the streets as strings trooped out to exercise. The gallops were already dotted with horses.

The Godolphin team was out on the Limekilns, where the trial gallop, a strip of land along the hedge used only during peak season, had been opened. Dubai Millennium, with Tony Proctor up, was working seven furlongs with Lockinge Stakes winner Fly To The Stars. Saeed bin Suroor accompanied them on the stable pony, while Simon Crisford and Tom Albertrani took the car.

They were still puzzling over one of Dubai Millennium's latest works. Godolphin had been filming a documentary video of the colt's performances, at the races and while working at Al Quoz and Newmarket. The day the cameramen came to film him in Newmarket, after the Prince of Wales's Stakes, he threw in an uncharacteristically lethargic piece of work. Although he eventually picked up, and came out of the breeze looking fine, they were still scratching their heads over it.

Today there were no cameras and the big colt was on his toes. Stretching out into an easy, powerful stride over the fresh ground, he shrugged off his work companion, a Group 1 miler, with effortless disdain. Proctor didn't even need to step on the pedal. When he pulled his mount out, the electrifying burst of speed was instantaneous, and in a flash, the work was all over.

The riders pulled up their horses at the bottom of the Limekilns, turned back and walked through a gap in the hedge and down toward the traffic lights, heading home to Moulton Paddocks. When they reached the lights, Proctor felt Dubai Millennium take a tender step, as if he'd trod on a stone. Bin Suroor rode up beside him. "How was he?" he asked the rider.

"He's fine, it was a good work for him," answered Proctor.

"No, he's not right – jump off," said bin Suroor.

Looking shocked, Proctor hopped off. It was immediately apparent that the horse's right hind leg was beginning to swell. With the rider leading the colt, they walked from the traffic lights back to the stables, a trip of about 20 minutes. The leg continued to swell, and the horse was now clearly lame. By the time he was home, he could scarcely walk. Proctor could feel his stomach turning, and bin Suroor didn't want to believe his eyes, but there was no doubt at all by now – this was a grave, career-threatening problem.

By now Crisford and Albertrani had been informed, and Crisford called Sheikh Mohammed at his home. The sheikh drove immediately to the stables.

"I remember he said, 'This is from the gods,'" said bin Suroor.

"He said, 'You can't do anything about it. It's happened now. And now we just want to save his life.'"

At his home in Stetchworth, just outside of Newmarket, Frankie Dettori was working out on his treadmill. Today was to be his comeback; he was riding two horses at Newmarket, Atlantis Prince for Sean Woods and Dim Sums for David Barron, but all he had been thinking of all summer while pushing himself to the limit to recover from his injuries and regain his fitness was one thing: riding Dubai Millennium in the Prix Jacques le Marois.

The phone rang and he stepped off the treadmill, which was still running. "I remember hearing the treadmill still going, and somebody said, 'Dubai Millennium broke down,'" he recalled. "I just couldn't get back on the treadmill. I thought, 'Why am I doing it? What's the point of getting back on it? The only reason I'm trying to come back is for him, and now he's gone, so why am I doing all this?'"

The gallop had taken place at 6.30am. By 8.00am, Dubai Millennium had been x-rayed and transported to Rossdale & Partners veterinary clinic in Newmarket, where a team led by Dan Hawkins, formerly from the prestigious veterinary team of Hagyard-Davidson-McGee in Kentucky and now the senior surgeon at Dubai Equine Hospital, would attempt to repair a lateral condylar fracture to the colt's right hind leg.

Godolphin's overarching concern was the horse's health, the number-one priority with any serious fracture being to save the patient's life. Horses are no longer shot automatically after breaking a leg, but that doesn't mean that breaks aren't still life-threatening.

Despite this worry, Simon Crisford couldn't help but feel dismay at the irony of it all: around the time that Michael Tabor was opening his morning paper to find Sheikh Mohammed's bold challenge to his horse, Godolphin already knew that Dubai Millennium's career was definitively over. Soon Tabor and the rest of the racing world would know too.

They hadn't heard yet, though, and by 9.00 the Duke of Devonshire, representing Ascot racecourse, was on the line to Crisford to say that Ascot would be happy to stage the showdown.

Because of the inevitable publicity from the match race challenge, there was little time to lose in bringing the public up to date, and within hours Godolphin had issued a press release.

"Dubai Millennium sustained a lateral condylar fracture of his right hind when working on the Limekilns at Newmarket this morning and will be retired to stud.

"The brilliant racehorse will require surgery and internal fixation for this serious injury which sadly means that his racing days are over. He will stand at Sheikh Mohammed's Dalham Hall Stud next year.

"The injury came just after Sheikh Mohammed offered a sporting challenge to Michael Tabor, the owner of the other great horse this year, Montjeu, to a match against Dubai Millennium over ten furlongs for six million dollars a side. Unfortunately, this match will not now take place."

Inevitably, there would be some people who called the whole deal a marketing ploy, cynics who surmised wrongly that the horse had been injured earlier and was being sent out with a PR salute worthy of the wiliest spinmeister. Those doubters had not come face to face with a dispirited Frankie Dettori, listening aimlessly to the grind of the treadmill as it ran on and on, or with a broken-hearted Tony Proctor, who was so devastated by what had happened that he left the Godolphin yard that day for a two-week break. Wandering off alone, leaving even Sam, his wife, behind, he drifted down to David

Elsworth's stable, where he had begun his riding career all those years ago, and in his own words "wallowed in my own self-pity".

The great disappointment to Godolphin was that Dubai Millennium would miss two historical challenges – the match race and the Breeders' Cup Classic. After that, the plan had always been for him to retire to stud. Had he beaten Montjeu in a one-on-one on turf, and then gone on to trounce America's finest on dirt, he would have been, indisputably, the first world champion on both surfaces.

Everyone on the team believed the colt had been finally rounding into optimum form. He had taken so long to develop, from a gangly, backwards yearling to an oversized two-year-old, to a headstrong three-year-old who didn't know how to channel his energy. Now, as Dettori noted in the World Cup, Dubai Millennium was learning to control his raw energy and use it to his advantage. Both Dettori and Tony Proctor, who knew the colt as intimately as anybody, wanted to tell the world, "You ain't seen nothing yet".

"The great regret that I've got up to this day," said Dettori, six years after the breakdown, "is that just as he was coming to be an absolute ultimate superstar, just as he managed to control his own power, he blew out. What a shame. I was looking forward to that match race so much. Because he was actually going to become what would have been an unbelievable horse. It took us so long to teach him to use the fantastic raw power that he had; it was a shame that he was just coming to his best. We've all been cheated of one of the fantastic racehorses of all time."

Said Proctor, "I don't think people ever saw the best of him. He just had such a short career. He was spoiled, really, because there was so much potential, so much ability there, it was unreal. You could almost say we could have been so confident going to the

Breeders' Cup, because he was exceptional. I've never seen a horse like him, and I probably never will. You were never going to get the same feeling again."

Dubai Millennium arrived at his new home on Sunday night, a day after the surgery. An equine ambulance carried him to Dalham Hall Stud and, using a hydraulic lift which precluded the need for the patient to walk down a ramp, delivered him to the corner box in which he was born. It was a quiet spot, under the shade of Dalham Hall's lofty trees and away from the main activity of what was now the stallion barn. Liam O'Rourke, in his ninth year as Dalham Hall's stud manager, would now take over day-to-day management of the stallion's career.

O'Rourke had about a century of equine experience packed into his thirty-odd years. He didn't like to brag, or even talk about it – "I hate developing that old jaded, boring story, it can't make good reading," he said – but he had done the "Irish U" course, working summers at the Curragh, graduating from the Irish National Stud's famed programme, doing stints on American racetracks from Saratoga to Monmouth to Del Mar.

Along the way – or perhaps it was a natural gift – he had learned something rare and valuable: equanimity. Whatever disasters were raining down upon him – and there were plenty on a stud with a dozen or so stallions and tens of broodmares and foals, not to mention the hundreds of visiting mares passing through each season – O'Rourke kept his head. Now his calm would be tested by a cantankerous and high-profile patient.

In the beginning his job with Dubai Millennium was simply to oversee intensive care in hopes that the horse would recover fully. Although equine medical treatment has come a long way from the days when a broken leg meant a bullet in the head, a displaced fracture is still a serious injury, and recovery is never guaranteed. A fractious patient can re-injure the broken limb, while the mere act of resting a full 1,000lb on the opposite leg can lead to laminitis, an excruciating condition in which the blood pools in the affected foot, causing necrosis of the surrounding tissue and rotation of the coffin bone inside the hoof. Laminitis often ends in death, as the horse can no longer stand. The old maxim 'No foot, no horse' is as true as ever.

Dubai Millennium was receiving medication every four hours around the clock, and O'Rourke and his men quickly found that he was not a willing patient. The colt was in pain and resented the constant intrusion of people with syringes and needles. The first night they treated him, he whipped his head round and took a big chunk off the stud manager's finger.

Godolphin had warned O'Rourke to put a chain over the colt's nose whenever he was handled, but that didn't seem to tame him in the box. The second night they treated him, O'Rourke was to meet the attending vet outside the barn at 1.30am. Another Irishman, a farmer's son who was remarkable for his astute powers of observation, was on the nightwatch shift. O'Rourke, who had arrived 15 minutes early, walked over to the box and saw Francis standing inside with Dubai Millennium, who had his head down and seemed alarmingly quiet.

"I thought, 'I hope he's all right'," O'Rourke remembered. "And then I saw that he'd clipped the chain on to the ring below the horse's jaw. And the horse just stood there. And the vet came in, and the horse never blinked; he injected him, and the horse never moved. And from there on we could handle him by not messing with him, by not putting the chain over his nose, because as soon as we did that he got quite upset. And that's all it was – he didn't like people fussing with him."

After that revelation Dubai Millennium became a model patient. Once his leg was stabilised, the fracture healed and the threat of laminitis lifted, the main job was to get him physically fit. Stallions at busy commercial studs like Dalham Hall work hard; although its demands are vastly different than those of racing, the stallion business requires significant energy, not least of which is libido. Exercise, nutrition and daily variety – turnout time or hand-walking – all contribute to a stallion's wellbeing and thus his efficiency.

Beginning on December 1, the Dalham Hall stallions begin a fitness regime to prepare them for the breeding season beginning in mid-February. The programme begins with an hour and a half or more of hand-walking each day, and when the horses are fit enough, 15 minutes of twice-weekly lunging – trotting and cantering in a circle on the end of a long line – is introduced. In Dubai Millennium's case the programme had to be curtailed to short periods of hand-walking, so it was hard to tell if he was getting fit enough for the season ahead, with a full book of 100 mares awaiting him. Any doubts were firmly answered after his first 'test' covering, though.

New stallions, like any athletic recruits, undergo a sort of testing and training period. Beginning in December and January, Dalham Hall introduces non-thoroughbred mares on whom the new stallions perform experimental covers. Not all stallions are natural Lotharios, but Dubai Millennium's test covers left no doubt: the horse's libido, like most of his attributes, was larger than life.

A stallion's hind legs are particularly subject to stress as he jumps on top of up to three mares daily, and the one remaining worry about Dubai Millennium was that he would re-injure the old fracture. However, the fears proved unfounded. A highly intelligent horse, he seemed to take care of himself despite his abundant sexual desire.

Ken Crozier, the Scotsman who had looked after Shareef Dancer, was the head stallion man. Dubai Millennium left a vivid impression on him.

"Coming down through the yard, he knew exactly where he was going," Crozier recalled. "You'd hear him shouting, coming in the door, hollering and rearing."

Indicating the double-wide door of the covering shed, he said; "When he came in there, he virtually filled the whole door up. His ears were up, and he was really ..." The small, wiry Crozier broadened his shoulders and made a roaring sound. "He knew exactly what he was doing. He was a real man."

The first mare that Dubai Millennium covered was Zelanda. One of the Darley mares, she had been a smart sprinter in her day for Sheikh Mohammed. Her background provided an interesting blend of speed and stamina; a daughter of the speed-injecting sire Night Shift, she had shown a blistering turn of foot herself. However, her dam was a mare called Zafadola, a product of the Aga Khan's stamina-rich breeding programme. Zafadola, by the stamina-influencing sire Darshaan, had been a classy stayer who finished third in the Irish St Leger for the Aga Khan.

Eleven months later, on January 13, 2002, Zelanda would give birth to Dubai Millennium's first foal, a chestnut colt, at Wimbledon Farms in Lexington, Kentucky. Named Rajwa, the colt would enter training, along with 25 of his paternal siblings, with Godolphin in 2004.

But that was two years hence. For now Dubai Millennium was busy in a new role he clearly relished. "His fertility was fantastic, and he didn't look back," said O'Rourke.

CHAPTER NINE

MATING
PLANS

Dubai Millennium would need to work efficiently to meet the demands of his first breeding season. While the dream hatched in the Carlton Tower was gone forever, just days had gone by after the fateful morning on the gallops when Sheikh Mohammed called another meeting, this time inviting his bloodstock advisers to his residence in Deauville, where Dubai Millennium and Dettori should have been defending the colt's title in the Prix Jacques le Marois.

Under the slanting light of a long Normandy summer evening, Sheikh Mohammed, accompanied by his eldest brother and constant confidant, Sheikh Maktoum, pulled forth another plan. It would be, in his inimitable style, a grand experiment, unprecedented in scope, scale, and the resources devoted to it. Dubai Millennium was the best, the most talented and charismatic horse, that Godolphin had ever raced. Now at stud, he would become the centre of the world's greatest breeding experiment.

Sheikh Mohammed's plan was to source the globe's elite mares, choosing 100 to mate with his stallion. However, the goal was more ambitious than simply to compile a book of mares that had won at the top level, or produced Group or Grade 1 winners. What the sheikh wanted was to achieve in one year what would normally take five. He and his advisers would draw a cross-section of every type of high-class mare, sprinters, milers, as well as winners of the mile-and-a-half Oaks; they would include American dirt performers, European turf stars, and South American mares, with their notorious toughness and durability. Thereby Sheikh Mohammed would find out which type, or types, of mare produced the best runners when crossed with Dubai Millennium.

The sheikh hammered home a point: in the past, a lot of the best-bred horses that he had put to stud had been patronised by a very similar type of mare. In the early days of Dalham Hall stallions Machiavellian and Ajdal, for example, the syndicate shareholders had chosen as mates for the young stallions what they considered their best mares. These were usually their Oaks winners. That was fine, if the stallion happened to have a genetic affinity for that type of mare. But how would you know? Only through trial and error. Moreover, you would not have the results for five years – by which time the first crop would be three-year-olds.

After five years, if it became clear that the Oaks mares weren't working, you might try another type of mare. But that would entail another five years of waiting ... it was an altogether inefficient process, the breeding of thoroughbreds.

Sheikh Mohammed's experiment was an attempt to speed up the process, while giving Dubai Millennium the optimum chance to succeed as a sire. The bloodstock advisers would have to act quickly. Luckily, if there was one thing to be thankful for about Dubai

Sheikh Mohammed discusses plans with trainer David Loder, who earmarked the unraced Dubai Millennium as "the best horse I've ever handled".

Tony Proctor keeping Dubai Millennium to an easy gallop at Al Quoz training centre the morning before the colt's devastating Dubai World Cup win.

Team Godolphin: from left to right, Frankie Dettori, Maktoum family advisor John Leat, Tom Albertrani, Sheikh Mohammed and Saeed bin Suroor at York. © Phil Smith

Dubai Millennium wins the Queen Elizabeth II Stakes with an overpowering display at Ascot, 26 September 1999, under Frankie Dettori.

Godolphin's best win ever: Dettori and Dubai Millennium achieve the ultimate dream as they cross the finish line of the 2000 Dubai World Cup in splendid isolation. © Trevor Jones

An injured Frankie Dettori and his able sub Jerry Bailey are all smiles after Dubai Millennium's eight-length win in the Prince of Wales's Stakes, 21 June 2000.

Dalham Hall Stud manager Liam O'Rourke (right) and head stallion man Ken Crozier prepare Dubai Millennium for his new career in November 2000. © Trevor Jones

Echo Of Light, Dubai Millennium's treble-Group-winning son out of Spirit Of Tara, at the Goffs Orby Sale where Sheikh Mohammed paid €1.2 million for him.

Sheikh Mohammed and his chief bloodstock advisor John Ferguson survey the scene at Dalham Hall Stud during the annual stallion parade in July.

A joyous moment, as Sheikh Mohammed and Princess Haya lead in Dubawi after his win in the Prix Jacques le Marois, also won by his sire. Kerrin McEvoy is up.

Simon Crisford casts a critical eye over the talented but wayward Rakti, one of Dubawi's main rivals in the QEII at Newmarket. Princess Haya is in the background.

Sheikh Mohammed bin Rashid Al Maktoum, with his wife Princess Haya bint Al Hussein, at the Arab Investment and Capital Markets Conference in Beirut, 2004.

Dubawi (left), given a controversial ride by Dettori, can't get past the imposing Australasian interloper Starcraft in the QEII at Newmarket, 24 September 2005.

Dubai Millennium surveys the world from his box at Moullon Paddocks, a week before his career-ending injury on the Newmarket gallops.

DUBAI MILLENNIUM
SEEKING THE GOLD ~ COLORADO DANCER
1996 ~ 2001
WORLD CHAMPION
EUROPEAN CHAMPION MILER AT 3
CHAMPION OLDER HORSE IN EUROPE, 2000
HORSE OF THE YEAR IN U.A.E., 2000
WINNER OF £2,752,580 AND
9 RACES FROM 10 STARTS,
including -
DUBAI WORLD CUP (G1)
QUEEN ELIZABETH II STAKES (G1)
PRIX JACQUES LE MAROIS (G1)
PRINCE OF WALES'S STAKES (G1)

Dubai Millennium's gravestone at Dalham Hall. It is next to the gravestone of his broodmare sire Shareef Dancer, and a few strides from the box where he was born.

Millennium's breakdown – aside from the fact that he had recovered – it was the timing. Mare owners would not decide their mating plans until later in the autumn. There was still time for an international recruiting blitz.

The mares would be chosen using both physical and pedigree criteria. The physical test mainly entailed filtering the athletes, mares with powerful physiques, be they big or small – although with his size, Dubai Millennium wouldn't need any particularly large mares to compensate in that area.

Pedigree was a more complex matter. There are all kinds of theories as to which bloodlines do or do not combine well. As a grandson of the legendary Kentucky stallion Mr Prospector on his sire's side, and with Northern Dancer as one of his great-grandsires on his dam's side, Dubai Millennium was already an example of one of the most popular and successful crosses of the times.

Many people believe that inbreeding to a particular ancestor is a good way of multiplying the beneficial influence of that ancestor, while others argue that inbreeding is harmful. Of course, the success of those theories may hinge on how closely inbred the individual is. In any case, inbreeding to Northern Dancer, the most successful transatlantic sire at the turn of the millennium, had become a particularly hot topic in breeding circles.

As it turned out, the mares selected for Dubai Millennium provided him with an unusually high number of Northern Dancer crosses. When an ancestor is repeated twice in the third generation, the individual is said to be inbred 3x3; if it is repeated twice in the fourth generation, the inbreeding is 4x4. The general incidence of Northern Dancer inbreeding, at a level of 4x4 or closer, in the foals of a high-profile stallion prospect who has Northern Dancer within three generations of his own pedigree, has not been studied.

However, a haphazard survey of some such stallions in Britain and Ireland found the 'normal' range among their foals to be about 30 per cent. In Dubai Millennium's progeny, it was nearly 60 per cent.

According to John Ferguson, Sheikh Mohammed's chief bloodstock adviser, the Northern Dancer inbreeding was part of the experiment – "If you were not to inbreed to Northern Dancer, you wouldn't know if inbreeding to him worked," was how he put it.

Attracting mares proved to be no problem. Breeders across the globe were impressed by Dubai Millennium's race record, his blue-blooded pedigree and his imposing physique. And most of them were amenable to the rather unusual terms Ferguson suggested.

The Maktoum family would provide about one-third of the mares for Dubai Millennium. As to the rest, Sheikh Mohammed proposed a foal-sharing system. Rather than pay the £100,000 fee that had been set for the stallion's services, breeders would give up a half-share in the foal to Darley, Sheikh Mohammed's breeding operation. Then when the foal had grown into a yearling, Darley could offer to buy them out.

Foal-sharing is not uncommon on commercial studs, but it is not the norm; the majority of stud services are paid for in cash. Sometimes a venerable older stallion, who at the end of his career is becoming less fertile and physically more fragile, might entertain a small book of mares on special terms. But it was certainly unusual for an entire book of mares for a high-profile, newly retired stallion advertised on the open market to consist entirely of foal shares.

However, the scheme suited Sheikh Mohammed's penchant for directing and controlling his projects. The terms were also favourable to breeders who might otherwise hesitate at the hefty price tag on Dubai Millennium's services.

There were additional perks that attracted breeders. Darley

would pay all costs for the mares involved, and provide overseas transport – a matter of thousands of pounds – for the numerous mates coming from abroad. Veterinary services, feed, bedding, shoeing – Darley would front all of these costs. On top of that, Sheikh Mohammed invited the breeders to first-class travel and hospitality for the 2001 Dubai World Cup, culminating in a return to England for a tour of Dalham Hall and a visit with Dubai Millennium.

David Mullins, one of the thriving band of breeders who left their native Ireland to sink deep and lucrative roots in central Kentucky, was thrilled to hear that the mare belonging to him and his American wife, Ginger, had been accepted by the admissions committee. For Mullins, the visit to Dalham Hall had special meaning; after leaving school, he had spent a spell working on the old Derisley Wood Stud, which had been part of the original Dalham Hall. Derisley was later parcelled off and packaged with another stud, Hadrian, and in 1986 Sheikh Mohammed added those properties to Dalham Hall, which he had bought five years earlier.

Mullins remembered the glory days of Great Nephew, the Prix du Moulin winner who had sired the 1975 and 1981 Derby winners, Grundy and Shergar – the latter horse, who had also won the Irish Derby and King George VI and Queen Elizabeth Diamond Stakes, made legendary by his mysterious kidnapping in 1983 from the Irish stud where he had retired as a stallion.

But all that was long ago, and now David and Ginger Mullins were preparing for the trip of a lifetime thanks to Sheena's Gold, a mare they had claimed off a Maryland racecourse for $5,000.

Although she had earned less than twice that in her racing career, Sheena's Gold came from a family whose stock had been rising for the last decade. It was a funny sort of family, with a strong odour of parvenu redeemed by a whiff of blue-chip about it. Afasheen, the dam of Sheena's Gold, came from 'old money', namely the Aga Khans, and she could boast some distinguished ancestors, including her sire Sheshoon. A top-class stayer, who had the ability to run long and fast over distances of up to two miles, he was Europe's champion sire of 1970.

However, as some distinguished families do, this one had fallen on lean times and Afasheen's 12 foals had yielded just one minor stakes performer. In her senescence, the mare had ended up in the United States; Sheena's Gold, born in 1990, was her last foal.

Sheena's Gold, like Dubai Millennium, was a grand-daughter of Mr Prospector. However, her sire, Fast Gold, was a few rungs down the ladder from Dubai Millennium's sire Seeking The Gold. Not long after Sheena's Gold was born, Fast Gold was exiled to Brazil, a growing market for stallions who weren't making the grade in Kentucky's competitive climate.

The filly's pedigree and physique did not excite buyers at either Keeneland's Fall Yearling Sale in Kentucky in 1991 or an auction for unraced two-year-olds in Florida the following year; she was sold for $19,000 at the former and $15,500 at the latter.

Racing on the minor mid-Atlantic circuit at Laurel and Pimlico, Sheena's Gold ran exclusively in claiming competition – races in which every runner has a price for which it can be 'claimed' prior to the start – and it was thus that David and Ginger Mullins acquired her on April 13, 1993, from trainer Barclay Tagg and Last Chance Stable.

The mile-and-a-sixteenth dirt track contest was the filly's last of ten starts, and she finished third, earning $638. But although she had failed to brighten the family's dulled lustre, recording a single win over two years of racing, David and Ginger were pleased with their purchase. She had shown ability, 'hitting the board' by finishing first, second or third four times, and she had been the betting favourite in four of her starts.

Moreover, some of her siblings were showing promise as broodmares. Her elder half-sister On The Tiles, by Thatch, won just one of three starts in Ireland, but On The Tiles's first foal, born three years before Sheena's Gold, became a Group 1 winner in France. Five years later, On The Tiles produced a colt named Stiletto Blade, who flashed enough talent to finish second in the Group 2 Royal Lodge Stakes for two-year-olds at Ascot.

Another of Sheena's Gold's half-sisters, Future Past, had been a hardy racemare, running 59 times and winning four races. Her total earnings of $33,961 bore witness that hers was not a high level of athleticism, but nonetheless, she was an athlete. Like On The Tiles, she found her niche in the breeding shed; the family genes that had been doing so little for her generation were once again put to good use. Future Past's fourth foal was All The Way, who had led nearly all the way in Dubai Millennium's Derby to finish fifth behind Oath. The next year All The Way had won the Emirates Singapore Derby for Sheikh Maktoum.

The Mullins' speculation proved sound as they sold Sheena's Gold's second foal (by the Kentucky sire Runaway Groom) for $52,000 after he was weaned. Resold twice, the colt, named The Groom Is Red, later won a Grade 1 race, the Champagne Stakes for two-year-olds, and earned more than $400,000.

That was in 1998, and now Sheena's Gold had the freshly minted credentials that all broodmare owners seek: she was a Grade 1 producer. David and Ginger first thought of breeding her to Dubai Millennium when they saw an advertisement posted by Reynolds Bell, a Kentucky bloodstock agent whose office was helping to collect suitable mares from the States. They happily agreed to the foal-sharing terms.

Other American mares who signed on included Fitnah, whose first foal, three-year-old Dreams Gallore, had recently won the Grade 1 Mother Goose Stakes and finished second in the Kentucky Oaks and Coaching Club American Oaks. There was also Eaves, a mare from the vaunted Claiborne Farm breeding programme, who was a half-sister to the young sire Boundary; Storm Song, bred by William S Farish and Ogden Mills Phipps, and named the champion US two-year-old filly of 1998 after winning the Breeders' Cup Juvenile Fillies; Sweet Willa, a half-sister to Grade 1 winners Will's Way and Willa On The Move; Jode, a half-sister to Kentucky Derby winner and Horse of the Year Spend A Buck; Cinnamon Sugar, a Grade 2 winner who also boasted multiple placings in Grade 1 races; and Parade Queen, a stakes winner on turf and dirt.

In Britain many of the big breeders were also keen to breed to Dubai Millennium. Among them was Juddmonte Farms – although the farm's owner, Prince Khalid Abdullah, declined to enter a foal-sharing agreement. Juddmonte's mare was Daring Miss, a young mare by Sadler's Wells who, like many of her sire's runners, was adept at middle distances – races over a mile and a half or so. Daring Miss had won the Group 2 Grand Prix de Chantilly, but she really sealed her fitness for a mating with Dubai Millennium by finishing second to Montjeu in the Grand Prix de Saint-Cloud just three weeks before Michael Tabor's star won the King George.

Prince Khalid was not the only one to hold out against the foal-sharing proposal. Other breeders who chose to pay the full stud fee included Trevor and Elizabeth Harris, who had recently purchased the historic Lordship Stud in Newmarket; Roger Baines, another relative newcomer in the breeding business, who owned Britton

House Stud; and two breeders with deeper roots, Philippa Cooper of Normandie Stud and Kilcarn Stud owner Pat O'Kelly.

The Harrises had applied with Hydro Calido. Like Daring Miss, she had been a high-class racing filly in France. Bred and raced by Greek shipping magnate Stavros Niarchos, Hydro Calido was also out of a mare by a son of Northern Dancer. Furthermore, she was a half-sister to one of Dalham Hall's best stallions, Machiavellian.

Baines sent yet another mare who was descended from a strong French family. However, Solo De Lune's best performance had come in Germany, where she was second in a minor stakes race. She had already proved her value as a broodmare, most notably with her daughter Cerulean Sky, who had won the Group 1 Prix Saint-Alary at Longchamp a year earlier.

Philippa Cooper sent in an application for Napoleon's Sister. Descended from yet another stallion from Northern Dancer's male line (Alzao), Napoleon's Sister had won the Lupe Stakes over a mile and a quarter. Even more notably, she was a half-sister to Oath.

Pat O'Kelly, whose Kilcarn Stud had a long and lucrative history in Ireland, nominated her mare Spirit Of Tara. Spirit Of Tara was also by Sadler's Wells, and she boasted one of the best pedigrees of any of the applicants: she was a sister to Salsabil, who had won both the 1,000 Guineas and the Epsom Oaks for Sheikh Hamdan before beating the boys in the Irish Derby. She had proved an exceptional producer since her retirement.

Spirit Of Tara was also a half-sister to Marju, who won the St James's Palace Stakes, one of Europe's top miling events, and finished second in the Derby. He too had become a valuable breeding commodity for Sheikh Hamdan, who had purchased both Salsabil and Marju from O'Kelly at public auctions in Ireland.

There was no doubt that Darley would like to have a share in

Spirit Of Tara's foal. However, O'Kelly was determined to pay for the nomination and keep control of the foal herself, at least until it was a yearling. Kilcarn was a commercial stud, and like Salsabil and Marju before him, this foal would eventually go on the market.

Ferguson and O'Kelly arranged to meet in Deauville to discuss the matter. "He was very keen to foal-share, and said he was surprised when I told him I didn't want to," said O'Kelly. "But I was sure the foal would be worth more than twice the stud fee, so I didn't mind paying it."

The applications were collected with lightning speed, and Sheikh Mohammed and his team pored over them. They wasted little time in sorting the 100 successful applicants. "It all happened in a matter of days," recalled Ferguson. "The actual matings happened very quickly, because everybody was so quick to send in their suggestions, and Sheikh Mohammed was very keen to foal-share with a lot of the mares. Therefore price didn't really come into it."

Among the British breeders who entered into foal-sharing arrangements were Anthony Oppenheimer's Hascombe & Valiant Studs, which sent the Coronation Stakes winner Balisada. It would be the second time that Balisada and Dubai Millennium had met; the first was at Ascot in 1999, when Oppenheimer's filly finished 30 lengths behind the Godolphin colt in the Queen Elizabeth II Stakes. This, it was hoped, would be a happier meeting.

From Ireland, Mrs Max Morris was sending Sheer Audacity. The mare was the dam of Oath, giving her obvious, if faintly ironic, appeal as a mate. A daughter of the 200th Derby winner, Troy, Sheer Audacity had also bred Pelder, a three-time Group 1 winner in Italy and France. Although she was getting on in years – she would be a 17-year-old when the breeding season rolled around – she was well qualified.

The Irish National Stud, too, was getting in on the act, sending the dam of Desert King, who had landed the Irish 2,000 Guineas/ Irish Derby double three years earlier. The mare, Sabaah, had never won a race but she was a half-sister to Maroof, who had beaten Breeders' Cup Mile winner Barathea in the Queen Elizabeth II Stakes, and her dam had won the Group 2 Ribblesdale Stakes at Royal Ascot. Sabaah was yet another mare descending from Northern Dancer; her sire was Northern Dancer's son Nureyev.

There was further international interest from France, where Jean-Luc Lagardere kept his substantial broodmare band. Lagardere's mare Miss Satamixa already had something in common with her mate-to-be: she had won the Prix Jacques le Marois.

From Japan, Katsumi Yoshida would send two mares purchased in Europe: Reve d'Oscar and Seazun. The former had been a top performer in France, where she won the Group 1 Prix Saint-Alary, a mile-and-a-quarter race for fillies, and she had later proved competitive against the opposite sex, finishing second in the Gran Premio del Jockey Club. For her final start, she had finished a close-up fifth in the Japan Cup.

Seazun, a precocious two-year-old runner, had won the Group 1 Cheveley Park Stakes, and she was by Godolphin's top-class two-year-old sprinter Zieten. Her grandsire was Danzig, another son of Northern Dancer.

The book was completed by a number of the Maktoum family's best mares, including Shadwell Stud's Elfaslah, the dam of 1999 Dubai World Cup winner Almutawakel. Darley, of course, was sending numerous mares, among them Walesiana, a classy German performer for Sheikh Mohammed, and her daughter, the Group 1 Nassau Stakes winner Zahrat Dubai. Cape Verdi, the

1,000 Guineas winner who had flopped in the Derby, was another; she was by Caerleon, a grandson of Northern Dancer.

Sheikh Mohammed's plan may have been to extend the scope of Dubai Millennium's mates beyond Oaks winners, but he wasn't going to say no to Zomaradah. The mare was owned by his cousin, Sheikh Mohammed Obaid Al Maktoum, who had also owned High-Rise when he won the 1998 Derby. Zomaradah had won the Oaks d'Italia, and her grandsires were the Derby winner Shirley Heights and Prix de l'Arc de Triomphe winner Dancing Brave (who was second in the Derby). Moreover, she was closely related to High-Rise. If Dubai Millennium's genetic make-up was at all suited to an Oaks type of mare, Zomaradah should be an ideal mate. In any case, the theory would be put to the test.

Now, for the theorists, it was a case of watching and waiting. The real work was handed over to O'Rourke and team during the busy breeding season at Dalham Hall.

CHAPTER TEN

THE UNLUCKIEST
BLOW

It had been a particularly wet spring in Newmarket. At Dalham Hall, Liam O'Rourke and his team were pleased to find some early grass in a shaded area that they could cut and hand-feed to the indoor horses, stallions as well as broodmares who for one reason or another weren't allowed turnout time.

"It was in order to try to keep the stallions' energy level up and keep their digestive systems right," explained O'Rourke afterwards. "We felt it would benefit them, in their coats and in their general health. Plus, they would really look forward to some fresh grass."

Dubai Millennium welcomed the new regime with typical enthusiasm, charging to the front of his box for the grass, taking great green bites and savouring the sweet, bright blades down to the last nibble.

"We'd been doing this for about five, six days, and you're talking about probably no more than three double handfuls," O'Rourke said.

On the morning of Monday, April 21, head stallion man Ken Crozier noticed something was wrong with Dubai Millennium. The stallion had covered his 8.00am mare, Hydro Calido, who was a half-sister to O'Rourke's favourite Dalham Hall sire, Machiavellian, and had been brought over for the morning from Lordship Stud on the other side of Newmarket. The covering had gone uneventfully, but after being put back in his box the stallion seemed to lack his normal bouncy energy. "I went down and saw him straight away, and I could see he was uneasy," said O'Rourke. "He'd gotten a little bit colicky after he'd covered his mare, but he seemed to settle down, and we thought maybe it was just gas."

Dubai Millennium was sent out for his routine morning exercise of hand-walking, and before taking his coffee break, Crozier checked in on him again. What he saw set alarm bells ringing in his mind.

"He was uneasy in his box, and he was sweating," Crozier remembered. Delineating the telltale signs of colic, he said: "Pawing the ground, sweating, going down for a roll, getting up, going around the box, down for another roll, getting up again ..."

Crozier had seen this many times before. But although colic is common, it can also be deadly, and at 10.30am he summoned O'Rourke. "I'm not happy with Dubai Millennium," he told the stud manager.

O'Rourke noted especially that the behaviour was most uncharacteristic of the stallion. He knew from his recuperation the summer before that this was a tough horse with a high pain threshold. That made his present distress all the more worrisome, and he and Crozier called Darley vet James Crowhurst.

By lunchtime Crowhurst had arrived. A tall, fair-haired man, he wore the perpetually harried air of someone faced with a hundred daily emergencies, but it was usually offset by a wry sense of humour. Today he looked worried, but not unduly so, as he gave Dubai Millennium a thorough going over, including a rectal exam to detect any signs of impaction that might be causing colic. Although the horse had some light patchy sweating on his flanks that concerned O'Rourke, Crowhurst felt that was not unusual in colic cases. He administered a painkiller and instructed the men to contact him if there was no improvement.

The painkiller failed to settle the stallion, and two hours later Crowhurst returned to Dalham Hall, where he met Huw Neal, the chief colic surgeon from Greenwood Ellis. "Although his condition wasn't alarming, he had failed to respond to the painkiller, and that is always concerning," said Crowhurst. However, he was encouraged to note that the horse's pulse and demeanour were good.

The vets decided to admit Dubai Millennium to the surgery in Newmarket for more detailed assessment. Following another physical exam, they opted to perform an exploratory laparotomy, in which they would look at the horse's stomach and intestines while he was under a general anaesthetic to try to determine the cause of the pain. The surgery took place at 4pm.

O'Rourke had meanwhile updated John Ferguson, who called Sheikh Mohammed in Dubai.

Disappointingly, the laparotomy revealed no obvious reason for stomach pain. More worryingly, Dubai Millennium's small intestine was pale and although it showed some movement, it was not the normal movement the vets were hoping to see. "My first impression was that grass sickness was a possibility," said Crowhurst of the surgery.

To a vet, it was the beginning of a diagnosis. But Crowhurst knew it was more than that. So did Neal, O'Rourke, Crozier and Ferguson. Grass sickness, which is caused by a toxin mysteriously acquired by some grazing horses, is most often tantamount to a death sentence. Although horses have survived the disease, they must first endure a slow and agonising recovery that requires a tube-fed diet of gruel for months, and they can suffer permanent nerve damage.

Practitioners recognise different degrees of grass sickness, which kills by destroying nerve endings, particularly in the victim's throat and gut, making it impossible for the animal to swallow and digest food. The forms range from acute, when the horse dies or has to be put down immediately; to sub-acute, in which the vets have a window of a few hours to attempt treatment; to chronic cases, marked by varying degrees of nerve damage.

Horses with acute grass sickness die. Horses with chronic grass sickness may survive, as they are able to move small amounts of liquid through their digestive tracts. If the horse's bowel maintains enough functional nerve endings to continue to move fluids, the horse can sometimes be saved through feeding, over a period of months, by stomach tube. Eventually the horse begins to drink water on its own, then to drink gruel, and finally to eat; recovery usually takes at least a year.

O'Rourke, in particular, had a sinking feeling after the surgery. "Knowing the vets as I did, I knew when they were suspicious about a case of grass sickness they had a 100 per cent record of being borne out," he said. "And although I didn't want to admit it to myself, I pretty much knew the symptoms were telltale."

During the surgery, the vets debated whether to take a piece of tissue from Dubai Millennium's gut to test for grass sickness. However, a biopsy would have been even more invasive than the laparotomy, and they did not want to risk upsetting his bowel still more. In any event, grass sickness officially remained an unlikely possibility, given the horse's low exposure to grass.

"He was a lovely horse to deal with, but he failed to make the recovery you can get from a laparotomy," said Crowhurst. Sometimes the vets found that, after they had opened up a colic case, examined the digestive tract and sewn things up again, the patient would make a seemingly spontaneous recovery. However, that was not the case with Dubai Millennium.

"Many of them will just get over it, which he didn't," said Crowhurst. "The possibility of grass sickness became more likely as other things were ruled out."

Dubai Millennium was kept at Greenwood Ellis overnight. While he was clearly in distress, his pain level was manageable. If indeed grass sickness were the culprit, the toxin which causes the disease would have hit the nerves of his throat and bowel, causing paralysis and distress, but not pain.

"It's a bit like someone who's paralysed in a wheelchair – their legs are living, but they can't feel them," said Crowhurst. "The bowel is actually alive, it has a blood supply that's not blocked, it has some movement, but the movement is not progressive, and it's not moving the contents along. It's just sort of going in and out and not really getting anywhere. Many horses with really profound grass sickness don't show a lot of pain, especially if you can keep the stomach decompressed."

Vets decompress a horse's stomach by passing a large tube up the nose, down the gullet, along the oesophagus and into the stomach. Because the small intestine of a grass sickness or colic patient stops emptying, fluid build-up becomes a problem. Horses salivate even when not eating, so large quantities of fluid flow continuously into the stomach. If the fluids can't move through the digestive tract, the stomach fills up with liquid, like a blocked drain. The situation is especially dangerous in horses because they can't vomit like humans, cats or dogs.

In the beginning, Dubai Millennium did not need decompression – a fairly encouraging sign. "He had a very early surgery, and we had moved on much of the contents of his small intestine into the large intestine," explained Crowhurst. "So we had got ahead of the game a little bit there.

"His stomach wasn't what we call refluxing; that is, we weren't getting stuff out of his stomach, which is a common thing in grass sickness. And the other signs of grass sickness – muscle twitching, patchy sweating, droopy eyelids, salivating mouth – weren't obvious either."

But within a day and a half it was clear that something more would have to be done. Dubai Millennium was not improving. On Wednesday morning the team again put the big bay horse on the table and cut him open. Again they noted pale, distended loops with little movement in the small intestine, but no other obvious problem. They also took a biopsy from the end of the small intestine to be tested for grass sickness, and bypassed the poorly working section of small intestine by plumbing the end of it into the junction between the small intestine and the large intestine, known as the caecum – an established procedure to deal with blockages of the digestive tract. Crowhurst noted afterwards: "The surgery went well, and the horse was very good to deal with."

The biopsy was rushed down the road to the Animal Health Trust, a charitable research and treatment facility that was the British thoroughbred industry's official diagnostic centre. Located four miles outside of Newmarket in stately Lanwades Park, the AHT was home to many of the country's top specialists in fields such as virology, epidemiology, microbiology, pathology, and genetics.

The results of the biopsy were definitive. More than 90 per cent of the nerves in Dubai Millennium's small intestine had been destroyed by the toxin. This was almost certainly a case of grass sickness – a lethal one.

"Certainly, from the veterinary point of view, we did not believe the horse could survive," said Crowhurst. "For most horses, that would have been enough to justify putting him down."

However, Dubai Millennium was still not refluxing, and he did not appear to be in much pain. He was also a very good patient, and an IV drip was providing him with vital nutrition. For the moment, he could be kept alive.

The week, only half over, was already wearing on everyone. Ken Crozier and the other stallion men had been taking it in turns to sit up with the patient, so that someone from the stud was with him 24 hours a day. Crozier was shocked by how quickly the horse lost condition – two days after careening into the breeding shed in his trademark fashion, with that air of broadening his shoulders and filling up space with his sheer, vibrant, irrepressible presence, he had become a docile, weakened animal, with tubes sprouting from his every orifice.

Like the others, Crozier had seen grass sickness kill before. But as with the others, he couldn't help hanging on to a shred of hope.

"On Wednesday morning, I went down there, and he looked that little bit brighter, and you couldn't help thinking 'just maybe'," Crozier recalled. "His eyes looked a bit brighter and his head was up. After that, there wasn't much ..." his voice tailed off.

As usual, it was Sheikh Mohammed's determination and

enthusiasm that kept everyone going – even, it seemed, his horse. The sheikh flew in from Dubai on Wednesday morning, bringing with him a team of vets including Dan Hawkins, the senior surgeon at Dubai Equine Hospital. He also brought with him a suggestion: that the patient might be moved to another clinic, possibly in another country. As with his racing stable, he was ready to ship the horse anywhere in the world, if better results could be had there.

"It was discussed, and we felt that there were no other countries that had such experience with grass sickness as Britain," said Crowhurst. "We felt that the team combined with the experience here made this the best place to treat the horse, which Sheikh Mohammed agreed with."

It did not appear to anyone that Sheikh Mohammed was ready to accept death as an option at this point. "Any case of grass sickness is probably going to be fatal," said Crowhurst. "Sheikh Mohammed was told that, but it's always difficult to take on board with a horse that is not in pain. And he is a man who believes that most problems can be fixed."

O'Rourke, too, felt torn between his own sometimes depressingly practical experience as a horseman and the power of his boss's belief. Sheikh Mohammed had, after all, made the seemingly impossible happen more than once, from constructing ski slopes in the desert and islands in the gulf to winning the Dubai World Cup with this very horse. But conquer grass sickness? You might as well announce an overnight cure for cancer.

"The writing, I'm afraid, was on the wall once we got the result of the test," said O'Rourke. "But Sheikh Mohammed just wasn't going to give in like that, and he went back and he organised

146

specialists from all over the world, who would liaise closely with the team of vets who began to assemble. There was a team of surgeons who really discussed this case around the clock."

Said Crowhurst: "It was quite an international effort. Huge support was gathered, and everything was being done that could help him."

Still, this was a horse who had not been allowed to eat or drink for days – and all the horsemen, vets and specialist researchers knew that could not go on forever.

On Thursday, the day after the second surgery, the scientists at the AHT arranged a presentation for Sheikh Mohammed and his team. After stopping in at Greenwood Ellis to visit Dubai Millennium, Sheikh Mohammed got back in his car and drove to Lanwades Park, where the experts described for him the most up-to-date studies on the disease and discussed its diagnosis, prognosis and potential treatment.

Ken Smith, the head of the pathology department, had set up a teaching microscope so that the sheikh could see for himself the damaged neurons in the biopsy. The two of them peered down the microscope lens together, head to head, Sheikh Mohammed intent on understanding the source of his horse's distress, Smith absorbed in explaining it to him.

Smith, a 13 year veteran of the AHT, was particularly impressed by Sheikh Mohammed's participation in the process, from the diagnosis to every step of the decision-making. "It was wonderful to see how involved the sheikh was with his favourite horse," he said later.

After the presentation Sheikh Mohammed returned to Dubai, leaving behind Hawkins to assist the Newmarket vets. Crowhurst still couldn't tell if he accepted that the horse would die, but like Smith he found the sheikh's personal involvement with the whole process remarkable.

"He had interrupted whatever schedule he had, and he had to get back to doing it," he said. "But I think it was great that he came over. He saw exactly what we were doing, and he wanted to be involved in it. He took it all in, and he held a lot of discussions with the Dubai team, and helped co-ordinate the team effort. And then he probably realised he couldn't contribute anymore. He had assessed the situation and made the decisions as to the care of the horse, and then he had to move on."

The team continued to relay updates to Sheikh Mohammed via Ferguson, who also made a handful of hastily scheduled public appearances to alert the press to new turns of events. He also began advising breeders whose mares were booked to the stallion to make alternative plans. The Darley nominations team hurried to rearrange schedules; Machiavellian in particular found his book suddenly swelling.

Once the vets had a diagnosis, Dubai Millennium's treatment became mainly a matter of nursing. He was given little bits of exercise, short walks to encourage him, ironically, to take bites of grass. However, the IV feeding regime continued so that his stomach would remain as empty as possible.

The vets were loathe to put him through a third operation, but by the weekend Dubai Millennium was deteriorating. He was clearly in pain now and he was refluxing a lot more – evidence that his small intestine was backed up with fluid. The team was having to drain his stomach every three hours, causing him still more distress. A crisis was approaching.

"He took it all absolutely brilliantly, but basically the clinical scenario was deteriorating," said Crowhurst.

On Sunday, Crowhurst proposed one more surgery, on the understanding that if nothing else could be done, they would put him down without letting him come out of the anaesthetic. The other surgeons agreed. None of them wanted him to die naturally, given the distress and pain he was in.

With the once majestic body laid open on the operating table yet again, the surgeons peered sombrely through the narrow gap between the surgical caps pulled low over their foreheads and the masks covering their mouths. The facial gear made the room feel close, and it was clear there would be no escaping the final verdict this time. The bypass was working perfectly and there was no sign of intestinal blockage, infection, or anything else that they could possibly fix. So this was it. Huw Neal said: "Let's not let him come round." After a short discussion with the sheikh in Dubai, it was agreed. The team bid goodbye to Dubai Millennium.

Reflecting on the week, Crowhurst said: "There'd been no other case where so much had been tried. The horse had been taken – of course he'd let us do it, he was such a lovely horse to deal with – beyond where most horses would have been allowed to. And everything was tried, and I think it was always felt that we were going into uncharted waters. But there was hope that the horse would respond to all that was being done for him, despite the pathology – in logical terms you'd feel that nothing was going to get over that. It was felt that, with all the effort, new ground was being broken, and therefore it was literally uncharted territory, and I think there was very much hope in everybody that the great horse would respond to that slightly against the expectation. And it was a hope more than anything, because more was done for him than for any other case of grass sickness."

"It was a long week for everybody connected with the horse," said O'Rourke. "Because you sort of felt that where there was life there was hope. But the last couple of days, he got into a downward spiral. There was just nothing more we could do for him."

The most poignant thing for O'Rourke was the horse's tenacious spirit. "He fought – he had that sort of spirit, he had resolve, and he fought it for as long as he could," he said. "In your average case, horses last hours. This fellow lasted – with a lot of help – a week. And I think that said as much about the horse as it did about the people around him."

To a man who had dedicated his life to the welfare of thoroughbreds, Dubai Millennium's suffering was almost too much. Reflecting on the stallion's ordeal, O'Rourke said: "You can sedate them, but you cannot render the motility back in their intestines. It just doesn't happen. And it's like passing a current through a rubber wire – you just can't get anything across it. The nerve endings are destroyed and that's that. There's no way back. It's a horrible thing to watch, and there's usually only one way out."

He had seen his fair share of illnesses and freak accidents, and knew of many more. The stallion Ajdal broke his leg at Dalham Hall before O'Rourke's tenure, and Reference Point had cracked his pelvis in the paddock while out for a roll. Shareef Dancer, the sire of Dubai Millennium's dam, broke his leg when he twisted awkwardly while dismounting a mare.

"You can't prevent those things – you do the best you can do but you can't actually prevent them," reflected O'Rourke. "You don't know what could happen to any of them, what could happen to anyone crossing the road – that's life. You do the best you can and you can't do any more.

"But this guy – it was the suddenness of it, and that it wasn't complete. When a horse breaks a leg there's nothing you can do for them. Generally speaking they have to be put down and it happens. We endured watching this fellow, wondering, can he fight his way out or not? It lingered. It lingered and lingered, and it was upsetting to watch that."

CHAPTER ELEVEN

THE MYSTERIOUS KILLER

On the morning of April 30, exactly one week after Dubai Millennium fell ill, the Animal Health Trust's brand-new high-security diagnostic facility, the Allen Centre, kicked into high gear.

The biosecure building, the best of its kind in Britain, had just been completed at a cost of £4 million. Designed to accommodate vaccine studies using highly pathogenic organisms, the centre also featured a custom-built room for carrying out equine post-mortems. The paint was still fresh on the walls as Dubai Millennium's body was wheeled in from the refrigerated storage area, and pathologist Katherine Whitwell, preparing to perform the autopsy, couldn't help but think what a curious twist of fate it was that the new centre should be christened by such a famous first subject.

The heavy body had been laid upon the stainless steel operating table with the help of electronic hoists on overhead tracking. The hoists guided the body into position, placing it on its back in the middle of the table, which was long and narrow, with a deep groove down the middle for fluids to run through.

As Whitwell, aided by pathologist Tony Blunden and a technician, removed the stainless steel side supports which had held the body in place during the short trip down a corridor between the storage room and the PM hall, she drew a deep breath. Whitwell had made a life out of cutting open and examining dead animals; she was used to seeing her patients for the first time lying upside down, cold and inert on clinical beds of steel. But she also loved animals, and this one moved her. Even in death, he had presence.

"An upside down Dubai Millennium was heart-rending," she said later. "He was so magnificent. Upside down and dead, all the rest of it, it really made me very sad. I'm not easily swayed, but he was amazing. He was put together like a statue, just marvellous-looking. No wonder he won all those races. He was the ultimate."

Everyone in the room was wearing white overalls covered by long plastic aprons. On their heads were disposable surgical covers, and their arms were sheathed in gauntlets topped by stretch gloves. Their feet were covered by rubber boots.

A routine autopsy of a large animal is messy; it entails systematic removal of all of the internal organs along with the head, so that each can be examined separately. Whitwell had received special instructions for Dubai Millennium's autopsy, though. "Please do as little damage as possible," she was told. So the pathologists cut through the stitches sewn along the midline of the horse's abdomen by Huw Neal's team after their earlier surgeries.

Whitwell's goal was to locate and remove a two-centimetre section of a large ganglion. The condition of the ganglia, structures containing dense clusters of nerve cells, is considered definitive in proving a diagnosis of grass sickness. Although the 90 per cent nerve damage found in the biopsy from the small intestine was a pretty clear indicator of the disease, the international team that had been treating Dubai Millennium wanted 100 per cent assurance that this was indeed a case of grass sickness. After all, the case history was unusual in that the horse had been fed just handfuls of grass, although that was not unprecedented: horses in training had been known to contract the illness having had no more than a pick of grass on the bridle after exercise.

Equally important was that this was Sheikh Mohammed's favourite horse, and more effort had been devoted to saving him than had been given to any grass sickness victim in history. Now was not the time to let even the smallest detail slip away.

On the other hand, Sheikh Mohammed wanted the body intact. It was an unusual request; although dog owners often asked to have their pets' physical appearance preserved, this was the first time the pathologists had received such instructions for a horse. But with this one's beauty it was easy to see why.

After removing, inspecting and replacing the bowel and its contents, Whitwell and Blunden, with some difficulty, identified a path to the largest ganglion, which lay hidden deep within the abdominal cavity by the left adrenal gland. As they worked, they removed small tissue samples and immersed them in a formalin fixative. Later these would be placed on slides for microscopic examination.

Then they placed everything back through the narrow abdominal opening and painstakingly sutured the wound back together. Hours went by in the cold, bright room as they tried to obscure traces of repeated surgical violations to the body, using tiny, careful stitches. Finally they finished, and Dubai Millennium's body was loaded into the lorry for delivery to Dalham Hall, where it would be buried next to Shareef Dancer's.

Whitwell's role in Dubai Millennium's brief story was done, but her work on grass sickness was a decades-long obsession. She was not involved in treating the illness, as the Newmarket vets were, or directly involved in determining its cause, as other scientists had sporadically tried to do over the last 100 years since its appearance in Britain. She had, however, spent upwards of 30 years documenting the disease's devastating effects, and she was always seeking new and better ways to diagnose it in live animals.

Whitwell had a dogged, methodical investigative style punctuated by flashes of quirky insight, a sort of Columbo or DI Frost of the farmland. Once, after she opened the door of her cottage home to a stranger, her laptop disappeared from the kitchen table. Rather than reporting the incident to the police, Whitwell began frequenting the local pubs, probing the regulars with questions – had they seen anyone new in the area, anyone fitting the description of the young stranger, anyone with meagre material means suddenly in possession of an expensive laptop? Finally someone steered her towards a lad who had recently been hired to work on one of the local farms. She tracked him down in the loft of a barn and recovered the laptop – unharmed except for the installation of several video games.

One day in 1989 she was called out to a local stud to examine a suspected grass sickness case. After processing a section of ganglion and taking a blood sample, she began carefully walking the field, a habit she had developed after each suspected grass sickness case was reported over the years. She was searching for clues – anything at all out of the ordinary. Although nothing of real interest had turned up yet, that was no reason to stop, in her book.

This particular stud had lost two mares and the owners were in a state of frantic worry. While nosing around, Whitwell fell into conversation with a couple of farm hands. "There is one funny thing," they told her. "We've noticed quite a lot of dead hares around recently."

"Oh, that's interesting – if you get any more bring them to me and I'll have a look," said Whitwell, not terribly intrigued.

Within ten days the men had brought her four hares. As she began to examine the first one, she felt her hair stand on end. There was a cement-like impaction in its intestines – just what she would find in a horse with grass sickness.

With the help of Joe Mayhew, a neurologist then working at the AHT, Whitwell carefully processed some tissue samples from the hare and extracted a piece of its tiny ganglion.

"I picked the slides up and looked at them, and I couldn't believe it," recalled Whitwell. "It was the same as the horse."

It was evening, and she immediately called Mayhew, who was still in his office. "You've got to come and have a look at this," she told him. "I don't know if I'm seeing things, but you've got to come over right now."

Mayhew's view concurred with Whitwell's. The pathology was the same in hares as in horses. It was an exciting discovery, because it was the first time that a grass sickness-like disease had been found in another grazing species. Of the four hares the men brought Whitwell from the stud, two had the disease.

She began spending more time looking for hares, which fortunately were prevalent in the area. The numerous large estates in Britain employ gamekeepers to rid the property of predators, such as foxes. Thus hares are free to populate the land, which they do in great numbers. However, Whitwell wasn't really getting the results she wanted – gamekeepers tended to feed the dead hares to their dogs – and she finally decided to push for funding for a proper study of hare deaths in East Anglia.

The results were startling. Of the first 100 dead hares she examined, the grass sickness-like disease was the second most common cause of death. The pathology was virtually identical to the disease in horses, except that the hares all seemed to be infected by a chronic version causing progressive wasting, rather than the acute version which often killed horses. However, her initial excitement over the ramifications for equine grass sickness was later dimmed. "I thought hares would be the sentinel species of grass sickness," she said. "However, a year or so down the line the penny finally dropped, and of course the horse is the sentinel for the hare. Because the horses get picked up on day one, and about three weeks later you'll start finding dead hares. So it's only association, and it's no help to anybody really."

More hopefully, she was later able to prove that the same disease afflicted wild rabbits. Because rabbits are much easier to breed and handle in captivity than hares, she is hopeful that the rabbit can be used as a research model for the horse.

Grass sickness has been a scourge in Britain since it was first reported sometime between 1906 and 1909 in Scotland. It made steady progress throughout the country but most especially in the east of Scotland, where some regions reported up to 20 per cent of their horse populations affected; in one year in the 1930s a reported 3,000 horses died of grass sickness in Scotland. Such was the impact of the disease that ways to control it were discussed in the houses of Parliament.

While the origins of grass sickness in Britain remain murky, there is a theory that it arrived along with millions of tons of guano imported from South America into Perthshire, in the north-east of Scotland, in the early 1900s, as the initial spread of the disease suggested dispersal by migrating birds from that area.

Although it is most common in Britain, the disease is also found throughout northern Europe, including Belgium, Denmark, France, Germany, Holland, Italy, Norway, Sweden and Switzerland. It is also prevalent in Chile, the Falklands and Patagonia. By some stroke of luck, it does not exist, beyond a handful of reported cases, in Australia, Ireland, or North America, where three of the major world centres of thoroughbred breeding are located.

Newmarket has a relatively low incidence of grass sickness, but the value of the local bloodstock, combined with the high profile of many of its residents (both horse and human) mean the impact of any case in the area is magnified. Before Dubai Millennium, the stallions Moorestyle and Mister Baileys had both been stricken while stabled on Newmarket studs. Moorestyle, a top sprinter who won the July Cup, the Prix de l'Abbaye de Longchamp, and the Prix de la Foret twice, died in 1984.

Just over ten years later the 2,000 Guineas winner Mister Baileys contracted the illness right before he was to have begun his first breeding season at the National Stud. He was fortunate in that he had a chronic, rather than acute infection, and he survived after a long recuperation period. But his system never recovered completely. Although an insurance company paid out a claim on his fertility, he was returned to stud, first in Kentucky and then in England. His fertility was always an issue though, and there was something else odd about him.

His handlers at the English stud, Whitsbury Manor, noticed that the hairs of his coat would stand on end when he was excited. Finally, he became completely infertile, and in 2003 he was gelded. Although neither the hairs nor the fertility problems were proven to have resulted from grass sickness, that was the general, if untested, hypothesis put forth by the people who worked with him.

It was a likely enough hypothesis. Whitwell had observed over time that nerve endings in the digestive tract and other parts of the body of grass sickness survivors were permanently damaged by the disease. She also documented peripheral damage, such as degeneration of the heart muscle.

The horrible symptoms of grass sickness result from damage to the autonomic nervous system, which controls normal bodily functions. The nerves associated with movement of the digestive tract, from the throat to the rectum, are particularly hard hit. Specific signs include depression, drooping eyelids, muscle weakness, sweating, tremors, weight loss and excessive salivation, as the horse is unable to swallow with its paralysed throat muscles. The victim may also colic, as Dubai Millennium did, and its stomach may become distended.

Susceptibility is one of the most frustrating mysteries surrounding the disease. It commonly strikes only one or two horses out of a full pasture, and incidents are sporadic. While it tends to recur in affected areas, it can also spring seemingly from nowhere – as in the case of Dubai Millennium, who was eating mere handfuls of cut grass. Dalham Hall had recorded two previous cases of grass sickness, but that was years earlier.

Among the factors associated with increased risk to the disease are recent changes of feed or pasture, time of year – spring being the peak season - and soil type, with sand or loam thought to be more risky than clay. Most victims, unlike Dubai Millennium, are on pasture full-time. Other risk factors include the presence of domestic birds or fowl, the removal of droppings by mechanical means (thereby turning up underlying soil) and low soil sulphur content (which is associated with low rainfall, typical of the Newmarket area). A 1998 study found that two-thirds of cases occurred after a period of two weeks of dry weather followed by rain.[1]

Perhaps counter-intuitively, another study found that although horses grazing in a pasture where the disease had occurred were more likely to develop it, horses exposed to a grass sickness victim were ten times less likely to do so – suggesting the possibility of acquired immunity.[2]

Age is also a significant factor. Young fillies and mares, along with recently retired racehorses aged three to five years, are stricken disproportionately, while foals and yearlings rarely succumb. One theory is that foals acquire immunity to the disease from their dams; another is that differences between a mature and immature gut contribute to susceptibility.[3]

The theory that immunity to grass sickness can be acquired has raised hopes that a preventative vaccine can be developed. The first person to attempt to do so was Dr James Fowler Tocher. Born in 1864, Tocher presented the first research on grass sickness, conducted for the Highland and Agricultural Society, at a meeting of the National Veterinary Medical Association in Perth, Scotland, on December 15, 1922. He also conducted the first, and to date only, field trial using a grass sickness vaccine.

Tocher had already noted many of the risk factors acknowledged by modern scientists, and by the mid-1920s had settled on the deadly toxin Clostridium botulinum, known at the time as Bacillus botulinus, as the most likely cause. A related toxin causes human botulism, which is contracted by ingesting contaminated food.

Tocher recruited over 2,000 horses to his project, inoculating half of them with a botulinus toxin/antitoxin mixture and leaving the other half as a control group. Over a two-year period, employing a stronger dose of vaccine the second year, he reported the incidence of grass sickness reduced from as much as ten per cent in the control group to 1.5 per cent in the group vaccinated with the stronger dose.[4]

Tocher must have thought he had a valuable product on his hands, as the incidence of grass sickness in parts of Scotland continued to hover above ten per cent, and horses were a vital cog in the agricultural machine that could ill afford to be lost. In March, 1923, the Veterinary Record ran a full-page advertisement for hermetically sealed vials of 'Wellcome' Botulinus Antitoxic Serum, produced at the Wellcome Physiological Research Laboratories and distributed by Burroughs Wellcome & Co. in London. However, Tocher was derailed completely the next year when a rival scientist, the veterinary pathologist Professor Gaiger, was given an appointment as chief investigator for the Animal Diseases Research Association and finagled the remit for grass sickness work from the local scientific community.

Professor Gaiger undermined Tocher's work with unsubstantiated claims that the vaccine was causing 'blind staggers' in some horses, and more to the point, that the scientist was barking up the wrong tree.[5] His own theory was that streptococcus was the disease agent.

However, whatever became of Gaiger's subsequent research has been lost to history. Grass sickness science fell into a black hole for the next several decades, perhaps partly due to the demise of the horse as a necessary agricultural tool. Tocher fell into obscurity.

Three-quarters of a century later, Tocher's work came back into vogue when Keith Miller published a paper establishing a link between botulinum toxin and grass sickness. Miller's 1999 work compared levels of the toxin found in the lower portion of the intestine of horses suffering from grass sickness with those in healthy horses; he found that the grass sickness animals had over ten times the level of toxin as the healthy animals.

This was the stage at which research sat at the turn of the new millennium, a century after the insidious arrival of grass sickness in

Britain. There had been brief flurries of interest after each stallion case in Newmarket, but science requires money, and none of any useful amount had been forthcoming. Until the death of Dubai Millennium.

A year and a half after the stallion's demise, international interest in grass sickness was revved into high gear with an injection of $1 million from Sheikh Mohammed. An international collaborative project was put together, headed by Dr Ulrich Wernery, scientific director of the Central Veterinary Research Laboratory (CVRL) in Dubai. Dr Scott Pirie from Edinburgh University was named the foundation's official vet.

Wernery, a German veterinary microbiologist, had taken an unlikely route to the head of Sheikh Mohammed's equine research foundation. He never could have imagined, 25 years earlier as a young researcher vaccinating cattle in Somalia, that one day he would be at the forefront of an international effort dedicated to preventing one of the most horrific and puzzling diseases in thoroughbred racehorses – let alone that he would be working directly for the most powerful man in the Emirates.

Wernery had moved to Dubai for one reason – the camels. While in Somalia he had fallen head over heels in love with the inscrutable mammals. Not so much the camel per se, but its fascinating physiology – after all, he was a laboratory researcher. There and then he decided that if ever a camel job came along, he would take it.

The opportunity came in 1986, when Wernery saw an advertisement in the *Veterinary Record* for a scientist to do camel research in Dubai. For an anxious nine months after he submitted his application, he heard nothing. Then a plane ticket arrived in the mail. There was a letter with the ticket: "We need you here tomorrow," it said.

"I just left everything and flew to Dubai," he recalled later. "And I would do the same thing today. It's a love story."

The set-up in Dubai, when Wernery landed with his wife Renate, a virologist, was nothing to write home about. Dubai itself was just a cow (or camel) town compared to what it is today. As for the lab: "There was nothing – we were in the desert," he said.

But as the high-rises and shopping malls rose about them, so the lab grew, eventually expanding from two to 90 people. Much of the work, to Wernery's delight, involved camels. Camel racing, along with falconry and of course horse racing, is one of Sheikh Mohammed's great passions, and Wernery takes pride in noting that during his tenure in Dubai, the top time for a ten-kilometre camel race has dropped from 20 minutes to 16.

The dramatic improvement in performance is a combination of the CVRL work in reducing disease, advances in veterinary and management techniques, and breeding, says Wernery. He also credits it to Sheikh Mohammed, who visits the lab regularly, and "understands that we need this". Incredibly, with all of the worldwide projects, investments and developments he directs, not to mention the political roles he plays, the sheikh still finds time to personally oversee his camel research.

Naturally, Sheikh Mohammed's own lab, with its dedicated virology team, was the place to lead a worldwide effort to solve the deadly riddle of grass sickness. On September 22, 2001, the Dubai Millennium Research Foundation was announced to the world, as 16 leading experts gathered in Dubai for a grass sickness conference. The initial target would be Clostridium botulinum type C. Hopes were high that a preventative, if not a cure, for the disease would be found within the five years designated for the project.

The working hypothesis that C. botulinum was indeed the

culprit was supported, it seemed, by the results of tests conducted on dozens of grass samples taken from Dalham Hall after Dubai Millennium's death. Labs in Germany and Dubai revealed high levels of C. botulinum in the samples. With this tentative evidence to hand, Sheikh Mohammed was taking no chances, and all of his horses in Britain and Dubai were vaccinated against the botulinum toxin. "We were desperate to do something," Wernery explained.

By 2006, however, the sense of optimism was gone. The project's goal had not been met and momentum had sagged. Wernery and his team were thwarted by two things: the complexity of a very strange disease, and lack of money. They had tried and failed to induce grass sickness using C. botulinum in trials conducted in Dubai. All they had managed to do was induce botulism.

So Wernery had abandoned the idea that a vaccine against C. botulinum would be of any use against grass sickness. He was quite sure the Clostridium toxin was not the sole cause of the disease (or not a cause at all), and was working through the process of eliminating other possible causes one by one. By this time he was convinced that many toxins, rather than a single one, were to blame.

Frustratingly – because he believed they were on the right track – the initial $1 million was gone. It hadn't taken long for the money to be sucked up by labs in several different countries.

Science grinds slowly towards truth, at a pace which is anathema to Dubai's time-lapse style. Wernery was still optimistic that he could meet what he called his life's challenge by cracking the disease – but he needed time, perhaps three to five more years, and only money, at least another million dollars, would buy that kind of time.

1.   *Wood et al.* 1998
2.   *Wood et al.* 1997
3.   *Tocher et al.* 1923

4. D. St. J. Collier, S.O. Collier, P.D. Rossdale, "Grass sickness – the same old suspects but still no convictions!" *Equine Veterinary Journal*, Equine vet. J. (2001) 33 (6) 540-542
5. Ibid.

CHAPTER TWELVE

CASTING HIS NET

SHEIKH MOHAMMED SWEEPS THE BLOODSTOCK
WORLD IN AN EFFORT TO CAPTURE
ALL OF HIS STALLION'S FOALS

The swiftness of Dubai Millennium's death cast a pall over both Dalham Hall Stud and Godolphin Stables. Watching the horse linger had been awful, and while one long night had seemed like a month to Ken Crozier, in hindsight it all seemed to have happened far too quickly. One day the big stallion had been in the peak of health, and a week later he was dead and buried. The illness had struck like the poison of some vengeful witch in a fairytale, disguised as innocuously fresh-cut grass but dusted with a deadly substance which would shortly strike the young prince a mortal blow. But this was real life, and there was no magic. Neither Sheikh Mohammed's passion for his horse, nor the tireless efforts of the greatest veterinary and scientific experts available, could breathe life into Dubai Millennium again.

"The mood at Godolphin had never been lower than in the days following his death. The light had gone out of our lives," Frankie Dettori said in his autobiography. "Twelve months earlier, the sky had been the limit for him. Now he was gone."

It would have been easy for the team to fall into a morose slump, but that was not Sheikh Mohammed's style. Almost immediately, the sheikh embarked on an ambitious new plan, and his employees were swept up by the same ineluctable momentum that fuelled all of his projects. John Ferguson observed, for the umpteenth time, "there's no hanging about with the boss," as just days after the horse's death Sheikh Mohammed summoned his bloodstock adviser with a plan: to buy as many of Dubai Millennium's just-conceived foals as possible. Not only that, Ferguson was to buy up most of the mares who were bred to him.

There was no telling what the sheikh's private grieving process was; a man given variously to bold statements, cryptic utterances and poetic expression, he kept his deepest feelings hidden even from the intimates of his team. In fact, he barely gave them time to draw breath before goading them into action again. Yet everyone knew he must have been keenly affected by Dubai Millennium's death; the hours he spent alone with the horse, including the final vigil, spoke his devotion more loudly than words.

Following his example, the team also kept their feelings to themselves. They had no option. "We had the shock, but we're over that, we've put it behind us," said Liam O'Rourke. "We put it behind us. Sheikh Mohammed particularly did. He led the way and said 'Look, we move on. Don't want to talk about it again.' He led from the front that way, and on we went."

So Ferguson set forth. Armed with a formidable bankroll and his boss's still more formidable willpower, he began making discreet enquiries as to whether the breeders who had wanted a Dubai

Millennium foal would now be willing to part, not only with the foal, but with the mare carrying it. The mares alone were worth millions, but Sheikh Mohammed was not looking to cut corners, and Ferguson prepared to make seven-figure offers.

His path had been smoothed by his boss's foresight. Sheikh Mohammed's penchant for control of his projects had led most of the breeders who sent mares to Dubai Millennium to sign foal-sharing agreements, and Darley was already a joint owner of most of the unborn foals that it didn't own outright.

Not surprisingly, most breeders, when offered a seven-figure sum for a foal in the early stages of foetal development, were happy enough to say yes. There were a few, though, who caused Ferguson headaches as they refused to yield to his repeated offers. One thing he did not want to have to do was tell the boss 'no'. So he kept up the pressure. In one case at least, he got his way.

Philippa Cooper owned Normandie Stud, a smallish operation with fewer than 20 mares located in West Sussex, near Goodwood racecourse. One of Cooper's favourite mares was Napoleon's Sister, who had won the Lupe Stakes at Goodwood in 1998, five months before Dubai Millennium made his stunning racecourse debut at Yarmouth. Napoleon's Sister was owned at the time by Anne Coughlan, who with her husband Sean bred thoroughbreds in Ireland, with some success; a year after Dubai Millennium's death, High Chaparral, a colt bred an subsequently sold by Sean Coughlan, would win the Derby.

The Coughlans had not bred Napoleon's Sister, though. They had bought her as a yearling from another very successful Irish breeder, Mrs Max Morris, whose earlier products included Oath, the colt who had beaten Dubai Millennium so comprehensively in the Derby. Napoleon's Sister was Oath's year-older half-sister.

The mare came by her unusual name through another filly Sean Coughlan had owned, named Ridgewood Pearl. Coughlan had asked trainer David Elsworth (Tony Proctor's first employer) to take Ridgewood Pearl as a young filly. Elsworth, a man known, among many things, for his strongly tendered opinions, categorically turned down the offer.

"But she's a sister to Ridgewood Ben," Coughlan reminded him. Ridgewood Ben was a talented colt who had won the Group 3 Gladness Stakes for the Coughlans while trained by John Oxx in Ireland.

"Well, who the hell was Napoleon's sister?" growled back Elsworth. So Ridgewood Pearl was sent to Oxx, for whom she won a string of Group 1s, beginning with the Irish 1,000 Guineas and culminating in the Breeders' Cup Mile.

Cooper had a fondness for small, tough fillies, along with a passion for the subject of Napoleon that began in her university days. In fact, Ferguson was to find that she fit the mould herself: a slender, finely framed woman, she was unusually single-minded when it came to getting what she wanted. Having finally landed both Napoleon's Sister and a fully paid up nomination to Dubai Millennium, she was determined to keep the foal. Especially after it was born.

A neat-sized bay born on April 4, the foal grew to be Cooper's kind of girl – a strong-minded filly who knew her way around a paddock. "She was exceptional. She was like a colt," she observed. She particularly liked the way the filly would boss the others in the field – "You know, every year you have one that's like a queen bee."

Well before the filly was born, though, Cooper resisted the idea of selling. In July, just four months after Napoleon's Sister and Dubai Millennium had their tryst, Ferguson made his first approach. Sheikh Mohammed had decided not to buy the mare. However, he wanted that foal.

"Certainly not. I don't do things that way – what if something was wrong with it?" Cooper responded initially. O'Rourke was also sent to cajole her, but with the same result – a resounding no. Throughout the autumn and the following year, the situation escalated into a battle of wills. At one point word came back to Cooper that Sheikh Mohammed had said she was "one tough lady".

"When it started to get to yearling time is when the pressure to sell became absolutely frantic," she recalled. "It wasn't just the phone calls – at the races or wherever I went someone would approach me, John Ferguson or people from his office. He thought I was playing cat-and-mouse."

By this time Ferguson's offers were no secret to the bloodstock world, and others – including John Dunlop, who was to train the filly – were advising Cooper to sell. After all, what were the odds that any unraced horse would ever be worth £1 million?

Two days before the filly was to arrive at Dunlop's stables in Arundel, Cooper allowed Ferguson to pay a last visit. He asked to see the filly trot and canter on a lunge line, and he liked what he saw. A new price was negotiated – £1.3 million. The phone call was made to Dunlop, and the filly joined Godolphin. She was later named Halle Bop, in honour of the comet.

One tough lady brought on-side, Ferguson knew he had another to deal with: Pat O'Kelly. A petite, independent Anglo-Irishwoman, O'Kelly had enjoyed great commercial success when selling yearlings bred at her Kilcarn Stud in County Meath at the Goffs sales in Kill and the Tattersalls sales in Newmarket. Particularly lucrative were the descendents of a mare named Welsh Flame.

Born in 1973, Welsh Flame won four races, but it was after her retirement that her true talent shone. Her best foal on the racecourse was a filly named Flame Of Tara. Sired by Artaius, the Kentucky-bred winner of the Eclipse and Sussex Stakes, Flame Of Tara won stakes races at ages two, three and four for O'Kelly. However, her most notable effort may have been when she was awarded second place on the disqualification of Tolomeo, while taking on colts in a hotly contested renewal of the Champion Stakes at Newmarket.

Like her dam, Flame Of Tara was even better in the breeding shed than on the racecourse. Her first foal, Nearctic Flame, won two races and finished third in the Ribblesdale Stakes at Royal Ascot, but there was still better to come.

Foal number two was Salsabil. Like Nearctic Flame, Salsabil was by Sadler's Wells, and Kilcarn Stud sold her to Sheikh Hamdan's Shadwell Estates at the Highflyer yearling sale for 440,000 guineas – the highest price for a yearling filly at Newmarket in 1988. Two years later, the price looked a bargain, as Salsabil piled up Group 1 trophies: the Ciga Prix Marcel Boussac as a two-year-old, and then the 1,000 Guineas, the Oaks, the Irish Derby and the Prix Vermeille. She was a rare filly, although British racing journalists ultimately preferred the sprinter Dayjur for their 1990 Horse of the Year – by a single vote.

Immediately after Salsabil came Marju. Also purchased by Shadwell as a 440,000 guineas yearling, this time at the Irish National Yearling Sale (where he was the second highest-priced colt), Marju proved a top-class miler by winning the St James's Palace Stakes, after finishing second to Generous in the Derby. He later became an influential sire under Shadwell's auspices.

The Maktoum family was thus well acquainted with Pat O'Kelly's equine family. When O'Kelly submitted the name Spirit Of Tara – Flame Of Tara's ninth foal – as a potential mate for Dubai Millennium, there was no debate. It was a perfect match.

However, after the stallion's death there was a hitch. O'Kelly, like Philippa Cooper, was one of the few breeders who had insisted on paying for a nomination, and she was not about to hand over the foal either, not even for a princely sum. In this case, Ferguson didn't waste much time fretting – he knew that Kilcarn, a commercial stud, would sell its yearlings at the Goffs Orby sale in September. Thus the Dubai Millennium – Spirit Of Tara colt gained the dubious distinction of being one of the very few foals for which Ferguson did not make an offer. He was sure he could get that yearling in time.

The time came on September 23, 2003. By now Sheikh Mohammed's heart was set on the colt, a strapping individual with more than a passing resemblance to his sire. O'Kelly thought he wouldn't be a two-year-old runner, because he was a big colt, bigger than most of the family. She did hold high hopes for him at three – perhaps he could emulate his grand-dam. But first there was a sale to get through. This colt had the potential to pay off a lot of bills.

John Magnier's Coolmore Stud was interested in the colt, too. They had bought Kilcarn's Danehill colt out of Flame Of Tara's half-sister Welsh Love for a sales-topping Ir£2,100,000 two years earlier. And it was no secret that Sheikh Mohammed was interested. The stage was set for a real showdown between the rival camps, and O'Kelly set her reserve, the minimum price she would accept for the colt, at half a million euros.

Nick Nugent, a dark-haired young Irishman whose Lambourn upbringing had erased all traces of a brogue, was the auctioneer at the podium when the colt, his coat burnished to a glowing rich brown, entered the ring at 5.57pm. Unusually, Nugent had not made any marks in his sales catalogue when he inspected the colt earlier in the day, although he noted mentally it was a typical, big-framed Kilcarn horse. Taking pre-sale notes is a routine procedure as auctioneers try to determine the strengths and weaknesses of each horse they will be selling, and estimate the final price. But this horse "was what he was. He was a horse who was going to be sold regardless," Nugent said later.

There was a surge of excitement accompanying the colt, as by now everyone on the grounds knew of Sheikh Mohammed's quest to acquire Dubai Millennium's foals. But Nugent also felt slightly let down, as neither John Magnier of Coolmore nor Sheikh Mohammed was there. "There's nothing better than the two titans face to face," he said.

Normally, Sheikh Mohammed would have been there. He relished the competition and excitement of the sales ring, and he liked to see the yearlings for himself. However, on this night he had an inescapable commitment: Dubai was hosting the annual meeting of the International Monetary Fund, and the presence of the Crown Prince was required. Nonetheless, he was on the phone with Ferguson as Pat O'Kelly's colt entered the ring. The IMF meeting could wait, while Ferguson was his eyes and ears.

The arena at Kill was packed to capacity. Everyone knew this would be the highlight of the sale, and there was little doubt that Sheikh Mohammed's man would be the buyer. If Magnier entered the fray, there would be real fireworks. But where was the Coolmore commander? Not in his usual spot at the foot of the balcony stairs.

Nugent's request for an opening bid of €300,000 went unanswered. The bidding finally kicked off at €100,000, but stalled again upon reaching €300,000. It wasn't what a nervous Pat O'Kelly wanted to see, but Nugent wasn't worried. He knew that when a horse had a reserve of half a million euros, the auctioneer could be on his own for the first few hundred thousand. Bidders don't like to enter the fray until they know the reserve has been reached.

Right on target, Ferguson entered the bidding at €600,000. Nugent noticed something unusual: he was standing high up on the balcony, near the press room, not in his usual spot opposite the auctioneer. Another odd detail: John Warren, a well-connected British bloodstock agent, was providing the opposition, and he was bidding much higher than his usual limit allowed. Rumour had it that Warren had recently become affiliated with Derrick Smith, a wealthy gambler who was developing a partnership with Coolmore. Could Warren's client be Smith? If so, it would explain the absence of Magnier et al. While auction houses and public galleries love a spectacle, the titans themselves sometimes prefer to keep a low profile. Egos can fuel a sale like diesel on a bonfire, and millions can be saved by avoiding a face-to-face clash.

In the event, Warren's client was not as determined as Sheikh Mohammed. Six minutes after the bidding started, Nugent's hammer came down and Ferguson switched off his phone. "Thank you, sir," he said. The colt was going to Godolphin.

The Goffs sale was by far the most exciting of the three public auctions of Dubai Millennium yearlings. The first was something of an anticlimax. It took place on a sultry September afternoon at the Keeneland sales complex in Lexington, Kentucky. This was the site of many historic episodes, including the sales of Shareef Dancer and Fall Aspen. The most famous to date, though, was when a partnership from the nascent Coolmore empire bid $13.1 million to deny American trainer D Wayne Lukas a Nijinsky – My Charmer colt. That was in July 1985, at the height of a bloodstock bubble that would burst before the end of the decade, leaving many stallion owners and breeders reeling. Seattle Dancer, the colt's eventual name, soon became synonymous with the unsupportable profligacy of the period.

There would be no repeat in September 2003. The Dubai Millennium colt, a bright chestnut with a noticeably short tail and quizzical half-moon-shaped star in the centre of his forehead, was the result of a foal-share with Saud B Khaled's Palides Investments NV. Ferguson had not tried to buy the colt's dam, Fitnah, but he had flown, along with a team of auxiliary advisers, to Chanteclair Farm in Kentucky in April to assess the young horse. Khaled's bloodstock adviser Ron Wallace rated the colt a "gorgeous" yearling, if slightly light in his hindquarter. Ferguson, too, liked what he saw and duly made his offer, but Khaled turned it down.

He preferred to send the colt to Keeneland and let the market decide. You never knew – he might make even more money there. By this time the yearling's half-sister, Dreams Gallore, had won the Grade 1 Mother Goose Stakes and his half-brother, Fateful Dream, had landed a Grade 3 race in California. Both were sired by sons of Mr Prospector, while Dubai Millennium was a grandson of Mr Prospector. This evidence that the cross worked would add even more value to the colt, who already had rarity and good looks on his side.

He was consigned to the sale by Lane's End, owned by William S Farish, at the time US ambassador to Britain. Lane's End was as well connected an establishment as you could find among the Lexington brethren, but Khaled's hopes were soon dashed.

Catalogued as lot 371, the colt entered the ring in mid-afternoon. He attracted just three bidders, including Ferguson, who was accompanied by Sheikh Mohammed. The bidding quickly jumped up to $1.6 million and the hammer fell, in Wallace's favour; he had bought back the colt for Khaled. "Sheikh Mohammed went to what he originally offered, and my guy bought him back," Wallace said tersely.

Khaled named the colt Ten Centuries and put him into training, but just days before he was to make his first start for trainer Bobby Frankel, he blew out a tendon. His career was over before it began.

The third Dubai Millennium yearling offered at auction was a bay filly out of Tony Ryan's mare Cloelia. Ryan, the founder of the wildly successful budget airline Ryanair, had recently set up a breeding operation in Kentucky called Castleton Lyons. However, he chose the Tattersalls Houghton Sales in Newmarket as the place to offer his filly, who was one of Dubai Millennium's last foals to be born. Like Philippa Cooper and Pat O'Kelly, Ryan preferred to do things his own way and had resisted the idea of a foal-share. And like Khaled, he preferred to gamble that the market would value his yearling even more highly than Sheikh Mohammed.

After Keeneland and Goffs, the sheikh's team decided on a different tactic. Ferguson's presence, especially when he was accompanied by his boss, could induce unrealistically high expectations on the part of sellers. The two would keep a low profile at Tattersalls and have a less obvious agent do the bidding. Charlie Gordon-Watson, man of many clients and a frequent representative of various Maktoum family interests, was selected, and when the Cloelia filly walked into the Tattersalls ring shortly after 7pm on October 2nd, the agent was ready. The bidding was not protracted, and the hammer went down in Gordon-Watson's favour at 1,200,000 guineas, with agent Michael Youngs the underbidder. The filly, later named Mille, joined Godolphin but was one of 20 of her sire's offspring never to race.

CHAPTER THIRTEEN

THE NEXT
GENERATION

On a late May day in 2004, the warm air at Godolphin Stables in Newmarket was tinged with the clean scent of cut grass and redolent of optimism. Interspersed throughout the brick and wood-panelled buildings, with their freshly bedded boxes, were 26 unraced two-year-olds. These were the sons and daughters of Dubai Millennium who had been selected, from the 48 ultimately acquired by Sheikh Mohammed, to join Godolphin.

The sheikh was paying them an afternoon visit, accompanied by his new bride, Princess Haya Bint Al Hussein of Jordan. The couple had been married only a month, although they were observed constantly in each other's company at horse sales beginning the previous September, when the sight of Sheikh Mohammed walking hand in hand with an exquisitely attractive young woman in blue jeans had precipitated immediate and fierce Google searches by several journalists at the Keeneland yearling sale.

Since then Princess Haya, who had an Oxford degree in politics, philosophy and economics and had competed in the Sydney Olympics showjumping competition, had become an integral part of Godolphin. At the same time as she took up a role among the decision makers of Godolphin, the princess had also developed a personal relationship with every horse, rider and groom in the organisation. To the racing world she was a welcome figurehead to the eclectic team, with her imposing command of languages and cultures overlain by a comfortably down-to-earth brand of diplomacy. Plus, she was a woman in what until then had been strictly a man's world. Somehow, Sheikh Mohammed seemed more approachable by her side. And the camera loved her.

Days earlier, Sheikh Mohammed had hosted a Godolphin open house, in which he spoke of his pleasure at the decision to have all of the two-year-olds trained in-house, under the wing of Saeed bin Suroor; no longer would the juveniles be parcelled out among outside trainers, as the young Dubai Millennium had been. Speaking to the press crews, the sheikh had proclaimed: "The best change I have made is to have the two-year-olds under our banner this year. I think we made a mistake by leaving them with somebody else before. Now we are bringing them along the way we want, not the way the trainers want. We can see every single one of them. Before it was like having your children living with someone else."

It was a Tuesday, the last in May, and the Oaks was coming up in three days, the Derby a day later. Godolphin had two well-fancied fillies aiming for the Oaks, Punctilious and Sundrop, and a colt, Snow Ridge, who would be among the favourites for the Derby. Sundrop and Snow Ridge had both been second in their respective Guineas at Newmarket a month earlier, while Punctilious had won the Musidora Stakes in May by a wide margin.

Godolphin also had a longshot, Rule Of Law, in the Derby. In his first race of the year, Rule Of Law had finished second in the Dante Stakes to a colt called North Light, who was owned by the same breeders, Ballymacoll Stud, who had sold Snow Ridge to Sheikh Mohammed last year.

The yard was humming with the quiet excitement that comes in advance of the Epsom Classics, and the ensuing summer season, a dizzying run of big races. Godolphin had so many top runners in the barns every year that the seasonal buzz was a part of the atmosphere, filling the air like the sharp scent of liniment or the treacle aroma of sweet feed.

This spring there was an added thrill in the air. On Friday, less than three hours after the Oaks, the late Dubai Millennium would be represented by his first runner – Zomaradah's foal Dubawi. The colt was the ninth of the group to be born, having come into the world on February 7 in Ireland, where his dam would be bred back to the Breeders' Cup Mile winner Barathea. In spite of Dubawi's early birthdate, the team was somewhat bemused that he had turned out to be the crop's first runner. His breeding did not scream precocity, what with an Oaks winner for a dam and the slowly maturing Dubai Millennium as a sire, not to mention the progressive middle-distance stars scattered throughout his pedigree.

On the other hand, he looked the type. Unlike many of his paternal siblings, he was small and compact, with a muscular build and an air of confidence about him. In size, in fact, he was nothing like his sire. Still, Sheikh Mohammed thought he could see a resemblance. As he explained to a visitor, while the young Dubawi stood unconcernedly on the end of a lead shank in the stable yard, the colt carried the same muscling in his shoulder and down the length of his hind leg that his sire had.

The royal couple, accompanied by Simon Crisford, moved slowly through the yard, Sheikh Mohammed drifting into reminiscences of Dubai Millennium, while Princess Haya stroked each horse as it came out, explained how they were named, and joked with the grooms. Belenus, a lengthy chestnut with a narrow white strip between his eyes, was also expected to be an early runner, although he had been born later and had a taller frame to fill than Dubawi. Further along was Rajwa, a bright chestnut colt out of Dubai Millennium's very first mate, Zelanda. He too had a more compact build than his sire. Born on January 13, Rajwa had been the group's intended first runner, but had been stymied by a minor training setback.

Sheikh Mohammed admired each colt, pointing out the similar musculature in shoulder and hip, and the depth of girth that they shared – all characteristics indicative of raw potential for racing ability. None of them seemed to have captured his heart, though. Hints of another horse kept intruding, and there was a feeling that the afternoon was building towards a crescendo as the sun moved closer to the horizon.

The sheikh quickened his pace as they neared a large 'American-style' barn, an enclosed building with the boxes facing a central breezeway. A dark-haired groom led out a big bay colt, and posed him with his left front leg slightly in front of the right front and his left hind just in back of the right hind, so that the clean line of all four limbs was clearly visible. This was Echo Of Light, the colt bred by Pat O'Kelly and purchased for €1.2 million at Goffs during the IMF meeting.

"He looks like Dubai Millennium. You see the look, the big eye. You can see it in his eye," Sheikh Mohammed said, gesturing.

Princess Haya explained the origin of the name: it was the term given by astronomers to the birth of a star. She, the sheikh and, Crisford discussed the colt. Sheikh Mohammed continued to admire his size, his muscle, his frame, and most of all his eye, which was large – perhaps exceptionally so – and had an intelligent, knowing look. Crisford noted critically that the colt seemed to have gone through a growth spurt lately. He and Princess Haya crossed their arms and contemplated Echo Of Light's size, which was indeed extraordinary for a horse of his age. "Yes, I think he's going through an ugly-duckling stage," concluded the princess, giggling. They all agreed he was unlikely to run soon, and, with typical horsemens' aversion to counting on any future event, stopped just short of saying that he would be aimed at next year's Derby.

Echo Of Light was returned to his box, and the conversation moved out on to a grassy area where some of the racehorses were enjoying an evening graze in the fine weather. Frankie Dettori showed up, and the talk turned to memories of Dubai Millennium's glory days. Eventually someone asked if Sheikh Mohammed ever expected to see another horse as good as Dubai Millennium. He answered philosophically. "All life is hope."

The Epsom Classics absorbed most of the British racing world's attention in the ensuing days, but more quietly, there was a growing curiosity about the Dubai Millennium offspring. While most in the thoroughbred industry expressed hope that the great horse would live on in his progeny, some of the mainstream press sensed a chance to fire up populist resentment against wealth and privilege. The last thing they wanted was to cheer on an oil-rich sheikh's dreams. "Dubai Millennium's kids will probably be slow as moles," sneered one of them.[1]

Godolphin was uncharacteristically reticent about the crop, perhaps sensing that to build up expectation could quite possibly end in embarrassment as well as disappointment. However, Sheikh Mohammed did grant another interview to the BBC's Clare Balding, which was aired just before the Prince of Wales's Stakes at Royal Ascot. In it, he chose just one horse to display on camera: Echo Of Light. With the colt again posing in the stable breezeway, the sheikh motioned towards his outstanding conformational points, the shoulder and frame, and the eye. "If I know anything about horses, I think this horse will be something special," he concluded.

With thousands of viewers watching the Royal Ascot programme, Sheikh Mohammed was hardly hiding his light under a bushel. By mid-July, with Echo Of Light still no closer to a run, the bookmakers had already installed him the 20-1 joint favourite for the next year's Guineas.

First, though, there was the matter of Dubawi's race on Friday. The team's main focus was at Epsom, where Sundrop, who had been bought as a foal in Japan, would bid to become the first Japan-bred winner of the race. It was something Godolphin specialised in, broadening the international appeal of racing, and Sundrop was a rare European runner bred from the legendary imported sire Sunday Silence. Punctilious, too, had a good chance; indeed Dettori had opted to ride the British-bred filly, sired by Coolmore's stallion Danehill.

Unfortunately for Godolphin, the field also included a lightly raced filly named Ouija Board. The sole horse raced by Lord Derby, Ouija Board looked like a model, albeit a well-fed one – long-legged and blessed with near-perfect physical harmony, she seemed bigger and more beautiful than anyone had a right to be. Ouija Board was stepping into this level of competition for the first time, having won her first stakes race, the Pretty Polly Stakes, by six lengths a month earlier.

At Epsom the dark bay filly gave notice that she was something special, routing the field by seven lengths. All Too Beautiful, raced by the Coolmore gang and a sister to their 2001 Derby winner Galileo, was second, with Punctilious another three lengths back. Sundrop faded to a well-beaten sixth under Godolphin's new Australian rider Kerrin McEvoy.

It was not entirely bad news for Sheikh Mohammed's crew, as Ouija Board was one of the first runners sired by Godolphin's top miler Cape Cross, now a Darley stallion. The publicity would boost Cape Cross's fortunes no end. Godolphin was still without a winner for the day, though.

With one Classic behind them, they moved on to Dubawi's race. Dettori was ferried directly from Epsom to Goodwood in time for the first race on the card, the Green & Black's Organic Chocolate EBF Maiden Stakes. The six-furlong race looked a decent enough contest, although in hindsight, like many maidens, it proved not to be much of a benchmark. Only two of Dubawi's four rivals subsequently won a race, and just one of those outside of maiden company.

It was, though, a historic event, as the *Racing Post* analyst noted in his track comments. "Notable as the race that saw the first of the great Dubai Millennium's offspring to hit the track and in what looked a hot little maiden, run at a searching pace, Dubawi came home in some style."

There was also a note of warning, a hint perhaps that the little colt had inherited something of his sire's feistiness. "He doesn't look the easiest ride and appeared to fight his jockey on several occasions."

Dettori summed up his ride more pithily. "He's a little bastard," he cheerfully informed Sheikh Mohammed and bin Suroor after dismounting. "He stops and starts and stops again. He wants to argue with everybody, even the starter."[2]

The smile on Dettori's face betrayed his real feelings, though, and he added: "There's a lot more in the tank."

It was a good thing Dubawi gave him something to smile about, as his Derby mount Snow Ridge was a flop the next day. Ironically, North Light – the horse Snow Ridge's breeders had retained – won the race, while Godolphin's other runner, Rule Of Law, was a surprisingly good second.

Dubawi's next test came a month later. Racing at Newmarket had moved from the wintry Rowley Mile racecourse, where the wind blew straight through man and beast, to the more protected July course, just a short hack across the downs but a world away in micro-climate. The evening meetings of mid-summer were held on the July course, where towering trees formed a deep green canopy above the spacious pre-parade ring, and champagne flowed inside tents arrayed opposite the old wooden grandstand. The July meeting was under way, highlighted by the Group 1 July Cup for Europe's top sprinters. The three-day meeting also featured a trio of Group races for two-year-olds, which, following the juvenile stakes at Royal Ascot, were important in establishing an early pecking order among the youngest generation of runners.

Dubawi was entered in the Superlative Stakes, a Group 3 race held on the same day as the July Cup. Godolphin had two horses in the big sprint – Kheleyf, who was coming off a Royal Ascot win and would be Frankie Dettori's mount, and Country Reel, who hadn't won since taking the Gimcrack Stakes for two-year-olds two years earlier. A longshot here, he would be ridden for the first time by Richard Hills.

The Superlative Stakes, off an hour before the day's feature, proved to be Godolphin's high point of the day. A much more competitive race than the maiden at Goodwood, it featured a field of 12 previous winners running over seven furlongs. It would test Dubawi's stamina just that little bit more.

The colt settled beautifully this time before the race, dispelling fears of a temperament problem and impressing paddock watchers with his muscular physique and imposing demeanour. Breaking from the far outside, he allowed Dettori to hold him well back off a moderate pace. Then he smoothly made up ground in the last two furlongs, responding to two cracks of the whip to force his way past Henrik, who had moved to the lead first, and win by a half-length.

Back in the winners' enclosure, Dettori remarked that Dubawi could have won by a bigger margin, but the colt was "cheeky". He was a determined little fighter and would battle it out to the end, but was not the type to blow the field away with his sire's panache.

"He loves a fight and wants to kill people," Dettori informed the press when they converged upon him. "He doesn't know when he's beat and you never know how much he has left, as he will never go and win his race by eight lengths. But pound for pound he'll give anybody a race."[3]

Scurrying into action, a trio of bookmakers priced the colt at 33-1 for the 2005 Derby. No doubt they were encouraged by bin Suroor's post-race comments. "I think we have a nice horse for the future," the trainer said. "A mile and a quarter or mile and a half will be no problem for him next year. He could be a Derby horse."[4]

After all the excitement generated by Dubawi, the July Cup turned into a damp squib for Godolphin, with Country Reel finishing 11th and Kheleyf 14th of the 20 runners. Frizzante, a five-year-old mare saddled by Newmarket trainer James Fanshawe, was the surprise winner under jockey Johnny Murtagh.

Never mind; Godolphin had plenty more irons in the fire, not least Dubai Millennium's colts and fillies. A number of them were being geared up for their first runs, and one of them, the tall chestnut Belenus, had already won. Ridden by Dettori, Belenus made his debut at the July meeting, two days before Dubawi's Superlative Stakes win. The race, the first on the card, was a historically strong maiden; in 1995, it had been the starting point for Sheikh Hamdan's top two-year-old Alhaarth and Godolphin's 2,000 Guineas winner Mark Of Esteem, then trained by Henry Cecil. The pair had finished within a neck of each other in the Newmarket maiden before taking their separate roads into racing's record books.

The public showed their faith in the horse, his sire and Godolphin's winning form, by making Belenus the warm favourite. He rewarded them by racing near the front of the pack to finish clear of a field of 15, and win the seven-furlong contest by a length and a half. Back in the winners' enclosure, "We have a two-year-old, sir," a beaming Crisford told Sheikh Mohammed.

The bookmakers took a longer view, entering Belenus in their books at a general 25-1 to emulate Mark Of Esteem in the Guineas.

With two first-time-out winners from two starters, and a Group winner by early summer, Dubai Millennium was off to an exceptional start at stud. There was more good news in mid-July, when Khalid Abdullah's filly Quickfire, out of Daring Miss – the mare who had been second to Montjeu in Paris – finished a close second to the Queen's filly Free Lift on her first run. It was another encouraging development, suggesting that Dubai Millennium's fillies could be as useful as his colts. It was also proof that the stallion's success was not just down to Godolphin, as Quickfire was trained by Sir Michael Stoute and ridden by Kieren Fallon.

By the end of July, Oude had added another first-time win. One of the Godolphin colts, Oude had been bred in Kentucky from the mare Chosen Lady, a daughter of the great Secretariat and the dam of an American Grade 1 winner named Well Chosen.

The mating had been one of the foal-shares, done in partnership with the Stonerside Stables of Robert and Janice McNair, well-known Texas philanthropists and the owners of the Houston Texans football team as well as a very successful racing and breeding operation. Although Robert McNair had sold his power company, Cogen Technologies, for $1.5 billion in 1999, he accepted John Ferguson's offer to buy both Chosen Lady and her unborn foal in the aftermath of Dubai Millennium's death. Now Sheikh Mohammed's purchase looked prescient as Oude made a most fetching impression.

Oude's race, like the others, took place on the July Course at Newmarket. Travelling sweetly for Dettori on rain-softened ground that his sire would have appreciated, Oude tracked a moderate pace and then kicked on smartly when asked to win by a cheeky neck.

The colt's style, coupled with his pedigree, caused the *Racing Post* analyst to sit up and take note. "In what could prove a hot heat, Oude was able to continue the irrepressible run of the Godolphin team with sons of Dubai Millennium," he wrote, adding: "Dubawi and Belenus had both done the business on their debut and this fine athletic colt looked a picture in the paddock and on the way to the start. He can only learn from this and looks sure to take high ranking in the pecking order of the Godolphin two-year-olds."

The Dubai Millennium vibes were growing stronger. By the end of July the late stallion's record was three winners and two runners-up from five starters, including the unbeaten Dubawi. Two days after Belenus won, Rajwa, the modestly sized but muscular colt who had been his sire's intended first runner, made his debut at Glorious Goodwood the prestigious summer meeting at the southern racecourse. Although he got the same dream trip that Belenus had, making seamless progress to lead close home, Rajwa finished a neck behind a 50-1 chance named Doctor's Cave.

Punters and pundits alike were picking up on the success rate, with one journalist noting: "The late Dubai Millennium has already stamped his progeny with his star qualities."[5]

The bookmakers as usual were taking no chances, and had priced up all of Dubai Millennium's colt runners for the next year's 2,000 Guineas, along with the unraced Echo Of Light. They disregarded bin Suroor's description of the colt as "big and weak", preferring to remember Sheikh Mohammed's televised optimism.

Godolphin remained oddly quiet on the matter of the crop as a whole. They also gave little publicity to a minor but historic event at the end of June. This was the first race of Dubai Millennium's brother, Dahjee.

A three-year-old colt, Dahjee had been unimpressive in his gallops. The most noteworthy thing about his young life was that he, like his famous elder brother, had been given a name change. Dahjee had originally been registered as Peer Gynt, the wayward protagonist for whom Henrik Ibsen's 19th century play was named. The name had reportedly been scrapped when someone found that Peer Gynt was rhyming slang for skint.

In the lingering light of a summer's evening, Dahjee and a troupe of well-bred colts lined up in the stalls for the 9.10 at Kempton. None had particularly fired the punters' imagination, and the Godolphin colt was the lukewarm favourite. The starter let his flag fall and the field set on their way, Dahjee breaking slowly, then moving into contention under Dettori. He idled in midfield, made up some ground and lost it again in the run to the wire, finishing fourth.

It was not a disgraceful debut, but it turned out to be Dahjee's only race. He was nothing like his brother.

Dahjee's brief career illustrated, yet again, the whims of genetics. Try as humans might, they could not predict the particular reassembling of chromosomes at each mating. After all this time, breeders could do little more than follow the old maxim: Breed the best to the best, and hope for the best. But such simple advice flew in the face of commercial dictates.

The Dubai Millennium breeding programme had turned into an unusual situation indeed. Sheikh Mohammed had intended it as an experiment, and now it retained a scientific purity about it, untainted by commercialism. This was most unusual in the case of a freshman sire; normally each win is trumpeted with advertisements in all the racing publications, press releases to editors, brochures for breeders and the inevitable rumours of an increase in next year's stud fee.

Because Dubai Millennium was dead, none of the commercial hype was applicable. It may have been accidental, but it was fitting. Sheikh Mohammed, a man celebrated for giving priority to sportsmanship over business by keeping his older colts in training rather than sending them straight to the breeding shed as three-year-olds, was now making the campaign decisions for this champion-sired crop of runners based purely on sportsmanship. Commercial dictates did not apply. The whole story was in direct contrast to the saga of Shareef Dancer.

Nonetheless, Godolphin held the crop in high regard. Shortly after Dubawi's Superlative Stakes win, Sheikh Mohammed's son, Sheikh Hamdan bin Mohammed, bought the runner-up Henrik in a private deal.

July segued into August, and summer into damp autumn. More and more of Dubai Millennium's runners were sent out, most of them finishing first, second, or third. Among the first-time winners was Descartes, a tall, dark bay colt whose dam was the French mare Gold's Dance. She was already the dam of a Group 1 winner, Goldamix, who had won the Criterium de Saint-Cloud for two-year-olds a year before Dubai Millennium's breakdown. She had been owned by the Wertheimer brothers, but they sold her to Sheikh Mohammed while carrying her foal.

The most prominent of the runners were colts, but more of the fillies began to appear too. Quickfire returned to win a maiden in September, and duly received a 25-1 quote for the 1,000 Guineas. However, this was mainly bookie-reflex action; the filly hung so badly in the final furlong that she ended up virtually on top of the stands' rail.

The fillies were puzzling. While they showed ability, none had the sort of pizzazz that Oude, Belenus, and most of all Dubawi had. The first of the females to win was Halle Bop, the filly that Philippa Cooper had so nearly refused to part with. Halle Bop was a close-up second on her first start, a six-furlong race on softish ground at Newbury in August, despite getting rather rattled in the warm-up. She returned two weeks later at Kempton, more settled this time, to win over the same distance on slightly firmer ground after leading from the outset.

Her Own Kind, a Darley-bred half-sister to Godolphin's 1999 St Leger winner Mutafaweq, made the frame in her first start and returned to win. So did Russian Revolution, a filly bred by Sheikh Maktoum's Gainsborough Stud. Although each made a favourable enough impression, neither fired up much excitement.

That task was left to Dubawi. He had pulled to the head of the full assemblage of Godolphin two-year-olds. Just recently, another colt had emerged who might one day give Dubawi a run for his money. Named Librettist, the colt was sired by Kentucky's premier son of Northern Dancer, Danzig, and he was a half-brother to Godolphin's 2003 Queen Anne Stakes winner Dubai Destination. None of that would have mattered, though – the stables were littered with similarly well-bred animals – if the colt couldn't run. Librettist was unbeaten in two starts, and he was under close observation as a potential Guineas contender.

As for Dubawi, the feisty colt was forced to bide his time through the summer. While he periodically wowed work-watchers on the Newmarket gallops, he did not race between July and mid-September. The Godolphin think-tank had come to the conclusion that he – and most of Dubai Millennium's runners – needed some give underfoot to be at their best. The firm summer ground was not good for them.

By the latter half of September, the rains came and the going softened. Godolphin had targeted one of two possible races for Dubawi – the Royal Lodge Stakes at Ascot, or the National Stakes at the Curragh. The case was decided after the colt put in a particularly stirring work against a six-year-old named Divine Task, and the €30,000 supplementary fee for the Irish race was handed over just five days before the race with a fair dose of confidence.

It was well justified. Although the National Stakes was a Group 1, the field did not include anything approaching Dubawi's talent on form. The main challengers appeared to be Democratic Deficit and Elusive Double, second and third respectively in the Group 2 Futurity Stakes at the Curragh. John Magnier's Ballydoyle stable had entered three of the seven runners, but only one appeared to have a legitimate chance – Russian Blue, who had been placing in Group races all summer, but had yet to win beyond five furlongs. The National Stakes was over seven.

With showers falling in Ireland for two days before the race, the ground softened to yielding. Conditions were just right for Dubawi, who surged through the spongy grass like a dolphin through waves. Allowing the speedy Russian Blue to set the pace, Dettori held his colt together until just over two furlongs out; when he finally set him down for the drive, the race was over. Berenson, previously a maiden winner, got up for second, with Russian Blue holding on for third. There was just a slight knot of worry when Dubawi ducked towards the rail after gaining the lead. However, Dettori put a positive spin on the incident.

"It was a good sign," he claimed. "When a horse does something like that it usually means he's not fully extended and has more to give. That was the case here and he's a great prospect for next year, when he might give me my first Derby win."[6]

All of a sudden, it was all about the Derby. The National Stakes had long since gained a reputation for producing winners of the Epsom race. Sinndar was the most recent example – the Aga Khan's colt had taken the 1999 National Stakes by a head nine months before winning the Derby.

Crisford ushered the speculation along with a post-race claim that Dubawi would get the mile and a half "standing on his head". The bookmakers made their usual evasive moves; Ladbrokes halved the colt's odds, making him the 10-1 favourite.

Dubawi was put away for the rest of the year, with big plans ahead of him. However, a number of his paternal siblings, who had been slower to develop, were sent out for their first runs in the autumn. The most closely watched of these was Echo Of Light, who made his debut at Newmarket in mid-October. The race drew a large field of 21 runners, including another Dubai Millennium colt, Muraabet, who was trained by John Dunlop for Sheikh Hamdan.

Crisford downplayed Echo Of Light's chances before the race, warning the press that this was just ground being laid for the future. And indeed there was no replay of Dubai Millennium's spectacular end-of-season debut at Yarmouth six years earlier – Echo Of Light finished fourth and Muraabet third in the field of 21. Later, this would prove to be a very useful maiden, with five subsequent stakes winners, two of them at Group 1 level, emerging from the field. For now, though, it was a satisfactory start for Echo Of Light.

The season was winding down. Soon the leaves would be falling and it would be time to pack up the horses and adjust to the less hectic rhythms of Dubai. As they left Newmarket behind, the Godolphin crew could breathe a sigh of relief, knowing that four of Dubai Millennium's foals figured prominently among the betting for the colts' spring Classics. The dream would continue next year, when Dubawi had a crack at the one race that had defeated his father.

1. Alan Fraser, "My Kingdom for a Horse", *Daily Mail*, 13 May 2004.
2. Simon Milham, "Goodwood: Dubai Millennium off the mark with Dubawi", *Racing Post*, 6 June 2004.
3. Tony Elves, "Newmarket: Dubawi lands Superlative in style and leaves Dettori dreaming of Derby glory", *Racing Post*, 9 July 2004.
4. Ibid.
5. Bruce Jackson, "Unraced Guineas favourite Echo 'needs time'", *Racing Post*, 22 July 2004.
6. Tony O'Hehir, "Godolphin in raptures as Dubawi romps home", *Racing Post*, 20 September 2004.

CHAPTER FOURTEEN

DUBAWI'S YEAR

With the top European racing yards in hibernation over the dark northern winter, Godolphin was allowed some respite from racing and its attendant press coverage while relaxing under a daily dose of sun.

Dubawi and the other Dubai Millennium progeny became three-year-olds on January 1. This would be their definitive season, the year they would, it was hoped, compete in the Classic races that define the best of the breed – the Guineas, the Derby and the Oaks. Each major racing nation in Europe holds its own version of these contests, but it is the British races that are valued most highly, and it is these on which the bookmakers begin totting up ante-post prices as soon as the first two-year-olds from the elite yards begin racing.

By March, the press had descended on Nad Al Sheba for the tenth running of the Dubai World Cup. The contest was now the centre of focus for a good cross-section of the racing world, although the international flavour this year was heavily biased towards

Americans, who were providing nearly half of the field. There were lone entries from Britain, Japan, and South Africa, and a smattering of middle-eastern-owned entries completed the field.

Sheikh Mohammed had no more than a host's interest in the race this year; Godolphin had not entered a single horse. Its focus would be on winning the British, and possibly American, Classic races. Dubawi was the leading contender for the Guineas and Derby, while Shamardal, a new acquisition, was being mooted for the Kentucky Derby.

Shamardal was one of two colts who could be a real threat to Dubawi in the British Classics. Fortunately, Godolphin now had control of him, and could direct his campaign so as to maximise opportunities for both colts.

While Dubawi's life was a continuation of Dubai Millennium's story, Shamardal had already compiled a most interesting history of his own. He was among the first crop of foals sired by Giant's Causeway, nicknamed "the Iron Horse" for his tenacity in battle. A year younger than Dubai Millennium, Giant's Causeway swept four of Britain's top races during the summer of 2000. He and Dubai Millennium would have met for the first time in the Breeders' Cup Classic, had fate not intervened. It would have been a match to savour, as Giant's Causeway, unlike Montjeu, was best over Dubai Millennium's optimum trips of a mile to a mile and a quarter.

As things turned out, Giant's Causeway was a close second to the Californian challenger, Tiznow, at the Breeders' Cup. It was an exceptional performance for a first attempt on dirt; it was also the colt's last race. After a single season at Coolmore Stud in Ireland, Giant's Causeway was moved to Ashford Stud, Coolmore's Kentucky satellite, where his handlers could woo American mares bred to run on dirt tracks.

Shamardal's dam Helsinki, who had travelled to Ireland for her rendezvous with the Iron Horse, was from a family dear to Sheikh Mohammed's heart; she was a sister to the sheikh's homebred colt Street Cry, who had given him another Dubai World Cup victory in 2002.

Helsinki had fallen out of Sheikh Mohammed's hands, however. Shamardal, her third foal, had been bred in the name of Brilliant Stable in Kentucky, and so highly had he been valued at birth that his owners insured him for a million dollars.

However, no-one was willing to offer that much for him when he was sent through the ring, shortly after being weaned from Helsinki, at the Keeneland November Breeding Stock Sale in 2002. The sale was recorded as RNA – reserve not attained – on a bid of $485,000.

Worse was to come as the foal soon developed co-ordination problems. By the time he was a yearling, he had been diagnosed with wobbler syndrome, a neurological disorder which is often progressive and can lead to death, as severely affected horses are put down.

Shamardal's case was so severe that the insurers paid out a mortality claim on him. But before the yearling colt could be put out of his misery, a Kentucky loss adjuster who had developed an interest in energetic healing techniques decided to take him on. Against the odds, the colt recovered; some people who worked with him thought it was a miracle, while others thought he had been misdiagnosed. In any case, he was healthy enough to travel to Newmarket for the Houghton yearling sale in October of 2003. It was there that a representative for Sheikh Maktoum bought him for 50,000 guineas, unaware of his medical history.

Like Dubawi, Shamardal won all three of his races as a two-year-old, culminating in victory in a Group 1 race – the Dewhurst Stakes. He had thus closed out his season as one of the top-ranked juveniles of 2004, while trained by Mark Johnston. Now, after various ownership adjustments, he was in the hands of Godolphin.

The other credible challenger to Dubawi's supremacy among the three-year-olds was Motivator. Owned by the Royal Ascot Racing Club, a well-heeled syndicate of more than 200 members, Motivator was also a product of the first crop of a top racehorse: the mighty Montjeu.

Motivator was a hot-headed animal, like his sire, but he was unbeaten in two starts. His big win had been in the Racing Post Trophy, one of the most prestigious end-of-season races for two-year-old colts. Unlike Godolphin, with its fluid plans for Shamardal and Dubawi, Motivator's trainer Michael Bell had mapped out a clear and careful campaign. He wanted to win the Derby. There was no secret about that, nor about the fact that Motivator, rather than Dubawi, was the press darling. Weekly reports on Bell's colt filled the racing pages as spring approached, while news of Godolphin's colt came through in punctuated briefs.

But here was Dubawi, two days before the Dubai World Cup, going through his paces at Al Quoz before a throng of cameras and reporters, much as his sire had done four years earlier. The work was impressive, leading to questions about his speed: did he have too much of it to be a legitimate Derby contender?

If the Godolphin executive had an opinion, they weren't letting on.

"We're very excited about him," Crisford told the swarm of reporters. "He has the right size, right attitude and tremendous acceleration. Whether he stays or not we will find out on Derby Day."

He added that Dubawi was "a very different type to Dubai

Millennium … He is much further forward, he was more precocious as a two-year-old, and everything is going well at the moment."1

Shamardal and Dubawi would soon have their first real tests of the year. Shamardal would run in the UAE Derby, a mile-and-a-quarter dirt race which had been conceived as Godolphin's own Kentucky Derby trial, on World Cup night. Dubawi would contest the traditional Godolphin trials over a mile, two weeks later.

The UAE Derby turned out to be a disaster for Shamardal. Previously a confident front-runner, the colt came undone on the sandy track when attempting to make the running. Dettori finally had to ease him; they were beaten 46 lengths by the winner, Godolphin's other entry, Blues And Royals.

So there would be no triumphant return to America for Shamardal, the comeback kid. It was a shame; had he managed to win the Run for the Roses, his story would have rivalled any up-from-his-own-bootstraps tear-evoking saga the country had yet produced. Moreover, it would have been a first Kentucky Derby win for Godolphin.

But it wasn't, and it was time to move on. Dubawi's trial took place on April 13. It was a formality, really, as the colt dispensed with his five hand-picked rivals – all of whom were maiden winners – before the watchful eyes of Sheikh Mohammed.

It hadn't been much of a test, but Dettori put a sunny spin on it: "He worked really well, everybody's happy, and he can only beat the horses you put in front of him."[2]

The bookmakers made their perfunctory moves, shortening Dubawi's odds for both Classics. Ladbrokes now quoted him at 5-1 for the Derby, and Motivator 7-1.

In spite of these shows of confidence, there was an undercurrent of doubt back in Britain. Gone were the days when the Dubai experiment was viewed as an unqualified success. Some people were beginning to grumble that subjecting horses to a long flight and a temperature change of 20C, mere days before asking them to exert the biggest athletic effort of their young lives, was not a recipe for success. It had been ten years since Mark Of Esteem's triumphant return in the Guineas was followed by Lammtarra's stunning success in the Derby. Since the year 2000, Saeed bin Suroor had saddled twenty Guineas contenders who had been nurtured in the desert sun, but Godolphin had celebrated a single winner – Kazzia in the 1,000 Guineas of 2002.

The Godolphin contingent touched down on British soil on the morning of 25 April, five days before the Guineas. Although it had been a dry spring in East Anglia, the forecast in Newmarket was for daily rain before the race on Saturday. It was chilly, too, the temperatures hovering below 15C. The cold wasn't welcome, but the rain, if it came, would help Dubawi's chances.

After his disaster on the dirt, Shamardal had been re-routed from Louisville to Paris, where he would tackle the French 2,000 Guineas. Motivator was bypassing Newmarket, Bell's sights still set unswervingly on the Derby. That left a field of 19 contenders for the 2,000 Guineas, but none of them looked world-beaters.

Among the most likely prospects were four colts who had finished within a hand's breadth of each other in the Craven Stakes, the Guineas trial held at Newmarket in mid-April. It had been a messy result in all, with two longshots, Democratic Deficit and Kandidate, finishing first and third, while a pair of short-priced horses, Rob Roy and Iceman, finished second and fourth.

Another interesting entry was Footstepsinthesand, owned by the Coolmore partnership of Sue Magnier and Michael Tabor. A son of

Giant's Causeway, he had easily won his only two starts as a two-year-old. This would be his first race since then, and no-one, outside of Ballydoyle, knew how good he might be. While Coolmore did not spirit their horses off to another country over the winter, they might as well have. Enshrouded in their mysterious cloak which wound tightly around the heart of County Tipperary, the Coolmore team conducted its own private rituals during the quiet months. Little news leaked out – and what did was deliberately leaked.

This was the kind of tangle the public was faced with, and the matter of Dubawi's fitness only snarled things further. Was he jet-lagged? Would he handle the footing, after the promised rains failed to materialise? And did the Dubai trial really mean anything, or was it just a publicised workout?

On April 30, they had some answers.

In defiance of the Met Office, it was a pleasant spring day, the wan sun just teasing the temperatures up into jacket-removal zone. The going was perfect for some horses – Iceman, for example, who had been fourth in the Craven Stakes and liked "to hear his feet rattle".

The officially rated good-to-firm ground would work against other horses, including Dubawi. Still, Dubai Millennium had managed to win on similar footing at Doncaster. There was only one shot at the Guineas, and Dubawi was ready to run. He would take his chance, ground worries or no.

The field was lined up in the stalls. Dubawi's ears were pricked, his muscles tight. Dettori closed his mouth, breathed through his nose, waited for the clang of the doors.

The stalls burst open, the horses dispersing across the broad grass track like so many seeds released in the wind. Party Boss, a tall grey colt who stood out in this field – until now he had been winning on all-weather tracks – surprisingly took the lead. Godolphin's second string, Satchem, under Kerrin McEvoy, was racing prominently, along with Iceman and Diktatorial, who was feeling keen on his first start of the year. Ranging up while under tight restraint from Kieren Fallon was the Ballydoyle threat, Footstepsinthesand.

Dubawi settled nicely for Dettori in mid-pack, with Rob Roy, the big bay colt who had closed ominously well in the Craven Stakes, just to his outside.

A half-mile had gone by already, and Party Boss still held the lead, enjoying his moment in the limelight. The experienced Kandidate, making his 11th lifetime start, was in second, giving his backers a thrill – he had been let go at 100-1, despite finishing a close-up third in the Craven. Close behind, Rob Roy and Dubawi were still matching strides, while Iceman dropped back. Footstepsinthesand began to move past him.

Gaining momentum as they headed into the Dip, Kandidate snatched the lead, with Tony James – unplaced since winning the Gimcrack Stakes the previous August – nearly beside him. But now Footstepsinthesand was rolling past them on the far side, away from the stands, Fallon's arms going like a pinwheel as he urged the bay colt on.

Dubawi began struggling, and Dettori tried to hold him together. Gone was the powerful stride, gone too the fierce resolution to win. Suddenly, the colt veered sharply left, towards the stands rail, carrying the Craven Stakes winner Democratic Deficit with him. Dettori cursed as both horses lost ground and momentum.

Out in the middle of the track, Footstepsinthesand was pulling clear. Once again, Godolphin's top jockey was doomed to watch Kieren Fallon's backside aboard a winner, while he swallowed the bitter taste of defeat on a favourite.

Every Guineas is subject to hyperbolic praise, then critical dissection. The winners are lauded even as the form is picked apart. So it was in 2004: Footstepsinthesand and Fallon were heroes. The win sealed Fallon's new relationship with Ballydoyle, for whom he had become stable jockey following high-profile break-ups with first Henry Cecil, then Sir Michael Stoute in the interim since Oath's Derby victory. The next day, as in a dream, Fallon, O'Brien and the Magnier/Tabor partnership repeated the feat in the 1,000 Guineas with Virginia Waters. It was 1999 all over again.

But in the days following, the 2,000 Guineas was open to scrutiny. Rebel Rebel, who had come from the back of the pack, and Kandidate had finished second and third, both priced at 100-1. The favourite, Dubawi, was a soundly beaten fifth, while Rob Roy had finished last.

The debate on Dubawi's Guineas preparation continued. While Godolphin first claimed he didn't handle the firm ground, they later added that he had been struck into. Others outside of the group continued to mutter about jet lag.

There was more head-scratching as the Irish 2,000 Guineas approached. There were three weeks between the Newmarket Classic and its equivalent at the Curragh. But while Dubawi signalled his readiness for round two with a strong seven-furlong work on the Al Bahathri gallop, the betting market foretold trouble with Footstepsinthesand.

In the new age of high-tech betting, the Classic races were sponsored with increasing frequency by gambling ventures – Ultimatepoker.com for the 2,000 Guineas, Boylesports for the Irish 2,000. So when Boylesports let on that punters weren't backing Footstepsinthesand, while his stablemate Oratorio – who had been fourth in the Guineas – was attracting lots of money, it was a sure sign that something was amiss. Would the 2,000 Guineas hero even make the line-up?

Ever cautious, Boylesports made him the favourite four days before the race, with Dubawi next and Oratorio third. Another Irish betting firm, Cashmans, had simply priced up the "Aidan O'Brien stable" as race favourite.

But a day later, the whispers proved correct: Aidan O'Brien announced that Footstepsinthesand would not run, due to a stone bruise that he had picked up at Newmarket. The Guineas hero, he revealed, had been galloping with a bandage on his foot since the race. No wonder the colt had been shaky in the market; even the invisible walls of Ballydoyle are penetrable to gossip mongers at the height of the season, especially with visual clues to fuel the rumours.

Things were going Dubawi's way. The Godolphin team knew it when a downpour began before the second race on Irish 2,000 Guineas day. The Curragh's emerald turf was softening by the moment, and their colt would be able to get his toe deep into it, lessening the impact on his joints and allowing his stride to reach its full length and power.

The race worked out like a dream, just as the National Stakes had on this same course the previous year. Moving fluently, Dubawi strode along with utter confidence, and when Dettori crouched down and pushed the reins up his neck, he took off like a shot, soaring straight down the centre of the track.

Suddenly, the colt headed to the right, tacking all the way across to the rail opposite the stands. This time there was no other horse outside of him, and he maintained enough momentum to win while eased down by Dettori.

Back in the winners' enclosure, the jockey performed his trademark flying dismount, then exchanged a few words with

Crisford. The two men went their separate ways but were stopped in their tracks by the press. They both expressed firm delight. "Dubawi doesn't need soft ground, but it was hard at Newmarket and he hated it," said Dettori. "Today he moved beautifully going to post and gave a massive display. He travelled super and showed a tremendous turn of foot."[3]

Crisford confirmed his jockey's assessment. "All great horses get beaten and what happened at Newmarket, where the ground was against him, was no disgrace."

He added that Dubawi's drift across the track had been directed by Dettori. "Today it was Frankie that took him to the far rail."[4]

Many onlookers remained unconvinced by this explanation. "If the electorate leaned to the right as much as the leading Derby candidates, Michael Howard would now be prime minister," proclaimed columnist James Willoughby, referring to the head of the Conservative party. Dubawi had obvious talent, but was he reliable enough to handle the infamous undulations at Epsom? And would he have enough stamina to last out the mile and a half? These were the questions left hanging over the Godolphin victory party as the son of Dubai Millennium was prepared for his next move.

Eight days before the Derby, summer arrived. Like a dinner guest knocking on the door an hour early, its unexpected presence provoked sudden dismay.

So sultry was it the first evening that trainer Michael Bell pulled off Motivator's protective night sheet. The next morning there was mild alarm in the yard – the colt's skin was marked with welts from an insect bite.

Moreover, the ground at Epsom was dry, and neither Godolphin nor Bell wanted it that way. The pride and joy of the Royal Ascot

Racing Club remained unbeaten, having won his only race of the season so far, the Dante Stakes. However, he too had moved these last few weeks under a cloud of uncertainty.

First, there was the issue of temperament. He had threatened to boil over in the preliminaries before the Dante, and after reaching the front had travelled sharply right, much like Dubawi at the Curragh. Second, he had never raced on anything other than soft ground. Third, he wasn't certain to stay the trip either. Although his sire had been a mile-and-a-half horse, his dam had speedier bloodlines.

A day before the five-day Derby entries were due in, Simon Crisford issued a warning. "We've made it very clear ever since the 2,000 Guineas that Dubawi will not be raced on ground that is too firm. It wouldn't matter what the race was, or what course we're talking about, he won't run, or even be trained, on a surface that we're not confident is suitable for him."

Bell also signalledto the clerk of the course that his horse was not a certain runner. "I'm worried about the ground and we're going to walk the track," he said. "Hopefully, they're putting plenty of water on. The ground needs to be safe. If it's safe, he'll run."[5]

The ground was duly watered. Dubawi was given the go-ahead after a late-night session between Sheikh Mohammed and Sheikh Maktoum, and the next day Crisford underlined the plan's import for Godolphin.

"The key thing is that the horse really deserves to have a shot at the Derby, and we're very excited about it," the racing manager said. "If you look at Godolphin's history you'll see we're not frightened to try new things and look at different horizons. Indeed, Sheikh Mohammed encourages us to have a positive outlook."[6]

Bell, too, pushed along by the enthusiasm of Motivator's 230 owners, chose to accentuate the positive. Both colts would take their chance. No, it wasn't the planned match race pitting Dubai Millennium against Montjeu. But here were the first-born sons, preparing to face off in the world's most famous race.

With so much at stake, it was no wonder Crisford added this caveat: "Obviously, we'll not find out until the race if he stays."

Loaded into the stalls at Epsom for his 13th Derby (and still looking for his first winner) Dettori briefly pondered his mission. He was to ride Dubawi conservatively, so as to save his mount's stamina. At least the colt was biddable, unlike his sire.

The jockey also gave a brief thought to Gypsy King. The Ballydoyle colt had emerged as another threat to Godolphin. Unbeaten on his only two starts, Gypsy King was now second favourite for the Derby, behind Motivator and ahead of Dubawi.

"They're off," came the call, timeless in its simplicity.

Hattan, a colt bred by Darley and raced by Saeed Manana, led the way. Motivator, breaking from an inside post, flowed into a handy tracking position. Dettori held Dubawi together, settling him in mid-pack.

Hattan continued to lead as they began climbing the hill. He was setting an easy enough pace, but Aidan O'Brien's phalanx of four was unhappy with the status quo. Almighty, the pacemaker of the quartet, had been outfooted early but now scooted around the field to apply pressure up front.

The pace increased as they neared the summit, Motivator still poised on the outside under Johnny Murtagh, Dubawi now tucked along the fence in fifth and beginning to tug at Dettori.

Heading downhill into Tattenham Corner, Almighty and Hattan continued to vie for the lead, Motivator breathing down their necks. On Gypsy King, Kieren Fallon moved off the fence, looked over his right shoulder and took aim at Murtagh's mount.

Motivator was having none of him, though. The wiry bay was travelling more strongly than ever. Dettori, who had Dubawi back on cruise control, kept his cool.

The leaders were already turning for home. A remarkably stubborn Hattan had regained the lead, but Motivator was now a wave coming to engulf him. Fallon still had Gypsy King in striking position, while Dettori began edging his mount closer, playing his speed like a finely tuned instrument.

And there went Motivator. In full drive now, the lean bay frame strode clear, three, four, five lengths in front of Dubawi as Gypsy King lost ground towards the outside.

It was a triumphant moment for Murtagh, Michael Bell and the Royal Ascot Racing Club, whose members were already spilling out of the grandstand as Walk In The Park passed a determined but stamina-sapped Dubawi to gain second place. The Godolphin colt was third, an impressive effort given the now indisputable knowledge that he did not stay a mile and a half. Still, it was a long walk down from the stands for Sheikh Mohammed's troops, as they watched the victory celebrations.

1. Tony Elves, "Magnificent Dubawi sets Derby trip poser", *Racing Post*, 24 March 2005.
2. Bill Barber, "Dubawi trial typical of what he's done all winter – Dettori", *Racing Post*, 14 April 2005.
3. Tony O'Hehir, "Dubawi returns to his brilliant best with tremendous Guineas win," *Racing Post*, 22 May 2005.
4. Ibid.
5. David Lawrence and Jon Lees, "Fast-ground fear over Dubawi's Derby challenge", 29 May 2005.
6. Lee Mottershead, "Dubawi given the go-ahead for Derby glory bid", 23 May 2005.

CHAPTER FIFTEEN

METEOR
SHOWER

Saeed bin Suroor ushered his star colts on to the Al Bahathri gallop, an artificial all-weather strip near the Rowley Mile racecourse, on a grey and clammy morning. It was the second week in July, but with the gallops abnormally quiet in the cold air, it could have been a dull winter's day. Newmarket's July meeting had just ended, and a lot of horses were having a short respite from the intense summer campaign.

Dubawi, unraced since the Derby more than a month earlier, was feeling fresh and fit. Today he was carrying Kerrin McEvoy, and he shone in a work against former South African hero Grand Emporium. Frankie Dettori was out with a broken collarbone, suffered in a fall at Sandown a week earlier. The accident had left an eerie sense of déjà vu; five years earlier, the jockey had narrowly survived the plane crash that killed Patrick Mackey on just such a day in Newmarket, and had focused his recovery on the thought of riding Dubai Millennium in the Prix Jacques le Marois.

Now he was in another race with time, aiming to win the same race aboard Dubawi. Had the colt's champion sire not been so cruelly stricken from the race five years before, he would have been rematched against Sendawar, France's leading miler who he beat so comprehensively at Royal Ascot.

In this year's Prix Jacques le Marois, Dubawi would confront the current French cynosure, Divine Proportions. Although small, the three-year-old was aptly named and had won all eight of her races so far, including both of the French fillies' Classics. Dettori did not want to miss the confrontation, which had the potential to be the highlight of the summer.

To be sure, the stars of the early season had ascended and faded as quickly as meteors before dawn. Footstepsinthesand had never run again after the 2,000 Guineas, a consequence, it was said, of the nagging hoof injury. Shamardal, after winning both of the French colts' Classics, had made a triumphant return to Britain with victory in the St James's Palace Stakes at Royal Ascot; but then he too had succumbed to injury on the eve of an intended clash with Motivator in the Coral-Eclipse Stakes. Motivator, for his part, had lost his unbeaten status in that race, when Ballydoyle's Oratorio finally came good.

Footstepsinthesand and Shamardal had already been packed off to Australia to get a head start on their stallion careers. Motivator's light had been dimmed. There was an opening for a hero and Dubawi was primed to fill it. Dettori flew back to Italy to rest, swim, and rebuild his strength for end-of-summer assault on the miling division, while Dubawi continued his preparations in Newmarket.

They went seamlessly, in the beginning. The colt was reaching a peak of fitness and wellbeing, trouncing his work partners with the same cheeky confidence he had shown from the beginning. Then, inexplicably, he threw in a dull gallop, his last before the big race.

Meanwhile, Dettori was struggling. The fractured collarbone wasn't healing as it should; an experimental climb aboard a pet horse at home left him gritting his teeth in pain. So it was McEvoy who made the trip to Deauville, amid slight misgivings about Dubawi's readiness.

Godolphin gave him all the help it could with a meticulously planned scenario, set out by Sheikhs Mohammed and Maktoum. There would be a pacemaker and a path to follow. The team had walked the track in the morning and, after a contentious debate, chosen a strip straight down the middle as the fastest. The plan was for Dubawi's pacemaker, Council Member, to take some of the sting out of Divine Proportions, who liked to track the front-runners before releasing her devastating turn of foot.

Divine Proportions wasn't the only threat; there were two other genuine challengers in the race: Valixir, winner of the Queen Anne Stakes at Royal Ascot a month earlier, and Divine Proportions' close relative Whipper, who had won this race a year before.

It was an important contest. More than a year had passed since Sheikh Mohammed and Princess Haya walked the rows of boxes at Godolphin Stables, pulling Dubai Millennium's sons and daughters from their boxes like newly unwrapped gifts, revelling in their novelty, dreaming of what might come. Despite the encouraging start the horses had made last year, it had been a disappointing summer for most of them. Echo Of Light had started the year promisingly enough by finishing second in a maiden race in May, but then returned to pull a dreadful stunt at Windsor on the first day of August. Ridden by Kerrin McEvoy, who was subbing for the injured Dettori, the big colt raced to the lead, but then hung to his left and suddenly ran off the course at an unfenced intersection a quarter-mile from the finish. He had never acted so atrociously at home, but the public, who had thought him a dead cert in the race, quickly labelled him a rogue. It was little comfort that the winner of the race was also owned by Sheikh Mohammed.

Many more of the crop were sitting out the season with nagging injuries, and the most promising of them, Belenus, had recently joined the sidelines.

The group had been winnowed down to this one horse; what was left of Dubai Millennium would be seen only in him. The sheikh and his wife were here to witness it, their dreams and binoculars focused on the small bay colt alone. Dubawi had a lot to live up to, but he didn't know it. He knew only what was in his heritage and in his training – to run fast and to win.

The plan worked to perfection. Council Member set a tepid pace and McEvoy settled Dubawi in behind him. With two furlongs to go the colt dug his hindquarters into the spongy Deauville turf and surged to the lead. Divine Proportions faded into fourth, while Whipper and Valixir made up some ground to finish second and third respectively.

Sheikh Mohammed and Princess Haya led the colt into the winners' enclosure, joy sparkling like raindrops on their faces. "This victory means the world to me," the sheikh declared. "Dubawi has followed in the footsteps of Dubai Millennium."

It was time to return to England. Six years ago a triumphant Dubai Millennium had travelled home from Deauville to prove to the world that he was Godolphin's best horse of all time. Dubawi would never be Godolphin's best horse, but he could make his sire's memory alive to the racing public and eternal in the breed.

He already had enough credentials to make a stallion. But the British and Irish racing elite were unlikely to remember the French race with the same fondness Sheikh Mohammed would. Even the National Stakes and the Irish 2,000 Guineas did not carry the cachet of a top British contest. It would take a race the calibre of the Queen Elizabeth II Stakes to stamp Dubawi's name indelibly on their memories.

The race, won with such a powerful run by Dubai Millennium at Ascot, had been moved to Newmarket while the Berkshire grandstand was undergoing a massive transformation. Being held on the Rowley Mile's straight course, with a sandy loam bottom and the infamous Dip, it wasn't, in essence, the same race contested in previous years. Nonetheless the Queen Elizabeth II Stakes of 2005, the unofficial championship for European milers, drew a vintage field.

The cast wasn't big but it featured two international stars, Rakti and Starcraft. Tall and dark, with an Italian past, Rakti could have been a Hollywood star – the kind who crashed cars, abused substances and left women crying. Rakti was an incorrigible rogue; his unpredictable temper tantrums were both eagerly awaited and dreaded by fans, who found the spectacle exciting, but knew it probably preceded the less pleasurable sight of their money going down the drain. But when he was good, Rakti was very, very good, and he had already collected six Group 1 scalps, including in this race a year earlier. He would be ridden by his regular jockey, Philip Robinson, and he was to be feared.

Starcraft had come to Newmarket via New Zealand and Australia. A winner of three Group 1 races over a variety of distances, he had arrived in early summer with a huge reputation and an equally imposing physique. Under a sun-burnished chestnut coat he was powerfully muscled, especially through his shoulders and haunch. A long blaze on his face, two evenly matched white stockings on his hind legs and a brand on each shoulder – Australasian thoroughbreds still being branded as a matter of course – completed the picture of a charismatic interloper.

Starcraft had also shown an alarming tendency to get excited in the parade ring, and his Newmarket trainer, Luca Cumani, had spent a good deal of time accompanying him to race meetings at which he wasn't running, so that he could experience the parade ring without the mind-rattling excitement of a race afterwards. The horse's personality was nothing compared to that of his owner, though; Paul Makin was given to outrageous public comments, which the press lapped up and regurgitated with fervour. So far, Makin had been fairly reticent on the Newmarket race, although his horse was coming off a win in France's other big mile race, the Prix du Moulin.

Starcraft would again be ridden by the jockey who guided him to victory in France, Christophe Lemaire, a 26-year-old who had never ridden at Newmarket before.

Dubawi's own past antics looked mild fare against these more battle-hardened competitors, and he would be the smallest horse and the youngest among these contenders. He was the only three-year-old in the field, which also included his experienced pacemaker, Blatant. On the plus side, Dubawi was on his home turf, rain had fallen a day earlier, and Dettori was back in the saddle.

If the stakes had been high in Deauville, they were a quantum leap higher here. This was almost certain to be Dubawi's penultimate race; the Breeders' Cup Mile was pencilled in next, and then, although it was not official, a new career at stud. If he could win this race, as his sire had, and then the Breeders' Cup – a target Dubai Millennium had been forced to miss – he would be a special horse indeed.

Nothing was left to chance. As in France, the Godolphin leaders had devised a clear and careful strategy, and Sheikh Mohammed delivered it to his jockey himself. Dettori was to follow his pacemaker along the stands' rail. They had an inkling that the tactically astute Robinson might steer Rakti down the middle of the course, in an attempt to draw Dubawi, with his wayward tendencies, with him; if this happened, Dettori was to remember above all, stay on the stands' rail.

A brilliant September sun was playing hide and seek with a roving band of clouds as the horses circled the pre-parade ring. Against the brick building housing the saddling boxes, Princess Haya stood serenely in a tailored cream coat, tilting her head slightly as she watched the horses circle round. Nearby, Sheikh Mohammed was all agitated movement, jamming a hand in his trouser pocket, then pulling it out again to clutch his racecard in both hands. His eyes moved left and right; he too was watching the horses.

Dubawi was wearing the type of leather-covered lip chain that had been used to calm Dubai Millennium. His upper lip wrinkled as he tried to wriggle it off, but he looked a tidy little package, compact and muscled but without an extra ounce of fat.

The opposition was each sporting his particular brand of headgear, Starcraft wearing a special rubber noseband to hold his bit in place, and a flashy browband in a red, blue and white diamond pattern. The extra schooling seemed to have worked, as he strode coolly around and around in the dappled light.

Crisford stepped in front of Princess Haya to give Rakti a critical glance as the horse walked by. There was something of the wild savage about Rakti – an untamed look in his eye, the proud crest of his neck. The impression was enhanced by the special headpiece he wore, a narrow rope device which exerted pressure on the tender spot behind his ears when pulled. Rakti's lad already had his hands full; he strode swiftly to keep up with the horse, but his shirt tail had come undone, and his cheeks flushed pink with effort, especially after Robinson was legged up.

As they headed out to the track, the lip chain gone now, Dubawi and Dettori looked a matched pair, both wearing oddly similar expressions: a mixture of confidence in their ability to do the task at hand, and impatience to get on with it.

They reached the grass verge and Dettori pointed his colt down the course, letting him break into a restrained gallop. Dubawi moved sweetly through the grass, enjoying the slight give underfoot.

Down at the start, horse and jockey were loaded into the stalls, just as they had been five months earlier for the Guineas. That disappointing day seemed years ago; today would be different. Dettori knew they could win this.

Another clang of the gates, and freedom as the padded metal doors burst open. The field of six split into two groups, with Blatant, Starcraft and Sleeping Indian taking the stands' rail. Rakti shot like an arrow up the middle, followed by Mullins Bay. Dettori sent Dubawi after them.

Up in Sheikh Mohammed's box, Crisford swore under his breath. Sheikh Mohammed directed a searing gaze at his racing manager, then his horse. Dettori had just committed the cardinal sin in Godolphin: he had disobeyed the boss. Whatever the outcome of the race, there would be a price to pay for this.

Blatant was setting a merry pace, and Starcraft, held up behind him, was enjoying a perfect trip. Dubawi was last of the six, held up behind the middle group. Dettori still had a tight rein on him when he looked over and saw that Starcraft's group, led by his own pacemaker, was moving better than his.

Cursing, he pulled on his left rein and began urging Dubawi forward while guiding him across the broad expanse of grass. They were entering the Dip now, and he knew his plight was critical as he asked the colt for his maximum effort.

Dubawi's powerful hindquarters were reaching deep under his body as his front legs stretched out gamely, but now they were on the stands' rail and Starcraft was making his own move. The massive chestnut frame dwarfed Dubawi, who was feeling the pressure and starting to lean towards his rival. Starcraft's tattooed shoulder was tantalizingly close as Dettori lowered himself into the colt's neck, arms pumping rhythmically and whip slashing, but the shoulder wasn't getting any closer. He was on a losing horse. Starcraft held his ground to win by a decisive margin – three-quarters of a length.

There was no flying dismount in the winners' enclosure. Dettori slid off his colt, reluctant to meet Sheikh Mohammed's steely gaze and Crisford's fury. He told the assembled press that Rakti and Mullins Bay had carried him out to the middle of the track, although he admitted that staying there was a costly mistake.

"It was a complete cock-up," Crisford said, implacable.

Dettori blamed himself, but he also blamed his draw in stall six. "If I'd been drawn better, it would have been easier for me to do what I'd wanted. I wish I could ride the race again."

But rare are second chances, as much in racing as in life. The jockey might have had a chance to redeem his awful mistake at Belmont Park, but in October Dubawi injured a hind ligament. He would not recover in time for the Breeders' Cup. Dubawi's retirement to Dalham Hall Stud was announced on 7 October.

CHAPTER SIXTEEN

THE BREEDING DREAM ANEW

The sun didn't look likely to push through the flat grey clouds blanketing Newmarket on a late May morning, but new life was pushing through everywhere. In the deepening fields on the perimeters of town, woolly lambs were interspersed with leggy young foals. Duchess Drive, a quiet road heading out into the Suffolk countryside, could have been named for the majesty of the great trees that formed a canopy over the asphalt, their newly green leaves suffusing the passage with a subterranean glow.

The road is used in springtime mainly by horseboxes delivering mares to the opulent studs obscured behind the trees. There the mares are mated with some of the world's best-bred thoroughbred stallions, as has been the tradition for a century on these acres.

Now, on this May morning, the stud was bustling quietly and efficiently as Dubawi prepared to cover his first mare of the day. It was only 8.00am, but everyone on the stud – horses, stallion men, stud hands bringing the visiting mares – had been up for hours. Dubawi, along with a dozen other Dalham Hall stallions, received his breakfast of sweet feed at 6.00am. An hour and a quarter later, he was groomed to a high polish and taken out for exercise – a brisk round of walking, led by his groom. Back in his spacious box, piled high with fresh straw, he was then clipped to the wall by a bit of twine fastened to his head collar, which was fitted over a smart leather bridle, minus the reins. The browpiece, in a pale blue and white triangular pattern, was adorned by a blue disc with his name, 'Dubawi' on it. (His mate would wear an identical disc, an extra measure to avoid last-minute confusion in the busy breeding shed.) The only item in the box not looking smart and expensive was the twine; it is used in place of leather or rubber because it will break if a horse panics and pulls back hard against the head collar as it is clipped to the wall.

Dubawi's date had arrived in good time for her 8.30 appointment, and waited in a holding box in the covering barn with her foal. In the days and weeks prior to her arrival here, she was assiduously checked by veterinarians to make sure that she would be on the cusp of ovulation today. If not, the mating would be in vain, an unnecessary expenditure of the stallion's energy as well as a needless risk to his health. Copulation between horses is a strenuously physical act that occasionally becomes violent. While stallions can be excessively forceful, one well-placed kick from a mare can end a stallion's season. Thus every effort is made to ensure that the mare is amenable to the whole situation, from using a twitch – a device that squeezes the flesh of the muzzle and so distracts her – to placing leather restraints, called hobbles, on her legs so that she can't kick.

There were two matings in line ahead of Dubawi, and his handler, a small-framed, bespectacled man named John Weldon, waited with him until the two large covering arenas were empty and the other stallions were put safely away before leading his charge out of his box. Dubawi danced lightly, like a boxer warming up for a fight or a tennis player bouncing in anticipation of his opponent's serve, as he approached the covering barn by way of an asphalt parking area. Weldon was dressed in standard Darley-issue gear: a blue jumper with 'Darley' embroidered over the left breast; khaki trousers; and a safety helmet with the name 'John' stitched on its cover, in a blue shade that matched the jumper. The helmet was for protection in case a horse's hoof should come crashing down in the wrong place. Humans as well as horses are vulnerable to the occasional brutality of the equine sexual act.

In spite of the precautions, Dubawi was not an imposing specimen as he bounced across the concrete. He had not grown since his racing days, although he had filled out, and his expression could best be described as mischievous.

Inside the dirt-floored arena, he stood calmly while waiting for his mare. From a glass-windowed viewing chamber above, the mare's owner and a handful of other people were watching, anxious that the moment of conception go without a hitch. It could be called a £25,000 moment – that was Dubawi's fee for covering a mare – but in fact, implicit in every mating is the dream that this one coupling of mare and stallion, the unique recombination of genes that will take place during fertilisation, will produce a special horse, one as good as its parents, or possibly better. If that were the case, this could be the £250,000 moment or the £2,500,000 moment. Then again, it could turn out to be the £2,500 moment.

The mare, a plain bay, entered. She was led by one stud hand while her foal was held by two others, who had their work cut out for them as the little animal whinnied and struggled to get back to its mother. Draped over her neck was a strange leather device with what looked like a handle, the type that male gymnasts use when working the pommel horse, near the crest. It is sometimes used for stallions who have a habit of savagely biting the mare's neck as they mount her, giving them a non-sentient object to sink their teeth into. But Ken Crozier, still the head stallion man at Dalham Hall, explained that in Dubawi's case, the leather handle was used to give the stallion something to hang on to, so that he didn't slide off before his job was finished.

The viewing room, which had been silent, filled with anxious mumbling as Dubawi began sniffing the mare. She responded by raising her tail and trying to stamp her feet, although the hobbles made this difficult. "Vet said she's ready. Oh oh, don't kick like the last time," they were saying, but suddenly Dubawi leapt up on his hind legs, dropped his forelegs down over the mare's neck and grasped the leather handle in his teeth. The alert handlers stepped in with lightning speed to guide him into place. The connection secured, he gave a few mighty thrusts with his hindquarters, and in less than a minute slid off again.

There were sighs of relief in the viewing room, and the mare's connections disappeared down the steps as the horses headed out of the arena.

Reunited with her foal, the mare was loaded into a horsebox to be driven back home. Dubawi, meanwhile, went back into his box where Crozier offered him a handful of carrots. Soon he would go out for another hour of hand-walking, followed by another polish, and at 1.00pm another covering. He would spend the afternoon relaxing in his box, with another meal served at 4.00pm, another mare at 7.00pm, and a final nighttime meal at 10.00pm.

The routine continued daily until June, when he would have a brief break spent mainly in quarantine before heading to Darley's

Australian base in the Hunter Valley. There the breeding process begins anew on southern hemisphere time. By the end of the year Dubawi will have covered more than 200 mares, and he will do the same the next year, and the next. It is a testament to human optimism – some might say foolishness – that every one of those matings carries with it the hope that this will be *the one*.

"We live in hope," Sheikh Mohammed says.

Liam O'Rourke believes that Dubawi gives the sheikh extra hope. But he believes that hope, unlike in Samuel Johnson's famous characterisation of marriage, is tempered by experience. "Dubawi's very special to Sheikh Mohammed," he said. "But I think the rapport that he had with Dubai Millennium was probably a one-off. It was absolutely unique. You know, the chances of duplicating that are so difficult."

As far as a repeat of Dubai Millennium, O'Rourke said: "I think the chances are slim." He added with a wry laugh: "We'll keep trying to produce it for him, anyway!" His face turning serious again, he said: "You know what you sometimes think are the good horses, the ones you expect something from, they don't always come up. Usually they don't. Usually they disappoint you."

Sheikh Mohammed and O'Rourke both know that Dubai Millennium was a once-in-a-lifetime phenomenon. Buy them or breed them, the chances of producing greatness are very slim. "Horses are blood and flesh, you know?" Sheikh Mohammed once said. "You buy them young, you try to train them, you spend all your time with them, and then they're no good. Or sometimes, a hero will come through."

Dubawi was almost good enough to be called a hero. In hindsight it was remarkable that his sire's one small crop should produce even a single stallion worthy of standing at Dalham Hall. By the time

Dubai Millennium's lone crop of runners had ended their four-year-old season, it was clear that it would be Dubawi's task, and his task alone, to carry on the line.

CHAPTER SEVENTEEN

EPILOGUE

On the whole, by the end of 2005, Godolphin had given up on the second generation – it had had its chance, and Dubawi was what it had come up with. Things could certainly be worse, but there was an unmistakable feeling of disappointment that they hadn't been better.

Take Echo Of Light, for example. The enigmatic colt had come back two weeks after his embarrassing stunt at Windsor to spread-eagle a field in a maiden at York, and three weeks after that he was equally impressive when winning a conditions race at Doncaster. The trouble was the timing – had he performed so well a year earlier, he would have been lauded as a top Derby contender. Now there was the question of where to run him next.

Godolphin chose the Champion Stakes – unwisely, as it turned out. The Champion Stakes is one of the toughest races of the year, pitting battle-hardened older horses against any three-year-olds strong enough to survive the season. It is the final Group 1 race of the year for three-year-olds and up in Britain, and a most prestigious title to win. In short, it was an ambitious target.

Echo Of Light was not up to the task. It was no surprise, really. Godolphin knew he had been pitched in over his head, and his jockey wore the white cap denoting second string. Frankie Dettori had opted to ride Godolphin's other horse, Layman, and it was he who carried the all-blue first colours.

Looking like a pacesetter run amuck, Echo Of Light grabbed the early lead, extending his margin to nearly a dozen lengths before the field swallowed him. He finished last by a long way.

So that was it. The experiment was over. Or was it?

The year 2006 was a hard one for Godolphin. Not that it was all bad – Electrocutionist won the Dubai World Cup, Bernardini would have been North America's Horse of the Year but for a second place in the Breeders' Cup Classic, Discreet Cat pounced on the New York scene as his worthy successor, and Librettist won two Group 1s in France.

It was a pretty dismal year in Britain and Ireland, though. To begin with the horses weren't right when they returned from Dubai. Something had upset their systems, to the extent that Godolphin pulled all its entries in the weeks before Royal Ascot. Highly priced acquisitions that had joined Godolphin over the winter disappointed when they finally reappeared in the blue colours. And the team's leading hope Iffraaj was beaten a heartbreaking head in the July Cup.

Slowly the stable regained form, but with its sights lowered. Horses were entered in lower-class contests, conditions races and handicaps, and sent to Germany and France for their Group races. Even Electrocutionist, the de facto leader by virtue of his win in Dubai, was not quite up to top competition. Then he died, of a heart attack in September. Godolphin finished the season without a single

Group 1 win in Britain or Ireland. Nor did they win a Breeders' Cup race. It was a far cry from the glorious period beginning in 1995, when Moonshell, Lammtarra, and Halling together swept the Oaks, Derby, Eclipse, King George and Juddmonte International Stakes, while So Factual added a top sprint, the Nunthorpe, and Classic Cliché the top distance race, the St Leger. In Dubai Millennium's heyday, Godolphin had plundered 14 British and Irish Group 1s with ten different horses.

No-one expected Dubai Millennium's progeny to save the day now. Dubawi might have done it, but he was otherwise engaged at Dalham Hall. But against expectations, Echo Of Light and Belenus between them added four British Group-race wins for Godolphin during that difficult season.

Their victories did not have the poignancy of Dubawi's three Group 1s. Even Echo Of Light, who remained special to Sheikh Mohammed, could not pull off a heartwarming finish to it all. His headstrong, quirky nature had not been subdued, and he nearly ran Dettori into the hedge at Longchamp when winning the Group 2 Prix Daniel Wildenstein towards the end of the year.

Godolphin gave Echo Of Light his chance, all right, but both times he was thrown into Group 1 competition, he fell back on his old trick of racing too freely. Ironically, he even made it to the Breeders' Cup, a goal that had eluded both Dubai Millennium and Dubawi. Visions of a fairytale ending to his career disappeared in a puff of reality about a minute and a half after the stalls opened at Churchill Downs, though. He pulled hard into a strong pace, faded and finished last.

That did complete the experiment. Dubai Millennium's only crop of 56 foals – three of whom were dead by now – had finished their racing careers. How did they stack up?

The answer is mixed. As a group, they performed exceptionally well in some key areas, compared to the averages for the breed. In others, they scored poorly.

The averages for the breed is a set of statistics, compiled by the Lexington, Kentucky publication *Thoroughbred Times*, based on worldwide performances of all named foals born in North America during a ten-year period. Although the most recent set predated Dubai Millennium's runners by a few years, the averages are still useful as a guideline by which to compare the results of a stallion's progeny against all others. Below are Dubai Millennium's results, set against those for all sires and those for the top one per cent of sires.

	Foals of 1989-1998	Foals by top 1% of sires	DM's foals
Starters/foals	70.40%	84.90%	61%
Winners/foals (starters)	47.5% (67.5)	65.9% (77.6%)	36% (58.8%)
Repeat winners/foals (starters)	36.5% (51.8%)	53.5% (63.0%)	17.9% (29.4%)
Stakes-placed/foals (starters)	5.6% (8.0%)	11.6% (13.6%)	3.6% (5.9%)
Stakes winners/foals (starters)	3.6% (5.1%)	8.7% (10.3%)	8.9% (14.7%)
Group/Grade SW/foals (starters)	0.8% (1.1%)	3.3% (3.9%)	5.4% (8.8%)
Gr1 SW/foals (starters)	0.2% (0.3%)	1.0% (1.2%)	1.8% (2.9%)
2yo starters/foals	34.50%	46.70%	39.30%
2yo winners/foals (starters)	11.6% (33.6%)	18.4% (39.5%)	19.6% (55%)
2yo SW/foals (starters)	1.0% (3.0%)	2.3% (4.9%)	1.8% (5.0%)
3yo starters/foals	60.50%	76.70%	46.40%
4yo starters/foals	46.00%	57.60%	12.50%
Average no. starts/foal	15	18	3.3
Average no. starts/starter	21	22	5.4
Average earnings/starter	$39,143	$85,598	$71,770
Average earnings/start	$1,853	$3,975	$13,262

In terms of producing winners to foals, Dubai Millennium lags well behind the average for the breed. In terms of repeat winners to foals, his results are shockingly bad. There was certainly a weakness to his stock, in that they tended to be big, slow to develop and prone to injury. On top of that, they needed soft ground to run on. However, he may have had more runners, and more repeat winners, if more of his progeny had been with trainers outside of Godolphin. Other owners and trainers with less emotional and financial investment in the horses might have been more inclined to run them at a lower level, or to persist with them.

Then again, perhaps not. Of the eight horses not in the possession of Sheikh Mohammed or his brothers, only three (Saeed Manana's Bahar Shumaal, Britton House Stud's Carisolo, and Khalid Abdullah's Quickfire) won races, and just two (Bahar Shumaal and Quickfire) were repeat winners.

However, the promise evinced by Dubai Millennium's two-year-olds was not a mirage. His ratio of two-year-old starters to foals is above average, and his ratio of juvenile winners to foals exceeds that of the top 1 per cent of sires. On top of that, his percentage of stakes winners to foals is exceptional – up there with the elite of the breed. His ratio of Group or Graded stakes winners to foals is well above that of the top one per cent, although his small sample size surely helped him here.

His average earnings index – which compares how much money his foals made on the racetrack with the average earnings of all runners during the same period – is excellent. The average for all runners in any given year is by definition 1.00, and his AEI of 3.24 puts him in an elite group. However, his comparable earnings index of 3.58 tells us that his foals actually earned less money than the foals his mares produced when mated to other stallions. In other words, the CI figure shows that his mares set a high standard, which he did not quite live up to. (The top 32 per cent of sires have an AEI higher than their mares' CI, which puts Dubai Millennium roughly in the lower two-thirds of all stallions – a broad category).

Dubai Millennium's foals were not a good investment in strict financial terms, especially considering what Sheikh Mohammed paid for them. Even based on the stallion's advertised stud fee of £100,000, they were a big financial loss. Their total earnings came to slightly more than £1,200,000. More than half of that was Dubawi's.

In more ways than one, the small bay colt rode to the rescue – not only did he earn accolades on the racecourse, but he is likely to turn a profit for the entire group by the end of his second year at stud. He covered 141 mares at a fee of £25,000 during his first season at Dalham Hall before heading to Australia (where his fee was A$33,000, or £13,242) for the southern hemisphere spring.

Dubawi is far and away the most prolific progenitor of Dubai Millennium's descendents, but he will not be the only one. Ten Centuries, the unraced colt out of Fitnah who Sheikh Mohammed bid on, but did not buy, at Keeneland, entered stud at Buck Pond Farm in Kentucky in 2007. His fee was set at $2,000. With his novelty value – he is the only son of Dubai Millennium at stud in America – his good looks and his strong family tree, the handsome chestnut is likely to draw a decent business, even in the highly competitive Lexington market.

There is also the female side to the equation. Most of Dubai Millennium's daughters will be cycled back into the breeding population. Being well bred top and bottom – on both their sire's and dams' sides – at least some of them should turn into valuable producers. How valuable? A hint came when Carisolo, the filly bred and retained by Britton House Stud from the French mare Solo De Lune, came on the market at Tattersalls December sales in 2006. Although she had won just one race and less than £16,000, Carisolo, a sleek dark bay with a small crescent star and a remarkable composure, had the bids showering down upon her. The final price was 1,000,000 guineas. The buyer was bloodstock agent Richard Frisby, bidding for an unnamed "international breeder".

Is it fair to draw a verdict on Dubai Millennium's performance as a sire? He did not have a lot of chances, compared to stallions with 100 runners in their first crops. He did, though, have every chance from his mares, a most accomplished set. Most of the leading sires of modern history had no better opportunity.

Take Hail To Reason, for example. After contesting 18 races as a two-year-old, the American-bred colt broke both his front sesamoids and was retired. This was 1960, and it was a different world. There were fewer mares in the world, and fewer humans breeding them, for that matter. Hail To Reason got only 13 foals from his first crop, but five of them were stakes winners, including the champion racemare Straight Deal and Belmont Stakes winner Hail To All. Hail To Reason went on to become an influential sire, his line carried on most successfully through his sons Roberto and Halo, and his grandson Sunday Silence.

As a sire, Dubai Millennium was no Hail To Reason, but he was not a flop either. He got two exceptional colts, Dubawi and Echo Of Light, from his one smallish crop. Both were probably better than their records show – especially Dubawi, who had excuses in the Guineas and the QEII, and could have progressed at four if he hadn't been retired, a decision based more on economic and personal considerations than on the horse's health.

In life and death, Dubai Millennium was defined by improbable extremes of good luck and bad luck. His life was brief and fantastic – it burned brightly and never had time to fade. For human athletes, this would be fulfilment enough. But for thoroughbred racehorses, success is measured in the perpetuation of a name, a bloodline, a chain of chromosomes down the generations. Siring Dubawi was pretty lucky, all in all. It gives Dubai Millennium a shot at immortality.

DUBAI MILLENNIUM'S PEDIGREE AND RACE RECORD

DUBAI MILLENNIUM (GB) (BAY 1996)	SIRE: SEEKING THE GOLD (USA) (BAY 1985)	MR. PROSPECTOR (USA)	RAISE A NATIVE (USA)
			GOLD DIGGER (USA)
		CON GAME (USA)	BUCKPASSER (USA)
			BROADWAY (USA)
	DAM: COLORADO DANCER (IRE) (BAY 1986)	SHAREEF DANCER (USA)	NORTHERN DANCER (CAN)
			SWEET ALLIANCE (USA)
		FALL ASPEN (USA)	PRETENSE (USA)
			CHANGE WATER (USA)

Race	Date	Distance	Going	Field size	FP	2nd	Margin	Odds	Trainer	Jockey
maiden-Yarmouth	28/10/98	1m	soft	18	1	Tabareeh	5	4/9F	D Loder	L Dettori
conditions-Doncaster	03/05/99	1m	GF	4	1	Ettrick	9	4/6F	S bin Suroor	L Dettori
Predominate S, L-Goodwood	18/05/99	1m2f	good	6	1	Red Sea	3.5	4/11F	S bin Suroor	L Dettori
Derby, G1-Epsom	05/06/99	1m4f	good	16	9			5/1F	S bin Suroor	L Dettori
Pr Eugene Adam, G2-ML	18/07/99	1m2f	good	5	1	State Shinto	3	7/10JF	S bin Suroor	L Dettori
Pr Jacques le Marois, G1-Deau	15/08/99	1m	v. soft	6	1	Slickly	2.5	14/10JF	S bin Suroor	L Dettori
QEII, G1-Ascot	26/09/99	1m	heavy	4	1	Almushtarak	6	4/9F	S bin Suroor	L Dettori
Maktoum Ch, List-NAS	02/03/00	1m2f	fast	6	1	Lear Spear	4.5		S bin Suroor	L Dettori
Dubai World Cup, G1-NAS	25/03/00	1m2f	fast	13	1	Behrens	6		S bin Suroor	L Dettori
Prince of Wales's S, G1-Ascot	21/06/00	1m2f	GF	6	1	Sumitas	8	5/4	S bin Suroor	J Bailey

Best RRP: 139, Timeform: 140 (at 3, 132); dam's Timeform: 122

AFRICANUS

DUBAI MILLENNIUM (GB) b 1996	SEEKING THE GOLD (USA)	**MR. PROSPECTOR (USA)**	RAISE A NATIVE (USA)
			GOLD DIGGER (USA)
		CON GAME (USA)	BUCKPASSER (USA)
			BROADWAY (USA)
	COLORADO DANCER (IRE)	SHAREEF DANCER (USA)	**NORTHERN DANCER (CAN)**
			SWEET ALLIANCE (USA)
		FALL ASPEN (USA)	PRETENSE (USA)
			CHANGE WATER (USA)
ASFURAH (USA) dkb/br 1995	DAYJUR (USA)	DANZIG (USA)	**NORTHERN DANCER (CAN)**
			PAS DE NOM (USA)
		GOLD BEAUTY (USA)	**MR. PROSPECTOR (USA)**
			STICK TO BEAUTY (USA)
	MATHKURH (USA)	RIVERMAN (USA)	NEVER BEND (USA)
			RIVER LADY (USA)
		MANAL (FR)	LUTHIER (FR)
			TOP TWIG (IRE)

Africanus (Ire) b c 5 Feb 2002.
Inbreeding: Mr. Prospector 3x4, Northern Dancer 4x4.
Breeder: Hadi Al Tajir
Owner: Godolphin
Trainer: Saeed bin Suroor

Race record:

Years	Starts	Wins	2nd	3rd	Earned (£/$)
1	2	0	1	1	£1,896 / $3,437

Best RPR: 74; Timeform at 3: 74; dam's Timeform: 108

ANTIQUE

DUBAI MILLENNIUM (GB) b 1996	SEEKING THE GOLD (USA)	MR. PROSPECTOR (USA)	RAISE A NATIVE (USA)
			GOLD DIGGER (USA)
		CON GAME (USA)	BUCKPASSER (USA)
			BROADWAY (USA)
	COLORADO DANCER (IRE)	SHAREEF DANCER (USA)	**NORTHERN DANCER (CAN)**
			SWEET ALLIANCE (USA)
		FALL ASPEN (USA)	PRETENSE (USA)
			CHANGE WATER (USA)
ANNA PALARIVA (IRE) ch 1995	CAERLEON (USA)	NIJINSKY (CAN)	**NORTHERN DANCER (CAN)**
			FLAMING PAGE (CAN)
		FORESEER (USA)	ROUND TABLE (USA)
			REGAL GLEAM (USA)
	ANNA OF SAXONY (IRE)	ELA-MANA-MOU (IRE)	PITCAIRN (IRE)
			ROSE BERTIN (GB)
		ANNA MATRUSHKA (GB)	MILL REEF (USA)
			ANNA PAOLA (GER)

Antique (Ire) ch f 8 Feb 2002.
Inbreeding: Northern Dancer 4x4, Native Dancer 5x6x5.
Breeder: Kilfrush Stud
Owner: Godolphin
Trainer: Andre Fabre/ Saeed bin Suroor

Race record:

Years	Starts	Wins	2nd	3rd	Earned (£/$)
3	8	2	1	1	£54,797 / $96,318

At 3, won Prix La Sorellina-L; 3rd Prix de Psyche-63, Deauville
Best RPR: 104; Timeform at 3: N/A; dam's Timeform: N/A

BAHAR SHUMAAL

DUBAI MILLENNIUM (GB) b 1996	SEEKING THE GOLD (USA)	MR. PROSPECTOR (USA)	RAISE A NATIVE (USA)
			GOLD DIGGER (USA)
		CON GAME (USA)	BUCKPASSER (USA)
			BROADWAY (USA)
	COLORADO DANCER (IRE)	SHAREEF DANCER (USA)	NORTHERN DANCER (CAN)
			SWEET ALLIANCE (USA)
		FALL ASPEN (USA)	PRETENSE (USA)
			CHANGE WATER (USA)
HIGH SPIRITED (GB) b 1987	SHIRLEY HEIGHTS (GB)	MILL REEF (USA)	NEVER BEND (USA)
			MILAN MILL (USA)
		HARDIEMMA (GB)	HARDICANUTE (GB)
			GRAND CROSS (GB)
	SUNBITTERN (GB)	SEA HAWK (FR)	HERBAGER (FR)
			SEA NYMPH (FR)
		PANTOUFLE (GB)	PANASLIPPER (IRE)
			ETOILE DE FRANCE (GB)

Bahar Shumaal (Ire) b c 9 March 2002.
Inbreeding: none in five generations.
Breeder: Airlie Stud & Sir Thomas Pilkington
Owner: Saeed Manana
Trainer: Clive Brittain
Acquired: privately

Race record*:

Years	Starts	Wins	2nd	3rd	Earned (£/$)
3	20	3	1	1	£50,081 / $98,129

Best RPR: 106; Timeform at 3: 104; dam's Timeform: 80
*still racing in 2007

BANCHIERI

DUBAI MILLENNIUM (GB) b 1996	SEEKING THE GOLD (USA)	MR. PROSPECTOR (USA)	RAISE A NATIVE (USA)
			GOLD DIGGER (USA)
		CON GAME (USA)	BUCKPASSER (USA)
			BROADWAY (USA)
	COLORADO DANCER (IRE)	SHAREEF DANCER (USA)	**NORTHERN DANCER (CAN)**
			SWEET ALLIANCE (USA)
		FALL ASPEN (USA)	PRETENSE (USA)
			CHANGE WATER (USA)
BELLE ET DELUREE (USA)	THE MINSTREL (CAN)	**NORTHERN DANCER (CAN)**	NEARCTIC (CAN)
			NATALMA (USA)
		FLEUR (CAN)	VICTORIA PARK (CAN)
			FLAMING PAGE (CAN)
	SOPHISTICATED GIRL (USA)	STOP THE MUSIC (USA)	HAIL TO REASON (USA)
			BEBOPPER (USA)
		CLOSE CONTROL (USA)	DUNCE (USA)
			SELF CONTROL (USA)

Banchieri (GB) b c 6 Feb 2002.
Inbreeding: Northern Dancer 4x3.
Breeder: Cheveley Park Stud Ltd & Darley
Owner: Godolphin
Trainer: Saeed bin Suroor

Race record:

Years	Starts	Wins	2nd	3rd	Earned (£/$)
2	9	1	1	2	£9,848 / $17,854

Best RPR: 82; Timeform at 2: 83 (at 3, N/A); dam's Timeform: N/A

BELENUS

		MR. PROSPECTOR (USA)	RAISE A NATIVE (USA)
DUBAI MILLENNIUM (GB) b 1996	SEEKING THE GOLD (USA)		GOLD DIGGER (USA)
		CON GAME (USA)	BUCKPASSER (USA)
			BROADWAY (USA)
	COLORADO DANCER (IRE)	SHAREEF DANCER (USA)	**NORTHERN DANCER (CAN)**
			SWEET ALLIANCE (USA)
		FALL ASPEN (USA)	PRETENSE (USA)
			CHANGE WATER (USA)
AJHIBA (IRE) ch 1996	BARATHEA (IRE)	SADLER'S WELLS (USA)	**NORTHERN DANCER (CAN)**
			FAIRY BRIDGE (USA)
		BROCADE (GB)	HABITAT (USA)
			CANTON SILK (GB)
	WELSH LOVE (IRE)	ELA-MANA-MOU (IRE)	PITCAIRN (IRE)
			ROSE BERTIN (GB)
		WELSH FLAME (IRE)	WELSH PAGEANT (FR)
			ELECTRIC FLASH (GB)

Belenus (Ire) ch c 22 March 2002.
Inbreeding: Northern Dancer 4x4.
Breeder: Gainsborough Stud Management Ltd
Owner: Godolphin
Trainer: Saeed bin Suroor

Race record:

Years	Starts	Wins	2nd	3rd	Earned (£/$)
3	6	3	2	1	£79,464 / $148,563

At 3, 2nd Steventon S-L, Hampton Court S-L, 3rd Predominate S-L; at 4, won Sovereign S-63
Best RPR: 110; Timeform at 3: 109; dam's Timeform: 110

BRIGHT MORNING

		MR. PROSPECTOR (USA)	RAISE A NATIVE (USA)
DUBAI MILLENNIUM (GB) b 1996	SEEKING THE GOLD (USA)		GOLD DIGGER (USA)
		CON GAME (USA)	BUCKPASSER (USA)
			BROADWAY (USA)
	COLORADO DANCER (IRE)	SHAREEF DANCER (USA)	**NORTHERN DANCER (CAN)**
			SWEET ALLIANCE (USA)
		FALL ASPEN (USA)	PRETENSE (USA)
			CHANGE WATER (USA)
SABAAH (USA) ch 1988	NUREYEV (USA)	**NORTHERN DANCER (CAN)**	NEARCTIC (CAN)
			NATALMA (USA)
		SPECIAL (USA)	FORLI (ARG)
			THONG (USA)
	DISH DASH (GB)	BUSTINO (GB)	BUSTED (GB)
			SHIPYARD (GB)
		LOOSE COVER (GB)	VENTURE (FR)
			NYMPHET (GB)

Bright Morning (GB) b f 19 March 2002.
Inbreeding: Northern Dancer 4x3.
Breeder: Irish National Stud & Darley
Owner: Godolphin
Trainer: Saeed bin Suroor

Race record:

Years	Starts	Wins	2nd	3rd	Earned (£/$)
1	2	1	0	1	£10,000 / $17,758

Best RPR: 65; Timeform at 3: 95p; dam's Timeform: 65

CARISOLO

		MR. PROSPECTOR (USA)	RAISE A NATIVE (USA)
DUBAI MILLENNIUM (GB) b 1996	SEEKING THE GOLD (USA)		GOLD DIGGER (USA)
		CON GAME (USA)	BUCKPASSER (USA)
			BROADWAY (USA)
	COLORADO DANCER (IRE)	SHAREEF DANCER (USA)	**NORTHERN DANCER (CAN)**
			SWEET ALLIANCE (USA)
		FALL ASPEN (USA)	PRETENSE (USA)
			CHANGE WATER (USA)
SOLO DE LUNE (IRE) b 1990	LAW SOCIETY (USA)	ALLEGED (USA)	HOIST THE FLAG (USA)
			PRINCESS POUT (USA)
		BOLD BIKINI (USA)	BOLDNESIAN (USA)
			RAN-TAN (USA)
	TRULY SPECIAL (IRE)	CAERLEON (USA)	NIJINSKY (CAN)
			FORESEER (USA)
		ARCTIQUE ROYALE (IRE)	ROYAL AND REGAL (USA)
			ARCTIC MELODY (GB)

Carisolo (GB) b f 7 March 2002.
Inbreeding: Northern Dancer 4x5.
Breeder: Britton House Stud Ltd
Owner: Britton House Stud Ltd*
Trainer: Sir Michael Stoute

Race record:

Years	Starts	Wins	2nd	3rd	Earned (£/$)
2	7	1	0	1	£17,997 / $32,626

Best RPR: 63; Timeform at 3: 71; dam's Timeform: N/A
* sold from Britton House Stud dispersal at 2006 Tattersalls December Sales for 1,000,000gns to Richard Frisby Bloodstock

CRIMSON YEAR

		MR. PROSPECTOR (USA)	RAISE A NATIVE (USA)
DUBAI MILLENNIUM (GB) b 1996	SEEKING THE GOLD (USA)		GOLD DIGGER (USA)
		CON GAME (USA)	BUCKPASSER (USA)
			BROADWAY (USA)
	COLORADO DANCER (IRE)	SHAREEF DANCER (USA)	NORTHERN DANCER (CAN)
			SWEET ALLIANCE (USA)
		FALL ASPEN (USA)	PRETENSE (USA)
			CHANGE WATER (USA)
CRIMSON CONQUEST (USA) ch 1988	DIESIS (GB)	SHARPEN UP (GB)	ATAN (USA)
			ROCCHETTA (GB)
		DOUBLY SURE (GB)	RELIANCE (FR)
			SOFT ANGELS (IRE)
	SWEET RAMBLIN ROSE (USA)	TURN-TO (IRE)	ROYAL CHARGER (GB)
			SOURCE SUCREE (FR)
		VELVET ROSE (USA)	ROUND TABLE (USA)
			PINK VELVET (USA)

Crimson Year (USA) ch f 28 Feb 2002.
Inbreeding: Native Dancer 5x6x5.
Breeder: Darley
Owner: Sheikh Marwan Al Maktoum
Trainer: Clive Brittain

Race record:

Years	Starts	Wins	2nd	3rd	Earned (£/$)
1	2	0	0	0	£0 / $0

Best RPR: 15; Timeform at 3: NA; dam's Timeform: N/A

DESCARTES

DUBAI MILLENNIUM (GB) b 1996	SEEKING THE GOLD (USA)	MR. PROSPECTOR (USA)	RAISE A NATIVE (USA)
			GOLD DIGGER (USA)
		CON GAME (USA)	BUCKPASSER (USA)
			BROADWAY (USA)
	COLORADO DANCER (IRE)	SHAREEF DANCER (USA)	NORTHERN DANCER (CAN)
			SWEET ALLIANCE (USA)
		FALL ASPEN (USA)	PRETENSE (USA)
			CHANGE WATER (USA)
GOLD'S DANCE (FR) 1991	GOLDNEYEV (USA)	NUREYEV (USA)	NORTHERN DANCER (CAN)
			SPECIAL (USA)
		GOLD RIVER (FR)	RIVERMAN (USA)
			GLANEUSE (FR)
	ANITRA'S DANCE (FR)	GREEN DANCER (USA)	NIJINSKY (CAN)
			GREEN VALLEY (FR)
		AZURELLA (FR)	HIGH HAT (GB)
			AZORELLE (FR)

Descartes (GB) b c 5 Feb 2002.
Inbreeding: Northern Dancer 4x4x5.
Breeder: Darley
Owner: Godolphin
Trainer: Saeed bin Suroor

Race record:

Years	Starts	Wins	2nd	3rd	Earned (£/$)
2	3	2	0	0	£18,393 / $34,293

Best RPR: 82; Timeform at 2: 90p (at 3, NA); dam's Timeform: N/A

DUBAWI

DUBAI MILLENNIUM (GB) b 1996	SEEKING THE GOLD (USA)	MR. PROSPECTOR (USA)	RAISE A NATIVE (USA)
			GOLD DIGGER (USA)
		CON GAME (USA)	BUCKPASSER (USA)
			BROADWAY (USA)
	COLORADO DANCER (IRE)	SHAREEF DANCER (USA)	NORTHERN DANCER (CAN)
			SWEET ALLIANCE (USA)
		FALL ASPEN (USA)	PRETENSE (USA)
			CHANGE WATER (USA)
ZOMARADAH (GB) br 1995	DEPLOY (GB)	SHIRLEY HEIGHTS (GB)	MILL REEF (USA)
			HARDIEMMA (GB)
		SLIGHTLY DANGEROUS (USA)	ROBERTO (USA)
			WHERE YOU LEAD (USA)
	JAWAHER (IRE)	DANCING BRAVE (USA)	LYPHARD (USA)
			NAVAJO PRINCESS (USA)
		HIGH TERN (IRE)	HIGH LINE (GB)
			SUNBITTERN (GB)

Dubawi (Ire) b c 7 Feb 2002.
Inbreeding: Northern Dancer 4x5, Raise A Native 4x5.
Breeder: Darley
Owner: Godolphin
Trainer: Saeed bin Suroor

Race record:

Years	Starts	Wins	2nd	3rd	Earned (£/$)
2	8	5	1	1	£699,341 / $1,256,932

At 2, won Superlative S-G3, Newmarket, National S-G1, Curragh
At 3, won Irish 2,000 Guineas-G1, Curragh, Prix Jacques le Marois-G1, Deauville; 2nd Queen Elizabeth II S-G1, Newmarket; 3rd Derby-G1, Epsom. Best RPR: 128; Timeform at 3: 129; dam's Timeform: 118

ECHO OF LIGHT

DUBAI MILLENNIUM (GB) b 1996	SEEKING THE GOLD (USA)	MR. PROSPECTOR (USA)	RAISE A NATIVE (USA)
			GOLD DIGGER (USA)
		CON GAME (USA)	BUCKPASSER (USA)
			BROADWAY (USA)
	COLORADO DANCER (IRE)	SHAREEF DANCER (USA)	NORTHERN DANCER (CAN)
			SWEET ALLIANCE (USA)
		FALL ASPEN (USA)	PRETENSE (USA)
			CHANGE WATER (USA)
SPIRIT OF TARA (IRE) b 1994	SADLER'S WELLS (USA)	NORTHERN DANCER (CAN)	NEARCTIC (CAN)
			NATALMA (USA)
		FAIRY BRIDGE (USA)	BOLD REASON (USA)
			SPECIAL (USA)
	FLAME OF TARA (IRE)	ARTAIUS (USA)	ROUND TABLE (USA)
			STYLISH PATTERN (USA)
		WELSH FLAME (IRE)	WELSH PAGEANT (FR)
			ELECTRIC FLASH (GB)

Echo Of Light (GB) b c 7 March 2002.
Inbreeding: Northern Dancer 4x3.
Breeder: Kilcarn Stud
Owner: Godolphin
Trainer: Saeed bin Suroor
€1,200,000 Goffs Orby yearling

Race record*:

Years	Starts	Wins	2nd	3rd	Earned (£/$)
3	11	5	1	0	£158,812 / $292,861

At 4, won Ladbrokes Summer Mile Stakes-G3, Lingfield, Strensall Stakes-G3, York, Prix Daniel Wildenstein-G2, Longchamp.
Best RPR: 121; Timeform at 3: 115; dam's Timeform: 106
*In training in 2007

ESQUIRE

DUBAI MILLENNIUM (GB) b 1996	SEEKING THE GOLD (USA)	MR. PROSPECTOR (USA)	RAISE A NATIVE (USA)
			GOLD DIGGER (USA)
		CON GAME (USA)	BUCKPASSER (USA)
			BROADWAY (USA)
	COLORADO DANCER (IRE)	SHAREEF DANCER (USA)	NORTHERN DANCER (CAN)
			SWEET ALLIANCE (USA)
		FALL ASPEN (USA)	PRETENSE (USA)
			CHANGE WATER (USA)
ESPERADA (ARG) gr 1995	EQUALIZE (USA)	NORTHERN JOVE (CAN)	NORTHERN DANCER (CAN)
			JUNONIA (USA)
		ZONTA (USA)	DR. FAGER (USA)
			SANTA TINA (IRE)
	ESMERADA (ARG)	FARNESIO (ARG)	GOOD MANNERS (USA)
			LA FARNESINA (ARG)
		ELYSEE (ARG)	EL GRAN CAPITAN (ARG)
			EMPIRIC (ARG)

Esquire (GB) b c 8 March 2002.
Inbreeding: Northern Dancer 4x4.
Breeder: Darley
Owner: Godolphin
Trainer: Saeed bin Suroor

Race record:

Years	Starts	Wins	2nd	3rd	Earned (£/$)
3	6	1	0	0	£6,841 / $12,330

Best RPR: 91; Timeform at 3: 92; dam's Timeform: N/A

FLAG OF TRUCE

		MR. PROSPECTOR (USA)	RAISE A NATIVE (USA)
DUBAI MILLENNIUM (GB) b 1996	SEEKING THE GOLD (USA)		GOLD DIGGER (USA)
		CON GAME (USA)	BUCKPASSER (USA)
			BROADWAY (USA)
	COLORADO DANCER (IRE)	SHAREEF DANCER (USA)	**NORTHERN DANCER (CAN)**
			SWEET ALLIANCE (USA)
		FALL ASPEN (USA)	PRETENSE (USA)
			CHANGE WATER (USA)
FLAGBIRD (USA) b 1991	NUREYEV (USA)	**NORTHERN DANCER (CAN)**	NEARCTIC (CAN)
			NATALMA (USA)
		SPECIAL (USA)	FORLI (ARG)
			THONG (USA)
	UP THE FLAGPOLE (USA)	HOIST THE FLAG (USA)	TOM ROLFE (USA)
			WAVY NAVY (USA)
		THE GARDEN CLUB (USA)	HERBAGER (FR)
			FASHION VERDICT (USA)

Flag Of Truce (GB) b c 6 Feb 2002.
Inbreeding: Northern Dancer 4x3.
Breeder: Darley
Owner: Godolphin
Trainer: Saeed bin Suroor

Race record:
Years	Starts	Wins	2nd	3rd	Earned (£/$)
1	1	0	0	1	£747 / $1,346

Best RPR: 81; Timeform at 3: 82p; dam's Timeform: 119

GROSVENOR SQUARE

		MR. PROSPECTOR (USA)	RAISE A NATIVE (USA)
DUBAI MILLENNIUM (GB) b 1996	SEEKING THE GOLD (USA)		GOLD DIGGER (USA)
		CON GAME (USA)	BUCKPASSER (USA)
			BROADWAY (USA)
	COLORADO DANCER (IRE)	SHAREEF DANCER (USA)	**NORTHERN DANCER (CAN)**
			SWEET ALLIANCE (USA)
		FALL ASPEN (USA)	PRETENSE (USA)
			CHANGE WATER (USA)
EMBASSY (GB) br 1995	CADEAUX GENEREUX (GB)	YOUNG GENERATION (IRE)	BALIDAR (IRE)
			BRIG ODOON (GB)
		SMARTEN UP (GB)	SHARPEN UP (GB)
			LANGUISSOLA (GB)
	PASS THE PEACE (IRE)	ALZAO (USA)	LYPHARD (USA)
			LADY REBECCA (GB)
		LOVER'S ROSE (IRE)	KING EMPEROR (USA)
			NONNIE (GB)

Grosvenor Square (Ire) b c 20 March 2002.
Inbreeding: Northern Dancer 4x5.
Breeder: Darley
Owner: Godolphin
Trainer: Saeed bin Suroor

Race record:
Years	Starts	Wins	2nd	3rd	Earned (£/$)
3	11	2	1	1	$36,051

Best RPR: 92; Timeform at 3: 93; dam's Timeform: 114

HALLE BOP

		MR. PROSPECTOR (USA)	RAISE A NATIVE (USA)
DUBAI MILLENNIUM (GB) b 1996	SEEKING THE GOLD (USA)		GOLD DIGGER (USA)
		CON GAME (USA)	BUCKPASSER (USA)
			BROADWAY (USA)
	COLORADO DANCER (IRE)	SHAREEF DANCER (USA)	**NORTHERN DANCER (CAN)**
			SWEET ALLIANCE (USA)
		FALL ASPEN (USA)	PRETENSE (USA)
			CHANGE WATER (USA)
NAPOLEON'S SISTER (IRE) b 1995	ALZAO (USA)	LYPHARD (USA)	**NORTHERN DANCER (CAN)**
			GOOFED (USA)
		LADY REBECCA (GB)	**SIR IVOR (USA)**
			POCAHONTAS (USA)
	SHEER AUDACITY (GB)	TROY (IRE)	PETINGO (IRE)
			LA MILO (GB)
		MISS UPWARD (GB)	ALCIDE (GB)
			AIMING HIGH (GB)

Halle Bop (GB) b f 4 April 2002. Race record:
Inbreeding: Northern Dancer 4x4;
  Sir Ivor 4x5.
Breeder: Normandie Stud Ltd
Owner: Godolphin
Trainer: Saeed bin Suroor

Years	Starts	Wins	2nd	3rd	Earned (£/$)
2	6	1	2	0	£9,263 / $16,620

Best RPR: 89; Timeform at 3: 92; dam's Timeform: 101

HER OWN KIND

		MR. PROSPECTOR (USA)	RAISE A NATIVE (USA)
DUBAI MILLENNIUM (GB) b 1996	SEEKING THE GOLD (USA)		GOLD DIGGER (USA)
		CON GAME (USA)	BUCKPASSER (USA)
			BROADWAY (USA)
	COLORADO DANCER (IRE)	SHAREEF DANCER (USA)	**NORTHERN DANCER (CAN)**
			SWEET ALLIANCE (USA)
		FALL ASPEN (USA)	PRETENSE (USA)
			CHANGE WATER (USA)
THE CARETAKER (IRE) b 1987	CAERLEON (USA)	NIJINSKY (CAN)	**NORTHERN DANCER (CAN)**
			FLAMING PAGE (CAN)
		FORESEER (USA)	ROUND TABLE (USA)
			REGAL GLEAM (USA)
	GO FEATHER GO (USA)	GO MARCHING (USA)	**PRINCEQUILLO (IRE)**
			LEALLAH (USA)
		FEATHER BED (USA)	JOHNS JOY (USA)
			SILLY SARA (CAN)

Her Own Kind (JPN) b f 12 Feb
  2002.
Inbreeding: Northern Dancer 4x4;
  Princequillo 4x5.
Breeder: Darley Stud
Management LLC
Owner: Godolphin
Trainer: Saeed bin Suroor

Race record:

Years	Starts	Wins	2nd	3rd	Earned (£/$)
1	2	1	1	0	£5,780 / $10,520

Best RPR: 93; Timeform at 3: 91p; dam's Timeform: 113

INTEND TO LEAVE

		MR. PROSPECTOR (USA)	RAISE A NATIVE (USA)
DUBAI MILLENNIUM (GB) b 1996	SEEKING THE GOLD (USA)		GOLD DIGGER (USA)
		CON GAME (USA)	BUCKPASSER (USA)
			BROADWAY (USA)
	COLORADO DANCER (IRE)	SHAREEF DANCER (USA)	NORTHERN DANCER (CAN)
			SWEET ALLIANCE (USA)
		FALL ASPEN (USA)	PRETENSE (USA)
			CHANGE WATER (USA)
SHEER AUDACITY (GB) b 1984	TROY (IRE)	PETINGO (IRE)	PETITION (GB)
			ALCAZAR (FR)
		LA MILO (GB)	HORNBEAM (GB)
			PIN PRICK (GB)
	MISS UPWARD (GB)	ALCIDE (GB)	**ALYCIDON (GB)**
			CHENILLE (GB)
		AIMING HIGH (GB)	DJEBE (FR)
			ANNIE OAKLEY (GB)

Intend To Leave (Ire) b c 20 Feb 2002.
Inbreeding: Alycidon 4x5.
Breeder: Mrs Max Morris
Owner: Godolphin
Trainer: Saeed bin Suroor

Race record:

Years	Starts	Wins	2nd	3rd	Earned (£/$)
1	1	0	1	0	£1,228 / $2,171

Best RPR: 76; Timeform: NA; dam's Timeform: N/A

KYDD GLOVES

		MR. PROSPECTOR (USA)	RAISE A NATIVE (USA)
DUBAI MILLENNIUM (GB) b 1996	SEEKING THE GOLD (USA)		GOLD DIGGER (USA)
		CON GAME (USA)	**BUCKPASSER (USA)**
			BROADWAY (USA)
	COLORADO DANCER (IRE)	SHAREEF DANCER (USA)	**NORTHERN DANCER (CAN)**
			SWEET ALLIANCE (USA)
		FALL ASPEN (USA)	PRETENSE (USA)
			CHANGE WATER (USA)
PARADE QUEEN (USA) b 1994	A.P. INDY (USA)	SEATTLE SLEW (USA)	BOLD REASONING (USA)
			MY CHARMER (USA)
		WEEKEND SURPRISE (USA)	SECRETARIAT (USA)
			LASSIE DEAR (USA)
	SPANISH PARADE (USA)	ROBERTO (USA)	HAIL TO REASON (USA)
			BRAMALEA (USA)
		NIJIT (USA)	NIJINSKY (CAN)
			BITTY GIRL (GB)

Kydd Gloves (USA) b f 28 Jan 2002.
Inbreeding: Buckpasser 4x5, Northern Dancer 4x5
Breeder: W S Farish et al
Owner: Godolphin
Trainer: Saeed bin Suroor

Race record:

Years	Starts	Wins	2nd	3rd	Earned (£/$)
1	3	2	0	0	£19,787 / £35,541

Best RPR: 95; Timeform at 3: 103+; dam's Timeform: N/A

LADEENA

		MR. PROSPECTOR (USA)	RAISE A NATIVE (USA)
DUBAI MILLENNIUM (GB) b 1996	SEEKING THE GOLD (USA)		GOLD DIGGER (USA)
		CON GAME (USA)	BUCKPASSER (USA)
			BROADWAY (USA)
	COLORADO DANCER (IRE)	SHAREEF DANCER (USA)	NORTHERN DANCER (CAN)
			SWEET ALLIANCE (USA)
		FALL ASPEN (USA)	PRETENSE (USA)
			CHANGE WATER (USA)
AQAARID b 1992	NASHWAN (USA)	BLUSHING GROOM (FR)	RED GOD (USA)
			RUNAWAY BRIDE (GB)
		HEIGHT OF FASHION (FR)	BUSTINO (GB)
			HIGHCLERE (GB)
	ASHAYER (GB)	LOMOND (USA)	NORTHERN DANCER (CAN)
			MY CHARMER (USA)
		GOOD LASSIE (GB)	MOULTON (GB)
			VIOLETTA (ITY)

Ladeena (Ire) b f 20 Feb 2002.   Race record:
Inbreeding: Northern Dancer 4x4.   Years   Starts   Wins   2nd   3rd   Earned (£/$)
Breeder: Shadwell Estate Co. Ltd   2   10   1   1   1   £6,536 / $11,940
Owner: Hamdan Al Maktoum   Best RPR: 77; Timeform at 3: 76; dam's Timeform: 116
Trainer: John Dunlop

MURAABET

		MR. PROSPECTOR (USA)	RAISE A NATIVE (USA)
DUBAI MILLENNIUM (GB) b 1996	SEEKING THE GOLD (USA)		GOLD DIGGER (USA)
		CON GAME (USA)	BUCKPASSER (USA)
			BROADWAY (USA)
	COLORADO DANCER (IRE)	SHAREEF DANCER (USA)	NORTHERN DANCER (CAN)
			SWEET ALLIANCE (USA)
		FALL ASPEN (USA)	PRETENSE (USA)
			CHANGE WATER (USA)
MAHASIN (USA) b 1989	DANZIG (USA)	NORTHERN DANCER (CAN)	NEARCTIC (CAN)
			NATALMA (USA)
		PAS DE NOM (USA)	ADMIRALS VOYAGE (USA)
			PETITIONER (GB)
	ICING (IRE)	PRINCE TENDERFOOT (USA)	BLUE PRINCE (USA)
			LA TENDRESSE (GB)
		CAKE (GB)	NEVER SAY DIE (USA)
			LA MARSEILLAISE (FR)

Muraabet (GB) b c 5 March 2002.   Race record:
Inbreeding: Northern Dancer 4x3.   Years   Starts   Wins   2nd   3rd   Earned (£/$)
Breeder: Shadwell Estate Co. Ltd   2   3   0   0   1   £1,102 / $1,987
Owner: Hamdan Al Maktoum   Best RPR: 81; Timeform at 3: 81; dam's Timeform: 90
Trainer: John Dunlop

MY DUBAI

DUBAI MILLENNIUM (GB) b 1996	SEEKING THE GOLD (USA)	MR. PROSPECTOR (USA)	RAISE A NATIVE (USA)
			GOLD DIGGER (USA)
		CON GAME (USA)	BUCKPASSER (USA)
			BROADWAY (USA)
	COLORADO DANCER (IRE)	SHAREEF DANCER (USA)	**NORTHERN DANCER (CAN)**
			SWEET ALLIANCE (USA)
		FALL ASPEN (USA)	PRETENSE (USA)
			CHANGE WATER (USA)
PASTORALE (GB) ch 1988	NUREYEV (USA)	**NORTHERN DANCER (CAN)**	NEARCTIC (CAN)
			NATALMA (USA)*
		SPECIAL (USA)	FORLI (ARG)
			THONG (USA)
	PARK APPEAL (GB)	AHONOORA (GB)	LORENZACCIO (IRE)
			HELEN NICHOLS (GB)
		BALIDARESS (IRE)	BALIDAR (IRE)
			INNOCENCE (GB)

My Dubai (GB) ch 11 March 2002.
Inbreeding: Northern Dancer 4x3.
Breeder: Darley
Owner: Godolphin
Trainer: Saeed bin Suroor

Race record:

Years	Starts	Wins	2nd	3rd	Earned (£/$)
1	1	0	0	1	£751 / $1,380

Best RPR: 70; Timeform at 2: 76p (at 3, NA); dam's Timeform: N/A

NOBLE DUTY

DUBAI MILLENNIUM (GB)	SEEKING THE GOLD (USA)	MR. PROSPECTOR (USA)	**RAISE A NATIVE (USA)**
			GOLD DIGGER (USA)
		CON GAME (USA)	BUCKPASSER (USA)
			BROADWAY (USA)
	COLORADO DANCER (IRE)	SHAREEF DANCER (USA)	**NORTHERN DANCER (CAN)**
			SWEET ALLIANCE (USA)
		FALL ASPEN (USA)	PRETENSE (USA)
			CHANGE WATER (USA)
NIJINSKY'S LOVER ch 1987	NIJINSKY (CAN)	**NORTHERN DANCER (CAN)**	NEARCTIC (CAN)
			NATALMA (USA)
		FLAMING PAGE (CAN)	BULL PAGE (USA)
			FLARING TOP (USA)
	LUV LUVIN' (USA)	**RAISE A NATIVE (USA)**	NATIVE DANCER (USA)
			RAISE YOU (USA)
		RINGING BELLS (USA)	BOLD LAD (USA)
			PRAYER BELL (USA)

Noble Duty (USA) b c 9 Feb 2002.
Inbreeding: Northern Dancer 4x3, Raise A Native 4x3.
Breeder: Darley
Owner: Godolphin
Trainer: Saeed bin Suroor

Race record:

Years	Starts	Wins	2nd	3rd	Earned (£/$)
3	5	0	1	1	$9,109

Best RPR: 82; Timeform at 3: 88; dam's Timeform: N/A

OUDE

		MR. PROSPECTOR (USA)	RAISE A NATIVE (USA)
DUBAI MILLENNIUM (GB) b 1996	SEEKING THE GOLD (USA)		GOLD DIGGER (USA)
		CON GAME (USA)	BUCKPASSER (USA)
			BROADWAY (USA)
	COLORADO DANCER (IRE)	SHAREEF DANCER (USA)	NORTHERN DANCER (CAN)
			SWEET ALLIANCE (USA)
		FALL ASPEN (USA)	PRETENSE (USA)
			CHANGE WATER (USA)
CHOSEN LADY (USA)	SECRETARIAT (USA)	BOLD RULER (USA)	NASRULLAH (GB)
			MISS DISCO (USA)
		SOMETHINGROYAL (USA)	PRINCEQUILLO (IRE)
			IMPERATRICE (USA)
	MINE ONLY (USA)	MR. PROSPECTOR (USA)	RAISE A NATIVE (USA)
			GOLD DIGGER (USA)
		MONO (USA)	BETTER SELF (USA)
			SIN IGUAL (USA)

Oude (USA) b/br c 16 March 2002.
Inbreeding: Mr Prospector 3x3.
Breeder: Darley & Stonerside Stable
Owner: Godolphin
Trainer: Saeed bin Suroor

Race record:

Years	Starts	Wins	2nd	3rd	Earned (£/$)
2	5	1	2	1	£29,088 / $52,288

Best RPR: 109; Timeform at 3: 110; dam's Timeform: N/A

PERFUMERY

		MR. PROSPECTOR (USA)	RAISE A NATIVE (USA)
DUBAI MILLENNIUM (GB) b 1996	SEEKING THE GOLD (USA)		GOLD DIGGER (USA)
		CON GAME (USA)	BUCKPASSER (USA)
			BROADWAY (USA)
	COLORADO DANCER (IRE)	SHAREEF DANCER (USA)	NORTHERN DANCER (CAN)
			SWEET ALLIANCE (USA)
		FALL ASPEN (USA)*	PRETENSE (USA)
			CHANGE WATER (USA)
SWEET WILLA (USA) 1989	ASSERT (IRE)	BE MY GUEST (USA)	NORTHERN DANCER (CAN)
			WHAT A TREAT (USA)
		IRISH BIRD (USA)	SEA-BIRD (FR)
			IRISH LASS (IRE)
	WILLAMAE (CAN)	TENTAM (USA)	INTENTIONALLY (USA)
			TAMERETT (USA)
		RACLETTE (CAN)	HOIST THE FLAG (USA)
			LAURIES DANCER (CAN)

Perfumery (GB) b f 8 Feb 2002.
Inbreeding: Northern Dancer 4x4x5.
Breeder: Darley
Owner: Sheikh Mohammed
Trainer: John Gosden

Race record:

Years	Starts	Wins	2nd	3rd	Earned (£/$)
1	3	0	0	0	£0 / $0

Best RPR: 60; Timeform at 3: 65; dam's Timeform: N/A

QAADMAH

DUBAI MILLENNIUM (GB) b 1996	SEEKING THE GOLD (USA)	MR. PROSPECTOR (USA)	RAISE A NATIVE (USA)
			GOLD DIGGER (USA)
		CON GAME (USA)	BUCKPASSER (USA)
			BROADWAY (USA)
	COLORADO DANCER (IRE)	SHAREEF DANCER (USA)	NORTHERN DANCER (CAN)
			SWEET ALLIANCE (USA)
		FALL ASPEN (USA)	PRETENSE (USA)
			CHANGE WATER (USA)
ZAHRAT DUBAI (GB) br 1996	UNFUWAIN (USA)	NORTHERN DANCER (CAN)	NEARCTIC (CAN)
			NATALMA (USA)
		HEIGHT OF FASHION (FR)	BUSTINO (GB)
			HIGHCLERE (GB)
	WALESIANA (GER)	STAR APPEAL (IRE)	APPIANI (ITY)
			STERNA (GER)
		WONDROUS PEARL (GB)	PRINCE IPPI (GER)
			WELTWUNDER (GER)

Qaadmah (Ire) b f 23 Feb 2002.
Inbreeding: Northern Dancer 4x3.
Breeder: Darley
Owner: Sheikh Ahmed Al Maktoum
Trainer: Michael Jarvis/ D. Selvaratnam

Race record:

Years	Starts	Wins	2nd	3rd	Earned (£/$)
1	5	0	0	0	£0 / $0

Best RPR: 70; Timeform at 3: 72; dam's Timeform: 114

QUICKFIRE

DUBAI MILLENNIUM (GB) b 1996	SEEKING THE GOLD (USA)	MR. PROSPECTOR (USA)	RAISE A NATIVE (USA)
			GOLD DIGGER (USA)
		CON GAME (USA)	BUCKPASSER (USA)
			BROADWAY (USA)
	COLORADO DANCER (IRE)	SHAREEF DANCER (USA)	NORTHERN DANCER (CAN)
			SWEET ALLIANCE (USA)
		FALL ASPEN (USA)	PRETENSE (USA)
			CHANGE WATER (USA)
DARING MISS (GB) b 1996	SADLER'S WELLS (USA)	NORTHERN DANCER (CAN)	NEARCTIC (CAN)
			NATALMA (USA)
		FAIRY BRIDGE (USA)	BOLD REASON (USA)
			SPECIAL (USA)
	BOURBON GIRL (GB)	ILE DE BOURBON (USA)	NIJINSKY (CAN)
			ROSELIERE (FR)
		FLEET GIRL (IRE)	HABITAT (USA)
			FLEET NOBLE (USA)

Quickfire (GB) b f 22 Feb 2002.
Inbreeding: Northern Dancer 4x3x5.
Breeder: Juddmonte Farms Ltd
Owner: Khalid Abdullah
Trainer: Sir Michael Stoute

Race record:

Years	Starts	Wins	2nd	3rd	Earned (£/$)
3	15	2	7	2	£78,766 / $143,211

Best RPR: 102; Timeform at 3: 103; dam's Timeform: 113

RAJWA

		MR. PROSPECTOR (USA)	RAISE A NATIVE (USA)
DUBAI MILLENNIUM (GB) b 1996	SEEKING THE GOLD (USA)		GOLD DIGGER (USA)
		CON GAME (USA)	BUCKPASSER (USA)
			BROADWAY (USA)
	COLORADO DANCER (IRE)	SHAREEF DANCER (USA)	**NORTHERN DANCER (CAN)**
			SWEET ALLIANCE (USA)
		FALL ASPEN (USA)	PRETENSE (USA)
			CHANGE WATER (USA)
ZELANDA (IRE) gr 1995	NIGHT SHIFT (USA)	**NORTHERN DANCER (CAN)**	NEARCTIC (CAN)
			NATALMA (USA)
		CIBOULETTE (CAN)	CHOP CHOP (USA)
			WINDY ANSWER (CAN)
	ZAFADOLA (IRE)	DARSHAAN (GB)	SHIRLEY HEIGHTS (GB)
			DELSY (FR)
		ZARAFA (IRE)	BLUSHING GROOM (FR)
			ZAHRA (IRE)

Rajwa (USA) ch c 13 Jan 2002.
Inbreeding: Northern Dancer 4x3.
Breeder: Darley
Owner: Godolphin
Trainer: Saeed bin Suroor

Race record:

Years	Starts	Wins	2nd	3rd	Earned (£/$)
2	4	0	3	0	£8,198 / $14,882

Best RPR: 93; Timeform at 3: 93+; dam's Timeform: 108

ROYAL GALA

		MR. PROSPECTOR (USA)	RAISE A NATIVE (USA)
DUBAI MILLENNIUM (GB) b 1996	SEEKING THE GOLD (USA)		GOLD DIGGER (USA)
		CON GAME (USA)	BUCKPASSER (USA)
			BROADWAY (USA)
	COLORADO DANCER (IRE)	SHAREEF DANCER (USA)	NORTHERN DANCER (CAN)
			SWEET ALLIANCE (USA)
		FALL ASPEN (USA)	PRETENSE (USA)
			CHANGE WATER (USA)
VIVID CONCERT (IRE) br 1989	CHIEF SINGER (IRE)	BALLAD ROCK (IRE)	BOLD LAD (IRE)
			TRUE ROCKET (IRE)
		PRINCIPIA (FR)	LE FABULEUX (FR)
			PIA (GB)
	VIVE LA DIFFERENCE (GB)	KNOWN FACT (USA)	IN REALITY (USA)
			TAMERETT (USA)
		VIVE LA LIBERTE (FR)	JIM FRENCH (USA)
			VALI (FR)

Royal Gala (GB) b f 15 Feb 2002.
Inbreeding: none in five generations.
Breeder: Darley
Owner: Sheikh Mohammed
Trainer: Andre Fabre

Race record:

Years	Starts	Wins	2nd	3rd	Earned (£/$)
1	7	1	2	1	£12,743 / $24,126

Best RPR: 81; Timeform at 3: NA; dam's Timeform: 73

RUSSIAN REVOLUTION

		MR. PROSPECTOR (USA)	RAISE A NATIVE (USA)
DUBAI MILLENNIUM (GB)	SEEKING THE GOLD (USA)		GOLD DIGGER (USA)
		CON GAME (USA)	BUCKPASSER (USA)
			BROADWAY (USA)
	COLORADO DANCER (IRE)	SHAREEF DANCER (USA)	**NORTHERN DANCER (CAN)**
			SWEET ALLIANCE (USA)
		FALL ASPEN (USA)	PRETENSE (USA)
			CHANGE WATER (USA)
RUSSIAN SNOWS (IRE) b 1992	SADLER'S WELLS (USA)	**NORTHERN DANCER (CAN)**	NEARCTIC (CAN)
			NATALMA (USA)
		FAIRY BRIDGE (USA)	BOLD REASON (USA)
			SPECIAL (USA)
	ARCTIQUE ROYALE (IRE)	ROYAL AND REGAL (USA)	VAGUELY NOBLE (IRE)
			NATIVE STREET (USA)
		ARCTIC MELODY (GB)	ARCTIC SLAVE (GB)
			BELL BIRD (GB)

Russian Revolution (GB) b f 14 Feb 2002.
Inbreeding: Northern Dancer 4x3.
Breeder: Gainsborough Stud Management Ltd
Owner: Godolphin
Trainer: Saeed bin Suroor

Race record:

Years	Starts	Wins	2nd	3rd	Earned (£/$)
1	2	1	0	1	£6,322 / $11,354

Best RPR: 81; Timeform at 3: 82p; dam's Timeform: 113

SPRING RAIN

		MR. PROSPECTOR (USA)	RAISE A NATIVE (USA)
DUBAI MILLENNIUM (GB) b 1996	SEEKING THE GOLD (USA)		GOLD DIGGER (USA)
		CON GAME (USA)	BUCKPASSER (USA)
			BROADWAY (USA)
	COLORADO DANCER (IRE)	SHAREEF DANCER (USA)	**NORTHERN DANCER (CAN)**
			SWEET ALLIANCE (USA)
		FALL ASPEN (USA)	PRETENSE (USA)
			CHANGE WATER (USA)
STORM SONG (USA) b 1994	SUMMER SQUALL (USA)	STORM BIRD (CAN)	**NORTHERN DANCER (CAN)**
			SOUTH OCEAN (CAN)
		WEEKEND SURPRISE (USA)	SECRETARIAT (USA)
			LASSIE DEAR (USA)
	HUM ALONG (USA)	FAPPIANO (USA)	**MR. PROSPECTOR (USA)**
			KILLALOE (USA)
		MINSTRESS (USA)	THE MINSTREL (CAN)
			FLEET VICTRESS (USA)

Spring Rain (JPN) b f 8 Feb 2002.
Inbreeding: Mr Prospector 3x4, Northern Dancer 4x4x5.
Breeder: Darley Stud Management Co. Ltd
Owner: Sheikh Mohammed
Trainer: Andre Fabre

Race record:

Years	Starts	Wins	2nd	3rd	Earned (£/$)
2	4	0	0	0	£1,550 / $1,988

Best RPR: 66; Timeform at 3: NA; dam's Timeform: N/A

THOUSAND ISLANDS

DUBAI MILLENNIUM (GB) b 1996	SEEKING THE GOLD (USA)	MR. PROSPECTOR (USA)	RAISE A NATIVE (USA)
			GOLD DIGGER (USA)
		CON GAME (USA)	BUCKPASSER (USA)
			BROADWAY (USA)
	COLORADO DANCER (IRE)	SHAREEF DANCER (USA)	NORTHERN DANCER (CAN)
			SWEET ALLIANCE (USA)
		FALL ASPEN (USA)	PRETENSE (USA)
			CHANGE WATER (USA)
MINISTER WIFE (USA) dkb/br 1992	DEPUTY MINISTER (CAN)	VICE REGENT (CAN)	NORTHERN DANCER (CAN)
			VICTORIA REGINA (CAN)
		MINT COPY (CAN)	BUNTY'S FLIGHT (CAN)
			SHAKNEY (USA)
	DOWERY (USA)	FULL POCKET (USA)	OLDEN TIMES (USA)
			DEAREST MOMMY (USA)
		VAGUELY ROYAL (USA)	VAGUELY NOBLE (IRE)
			SHOSHANNA (USA)

Thousand Islands (GB) b f 13 Feb 2002.
Inbreeding: Northern Dancer 4x4.
Breeder: Darley
Owner: Sheikh Mohammed
Trainer: Andre Fabre

Race record:

Years	Starts	Wins	2nd	3rd	Earned (£/$)
1	6	2	2	0	£29,893 / $56,479

Best RPR: 82; Timeform at 3: NA; dam's Timeform: N/A

VAULTING

DUBAI MILLENNIUM (GB) b 1996	SEEKING THE GOLD (USA)	MR. PROSPECTOR (USA)	RAISE A NATIVE (USA)
			GOLD DIGGER (USA)
		CON GAME (USA)	BUCKPASSER (USA)
			BROADWAY (USA)
	COLORADO DANCER (IRE)	SHAREEF DANCER (USA)	NORTHERN DANCER (CAN)
			SWEET ALLIANCE (USA)
		FALL ASPEN (USA)	PRETENSE (USA)
			CHANGE WATER (USA)
EAVES (USA) b 1987	COXS RIDGE (USA)	BEST TURN (USA)	TURN-TO (IRE)
			SWEET CLEMENTINE (USA)
		OUR MARTHA (USA)	BALLYDONNELL (GB)
			CORDAY (USA)
	EDGE (USA)	DAMASCUS (USA)	SWORD DANCER (USA)
			KERALA (USA)
		PONTEVECCHIO (USA)	ROUND TABLE (USA)
			TERENTIA (USA)

Vaulting (USA) br f 28 March 2002.
Inbreeding: Swaps 5x5.
Breeder: Darley & Angus Glen Farm
Owner: Sheikh Mohammed
Trainer: Andre Fabre

Race record:

Years	Starts	Wins	2nd	3rd	Earned (£/$)
1	1	0	0	0	£0 / $0

Best RPR: 46; Timeform at 3: N/A; dam's Timeform: N/A

VIP

		MR. PROSPECTOR (USA)	RAISE A NATIVE (USA)
DUBAI MILLENNIUM (GB) b 1996	SEEKING THE GOLD (USA)		GOLD DIGGER (USA)
		CON GAME (USA)	**BUCKPASSER (USA)**
			BROADWAY (USA)
	COLORADO DANCER (IRE)	SHAREEF DANCER (USA)	**NORTHERN DANCER (CAN)**
			SWEET ALLIANCE (USA)
		FALL ASPEN (USA)	PRETENSE (USA)
			CHANGE WATER (USA)
DANISH (IRE) b 1991	DANEHILL (USA)	DANZIG (USA)	**NORTHERN DANCER (CAN)**
			PAS DE NOM (USA)
		RAZYANA (USA)	HIS MAJESTY (USA)
			SPRING ADIEU (CAN)
	TEA HOUSE (IRE)	SASSAFRAS (FR)	SHESHOON (GB)
			RUTA (FR)
		HOUSE TIE (IRE)	BE FRIENDLY (GB)
			MESOPOTAMIA (GB)

Vip (GB) ch c 24 March 2002.
Inbreeding: Buckpasser 4x5, Natalma 5x5x5, Northern Dancer 4x4.
Breeder: Darley
Owner: Godolphin
Trainer: Saeed bin Suroor

Race record:

Years	Starts	Wins	2nd	3rd	Earned (£/$)
1	1	0	0	0	£323 / $591

Best RPR: 65; Timeform at 3: NA; dam's Timeform: 117

WATCHTOWER

		MR. PROSPECTOR (USA)	RAISE A NATIVE (USA)
DUBAI MILLENNIUM (GB) b 1996	SEEKING THE GOLD (USA)		GOLD DIGGER (USA)
		CON GAME (USA)	BUCKPASSER (USA)
			BROADWAY (USA)
	COLORADO DANCER (IRE)	SHAREEF DANCER (USA)	**NORTHERN DANCER (CAN)**
			SWEET ALLIANCE (USA)
		FALL ASPEN (USA)	PRETENSE (USA)
			CHANGE WATER (USA)
BALISADA (GB) ch 1996	KRIS (GB)	SHARPEN UP (GB)	ATAN (USA)
			ROCCHETTA (GB)
		DOUBLY SURE (GB)	RELIANCE (FR)
			SOFT ANGELS (IRE)
	BALNAHA (GB)	LOMOND (USA)	**NORTHERN DANCER (CAN)**
			MY CHARMER (USA)
		ON SHOW (GB)	WELSH PAGEANT (FR)
			AFRICAN DANCER (GB)

Watchtower (Ire) ch c 25 Feb 2002.
Inbreeding: Native Dancer 5x5, Northern Dancer 4x4.
Breeder: Hascombe & Valiant Studs & Darley
Owner: Godolphin
Trainer: Saeed bin Suroor

Race record:

Years	Starts	Wins	2nd	3rd	Earned (£/)
2	7	0	2	2	£13,364 / $26,774

Best RPR: 69; Timeform at 3: NA; dam's Timeform: N/A

INDEX

Henbit 59
Henrik 187, 191
Her Own Kind 192
Hern, Major Dick 59
High Chaparral 169
Highclere Thoroughbred Racing
 71
Highest Honor 36
Highland and Agricultural
 Society 161
High-Rise 67, 87, 138
Hills, Michael 66
Hills, Richard 186
Hobb Alwahtan 36, 37
Holland, Darryll 103
Hollywood Gold Cup 23
Housemaster 71, 72, 73
Hovdey, Jay 26
Howard, Michael 207
Hydro Calido 135, 140

Iceman 202, 203, 204
Iffraaj 228
inbreeding 129-130
Indigenous 90, 92
International Cricket Club (ICC)
 13-14
International Monetary Fund
 (IMF) 174

International Thoroughbred
 Breeders 34
Irish 1,000 Guineas 170
Irish 2,000 Guineas 69, 103, 137,
 205-207
Irish Derby 31, 79, 109, 137, 172
Irish National Stud 137
Irish National Yearling
 Sale 172
Irish St Leger 125
Island Sands 56, 57, 59, 64

James, Tony 204
Jamison, David 35
Jode 134
Johnston, Mark 200
Jones, Gill 95
Jones, Trevor 95
Juddmonte Farms 134
Jumeirah Group 113

Kalanisi 103
Kammtarra 88
Kandidate 202, 204, 205
Kazzia 202
Keeneland sales 34, 35, 175-177,
 199
 Fall Yearling Sale 132